Starting to Teach in the Secondary School

This completely updated edition of *Starting to Teach in the Secondary School* tackles all the issues that new teachers find difficult. It builds on the skills and knowledge you have developed during your initial teacher education course and offers a planned process of professional development.

The book is divided into four parts comprising nineteen chapters, each of which has practical advice as well as theoretical underpinning. Each section addresses the different stages an NQT might go through during their first year of teaching.

- Part I addresses immediate needs, helping you to manage your workloads and settle into your academic role.
- Part II focuses on teaching and learning; it also includes a section on your pastoral role.
- Part III covers a range of teaching and learning issues as well as wider school and curriculum demands; it includes assessment, language, special needs, key skills and vocational and post-16 education.
- Part IV discusses the importance of using research data for further professional development.

The book can be used either as a standalone companion for newly qualified teachers, or as a follow-on from the editors' successful textbook, *Learning to Teach in the Secondary School*, 3rd edition or the relevant subject book in the *Learning to Teach* series.

Susan Capel is Professor and Head of the Department of Sport Sciences at Brunel University. **Ruth Heilbronn** is Lecturer in Education at the Institute of Education, University of London. **Marilyn Leask** is Head of Effective Practices and Research Dissemination for Initial Teacher Training at the Teacher Training Agency in England. **Tony Turner**, now retired, was a Senior Lecturer in Education at the Institute of Education, University of London.

Related titles

Learning to Teach Subjects in the Secondary School Series

Series Editors
Susan Capel, Marilyn Leask and Tony Turner

Designed for all students learning to teach in secondary schools, and particularly those on school-based initial teacher training courses, the books in this series complement *Learning to Teach in the Secondary School* and its companion, *Starting to Teach in the Secondary School*. Each book in the series applies underpinning theory and addresses practical issues to support students in school and in the training institution in learning how to teach a particular subject.

Learning to Teach English in the Secondary School
Jon Davison and Jane Dowson

Learning to Teach Modern Foreign Languages in the Secondary School, 2nd edition
Norbert Pachler and Kit Field

Learning to Teach History in the Secondary School, 2nd edition
Terry Haydn, James Arthur and Martin Hunt

Learning to Teach Physical Education in the Secondary School, 2nd edition
Edited by Susan Capel

Learning to Teach Science in the Secondary School
Tony Turner and Wendy DiMarco

Learning to Teach Mathematics in the Secondary School
Edited by Sue Johnston-Wilder, Peter Johnston-Wilder, David Pimm and John Westwell

Learning to Teach Religious Education in the Secondary School
Edited by Andrew Wright and Ann-Marie Brandon

Learning to Teach Art and Design in the Secondary School
Edited by Nicholas Addison and Lesley Burgess

Learning to Teach Geography in the Secondary School
David Lambert and David Balderstone

Learning to Teach Design and Technology in the Secondary School
Edited by Gwyneth Owen-Jackson

Learning to Teach Music in the Secondary School
Edited by Chris Philpott

Learning to Teach in the Secondary School, 3rd edition
Edited by Susan Capel, Marilyn Leask and Tony Turner

Learning to Teach ICT in the Secondary School
Edited by Steve Kennewell, John Parkinson and Howard Tanner

Learning to Teach Citizenship in the Secondary School
Edited by Liam Gearon

Starting to Teach in the Secondary School, 2nd edition
Edited by Susan Capel, Ruth Heilbronn, Marilyn Leask and Tony Turner

Starting to Teach in the Secondary School

A companion for the newly qualified teacher

Second edition

**Edited by
Susan Capel, Ruth Heilbronn,
Marilyn Leask and Tony Turner**

RoutledgeFalmer
Taylor & Francis Group

LONDON AND NEW YORK

First edition published 1997 by RoutledgeFalmer

This edition published 2004
by RoutledgeFalmer
2 Park Square, Milton Park, Abingdon, Oxon OX14 4RN

Simultaneously published in the USA and Canada
by RoutledgeFalmer
270 Madison Ave, New York, NY 10016

RoutledgeFalmer is an imprint of the Taylor & Francis Group

© 1997, 2004 Susan Capel, Ruth Heilbronn, Marilyn Leask and Tony Turner
for editorial material and selection. Individual chapters © the contributors

Typeset in Bembo by
HWA Text and Data Management, Tunbridge Wells
Printed and bound in Great Britain by
TJ International, Padstow, Cornwall

British Library Cataloguing in Publication Data
A catalogue record for this book is available from the British Library

Library of Congress Cataloging in Publication Data
A catalog record for this book has been requested

ISBN 0–415–33817–4

Contents

EAL → 126-127

SUPPORTING → 141
LEARNERS

EAL, SEN

DIFFERENTIATION → 146

Illustrations

TABLES

FIGURES

REFLECTIVE TASKS

Contributors

Ahmad Al-Mohannadi is currently a PhD student in the Department of Sport Sciences at Brunel University. His dissertation is looking at causes of stress in Physical Education teachers in Qatar and the effects of stress on Physical Education teachers' attitudes towards teaching their curriculum. Ahmad has an MSc in Curriculum Instruction from the Arizona State University, USA and a BSc in Physical Education from Qatar University. He has taught Physical Education in primary and secondary schools in Qatar.

Kelly Ashford is currently a PhD student in the Department of Sport Sciences at Brunel University. Her dissertation looks at aspects of self-consciousness in sport and their effects on performance. She has a BSc in Sport Sciences from Brunel University – the dissertation for which was on team cohesion/leadership and goal orientations. She is a teaching assistant on the undergraduate Sport Sciences programme, specialising in sport and exercise psychology and research methods; she also teaches swimming at a local club to help fund her studies.

David Balderstone is Lecturer in Geography Education at the Institute of Education, University of London. He is Subject Leader for the initial teacher education course in Geography and conducts professional development courses for practising teachers. He was formerly Head of Geography and Senior Teacher at a large comprehensive school. He is active in the Geographical Association and has written school textbooks and several articles on the teaching of Geography and its assessment. He is co-author of *Learning to Teach Geography in the Secondary School* (2000), published by RoutledgeFalmer.

Judith Brooks is a lecturer at the Institute of Education, University of London, where she is Course Leader for the Certificate in Education and a tutor on the Postgraduate Certificate in Education (PGCE) Post-Compulsory Course. She taught in the secondary and further education sectors before becoming a curriculum manager in a tertiary college. Her main professional interests are the post-16 curriculum, assessment and quality assurance issues. She was for many years an examiner and moderator for English and Communication and is currently an editor for the Qualifications and Curriculum Authority key skills external assessments.

Tony Burgess is Reader in Education at the Institute of Education, University of London. His research has been in writing and in language diversity; and more briefly, in the assessment of English at Key Stage 3. He has written widely about English teaching and about language-linked issues in schools and classrooms.

Diana Burton is Professor and Dean of the Faculty of Education, Community and Leisure at Liverpool John Moores University (LJMU). A secondary school teacher for 11 years, Diana held a number of posts within teacher education at Manchester Metropolitan University before moving to LJMU. Diana contributed chapters to a number of texts on initial and continuing teacher education and has co-authored two recent books on Education Studies. She has published a number of papers on aspects of learning and teaching and is currently co-writing a book for teachers on practitioner research. Her current research focuses on performance management for teachers.

Susan Capel is Professor and Head of Department of Sport Sciences at Brunel University. She was previously Reader in Education and Director of the Academic Standards Unit at Canterbury Christ Church University College. Prior to that she was Programme Director for a secondary PGCE course. Before entering higher education she taught Physical Education and Geography in the UK and Hong Kong. She has a PhD in Physical Education and has published widely in a range of areas. She is a co-editor of this book, *Starting to Teach in the Secondary School*, and its companion volume, *Learning to Teach in the Secondary School*, 3rd edition (both published by RoutledgeFalmer). She is also co-editor of *Issues in Physical Education* and editor of *Learning to Teach Physical Education in the Seconday School*.

Kit Field is Head of the Department for Professional Development at Canterbury Christ Church University College. Kit has a background in Modern Foreign Languages teaching and has published in that field. More recently Kit has researched, published and developed provision in the field of subject leadership and middle management. Other recent publications include the *Portfolio of Professional Development: Recording and Structuring Teachers' Career Development*.

Philip Garner is currently Professor of Education at Nottingham Trent University. He has taught in mainstream and special schools for 17 years and was previously Director of Research in the School of Education at Brunel University. He has published widely on issues relating to special educational needs and emotional and behavioural difficulties. Indicative examples include *Pupils with Problems* (Trentham Books, 1999), *Special Educational Needs: A Companion Guide for Student Teachers* (David Fulton Publishers, 2001) and *The International Handbook of Emotional and Behavioural Difficulties* (Sage, 2004). He is currently directing the Teacher Training Agency's Initial Teacher Training Professional Resource Network (IPRN) on behaviour and classroom management.

Graham Haydon is Lecturer in the Philosophy of Education at the Institute of Education, University of London. He has experience of initial teacher education at the Institute over many years and through several changes of format of teacher education: at the receiving end as a student there himself; as a course tutor in professional studies and in optional courses; and for several years as Co-ordinator of the Issues in Education component of the Institute's PGCE. He now runs a professional development course at masters' level in Values in Education, including personal, social and health education and citizenship issues, and many of his publications, including *Teaching about Values: A New Approach* (Cassell, 1997), have been in these areas.

Jeremy Hayward is Lecturer in Citizenship Education at the Institute of Education, University of London. He is the subject leader for the Citizenship PGCE and runs a Citizenship course at masters' level. He is co-author of a number of books including *Exploring Ethics* (John Murray, 2000), *Sartre's Existentialism and Humanism* (John Murray, 2003) and *The Citizenship Co-ordinator's Handbook* (Nelson Thornes, 2003). Jeremy has also authored textbooks in the field of Citizenship Education and recently co-authored a chapter in *Learning to Teach Citizenship in the Secondary School* (RoutledgeFalmer, 2003). Jeremy was a teacher and lecturer at a number of London schools and colleges and is currently a Department for Education and Skills citizenship advisor for continuing professional development in the south east.

Ruth Heilbronn is Lecturer in Education at the Institute of Education, University of London, where she is currently Subject Leader for the PGCE in Modern Foreign Languages. She taught French and Spanish for many years in London comprehensive schools, where she was involved in a number of curriculum developments, including a language awareness programme, published as *The World Languages Project* (Hodder & Stoughton, 1989). She has been widely involved in in-service education and training and research on induction for many years. Published work includes co-editing *New Teachers in an Urban Comprehensive* (Trentham Books, 1997) and co-authoring *Improving Induction: Research Best Practice for Schools* (RoutledgeFalmer, 2002). Research includes being a member of the team which evaluated the effectiveness of the induction year for newly qualified teachers, 2001–3.

Sheila King is Secondary PGCE Course Director: Partnerships at the Institute of Education, University of London and is also Course Leader of the MA in Geography in Education. Before joining the Institute she taught for 17 years in various schools in the south-east of England and was Head of Humanities in one of the largest comprehensive schools in London. She has been a General Certificate in Education A-level examiner and written school texts, e.g. *Geography to 14* (Key Stage 3) and *BBC Bitesize* (Key Stage 4), as well as academic articles.

Julia Lawrence is currently a PhD student in the Department of Sport Sciences at Brunel University. Her dissertation addresses the transition from Key Stage 2 to Key Stage 3 and its impact on attitudes, self-esteem, self-motivation and attainment in Physical Education. She has a BEd (Hons) in Physical Education from Bedford College of Higher Education (De Montfort University). She has taught Physical Education in secondary schools in Luton and Milton Keynes, and currently contributes to both primary and secondary initial teacher education courses at Brunel University. Julia has undertaken consultancy work for the Teacher Training Agency (TTA). She is a member of the executive committee of the Physical Education Association of the United Kingdom.

Marilyn Leask is Head of Effective Practices and Research Dissemination for Initial Teacher Training at the TTA in England. In this book, she is contributing in her personal capacity. She has had substantial teaching, lecturing, research and administrative experience in schools across sectors both rural and urban, in local education authorities, in initial teacher education and teacher professional development programmes. Her academic research is built on an extensive study of change in national systems, with projects in many countries, and processes for embedding new knowledge in professional practice including the use of information and communications technology. Supporting initial teacher education staff in establishing and improving the quality of the professional knowledge base, e.g. through the systematic reviewing of evidence, and in the collaborative construction of new knowledge through networking and web publication is a key feature of her current work. She is co-author of the companion text *Learning to Teach in the Secondary School* (RoutledgeFalmer), now in its 3rd edition, which is the most popular text for initial teacher education at the secondary level in the UK. She is also co-editor for the accompanying *Learning to Teach* series of texts for student teachers covering all subject areas in the secondary curriculum, also published by RoutledgeFalmer. As well as research reports she has published many other texts which particularly focus on the application of research and evidence to educational practice.

Norman Lucas is Director of Post-Compulsory Education at the Institute of Education, University of London. He has experience of initial teacher education both in secondary schools and further education colleges. His research and publications include initial teacher education issues, post-16 curriculum developments, the professional practice of further education college teachers and policy developments in further education. His present research focuses on new developments for the education of teachers who teach Adult Literacy, Numeracy and English as a Second Language.

Norbert Pachler is Senior Lecturer in Education and Assistant Dean: Continuing Professional Development at the Institute of Education, University of London. His particular interests are in foreign language pedagogy, new technologies in education and teacher education. He has published extensively in these fields. He is co-author of *Learning to Teach Modern Foreign Languages in the Secondary School* (RoutledgeFalmer, 2001), *Learning to Teach using ICT in The Secondary School* (Routledge, 1999) and editor of *Teaching Modern Foreign Languages at Advanced Level* (Routledge, 1999). In addition, he is joint editor of the *Language Learning Journal* and of *German as a Foreign Language* an online journal available at http//www.gfl-journal.de published three times a year.

Richard Rose is Professor of Special and Inclusive Education and Head of the Centre for Special Needs Education and Research (CeSNER) at University College, Northampton. He has taught in schools in several parts of England, and has held posts as a head teacher and education inspector. Richard has published widely in the field of special education; his most recent works include *Strategies to Promote Inclusive Practice* (RoutledgeFalmer, 2002) and *Encouraging Voices* (Ireland: NDA).

Alexis Taylor is Lecturer in Education at Brunel University, where she is Assistant Head of the Education Department. Prior to this, she held positions of Head of the Religious Education Department and Head of Year in a secondary school in south-west London. She has a doctorate in education and her current research interests include recruitment into initial teacher education; student teacher perceptions of special education; and learning and teaching in initial teacher education.

Tony Turner was, until retirement in September 2000, Senior Lecturer in Education at the Institute of Education, University of London in the Science and Technology Department. He is co-author of *Learning to Teach Science in the Secondary School* (RoutledgeFalmer, 1998) and with colleagues is currently undertaking the revision of that book. He is co-editor of *Learning to Teach in the Secondary School*, 3rd edition (RoutledgeFalmer, 2001) and co-editor of *Starting to Teach in the Secondary School*, 1st edition (RoutledgeFalmer, 1997).

Acknowledgements

The ideas in this book have been influenced by the pupils, student teachers, teachers and teacher-educators with whom we have worked over the years. As it is impossible to thank them all individually, we should like to take this opportunity to acknowledge their influence on our thinking. We also thank our colleagues who have contributed.

We are pleased to have the opportunity to update the first edition of this book to accommodate the new demands of Induction for Newly Qualified Teachers in England in particular. Anna Clarkson from RoutledgeFalmer has provided continuing support and encouragement in the development of the *Learning to Teach in the Secondary School* series of texts, of which this text forms a part.

We wish to thank the publishers for permission to use extracts from A. Howe, *Making Talk Work*, 1992, C. Sutton, *Communicating in the Classroom* (1991) and R. Carter (Ed.), *Knowledge about Language and the Curriculum; The LINC Materials,* 1990, all published by Hodder & Stoughton and reprinted by permission of Hodder Arnold; M. Beveridge, M. Reed and A. Webster, *Managing the Literacy Curriculum,* 1996 (RoutledgeFalmer), reprinted by permission of Taylor & Francis; and N. Ratcliffe, *Issues from the National Writing Project Perceptions in Writing,* 1989/90, reprinted by permission of and published by Nelson Thornes.

Introduction

This book is part of the *Learning to Teach in the Secondary School* series of texts published by RoutledgeFalmer, which are written for teachers in initial teacher education and newly qualified teachers by experienced teachers and teacher-educators. They are intended to provide access to ideas, advice, support and resources for teachers starting out in the profession and may be useful to a wider audience of teachers. This text, *Starting to Teach in the Secondary School*, is intended particularly to support newly qualified teachers moving to their first post in a school.

Teaching is becoming more of a research- and evidence-based profession, but the fundamentals of good teaching remain the same:

- respect and a concern for meeting the individual needs of learners;
- the ability to create learning environments which engage and enthuse pupils and in which learners with particular preferences for learning (e.g. auditory, visual, kinaesthetic) and learners with particular special educational needs can be supported;
- the ability to explain difficult concepts in your subject in different ways to enable learners to understand such concepts;
- an attitude to learning which means that you are prepared to continue learning throughout your professional life;
- an enthusiasm and active interest in your subject and a willingness to share that enjoyment with others.

Technology and the extensive provision of in-school support from adults other than teachers create a working environment not available to previous generations of teachers. The publishing on the web of materials supporting your classroom practice with different types of learners is likely to continue to grow over the coming decades, as is your access to technology in your classroom. The research and evidence base supporting teachers' decisions about how they choose to teach particular topics and how they construct learning environments for children with particular needs can be expected to become stronger as each year passes.

When the first edition of this book was published, the development of the internet for educational purposes was at an embryonic stage. One of the challenges facing new teachers is how to access these proliferating resources and sift the useful from the unsuitable as well as establish which are valid and reliable sources.

The early years of teaching are very demanding as new routines have to be internalised, which in later years enable you to walk into any situation and command the attention of those present.

Young people expect their teachers to demand high standards but this does not stop them from testing you as a teacher new to their school to see what you expect and what you are prepared to do if they do not meet your expectations. A sense of humour and understanding of the challenges faced by adolescents is essential. If coupled with a constant expectation of getting the best from your pupils, a belief in your own authority and your right to create an environment supporting learning in your classroom, these attitudes should help see you through the testing time all teachers new to a school face, whether they are newly qualified or not.

This text is intended to help you as a newly qualified teacher to reflect on your practice in order to improve throughout your induction period. It is designed to support you through these stages of early professional development into a career that must be one of the most rewarding our society offers. The text is designed to support your reflection on your progress and to extend your understanding. For this purpose, each chapter includes reflective tasks and further readings. We also include cross-references to the generic book in the series, *Learning to Teach in the Secondary School*, 3rd edition, where relevant.

Throughout this book we use the term 'pupil' to refer to the learner, although we acknowledge that young learners aged 16 and over are referred to as 'students' and that some 11–18 schools use the term 'students' for all learners.

We wish all the best for your career in education. We welcome feedback about how the next edition of the text can be improved and we can be contacted through the publishers.

Susan Capel
Ruth Heilbronn
Marilyn Leask
Tony Turner

Part I

Being a Teacher

1 From Trainee to Newly Qualified Teacher

Your Immediate Professional Needs

Ruth Heilbronn

As a Newly Qualified Teacher (NQT) you already bring many skills to your new profession from your previous experience and from your initial teacher education. You may be embarking on a period of formal induction training and assessment, with an established induction tutor, or going through your school's in-service training programmes. The foundations you lay down for your professional development will support you throughout your career. As an NQT you should be attached to a mentor who supports you at this stage of development.

In England and Wales all NQTs have to complete a statutory induction period amounting to a school year if full time (or the part-time equivalent) in order to be able to teach in state maintained schools. Some form of support for the induction period is also in place in many countries, for example in most states in the United States of America (USA) and in Australia and New Zealand. At the time of writing, Jersey, Guernsey, the Isle of Man and Gibraltar follow the regulations for England and Wales. Scotland has a two-year probation period and Northern Ireland has an induction stage in their teacher education programme. Qualified Teacher Status (QTS) with Induction in these countries is recognised in England and Wales and vice versa. The requirements to follow these regulations in the countries stipulated will henceforth be referred to as 'statutory induction'.

The statutory induction policy has two main principles:

- a national entitlement for NQTs for support and professional development;
- assessment of NQTs against defined national standards.

The statutory induction period is intended to provide NQTs with a 'bridge' between initial teacher education and the role of an established professional (Department for Education and Employment [DfEE] 1999a, para. 1). Evaluation of the first two years of the policy showed that it has helped NQTs to become more effective teachers in terms of their own feelings of confidence in their growing professional expertise (Department for Education and Skills [DfES] 2002d).

At the end of the statutory induction period NQTs are assessed against induction standards and have to show that they still meet the standards for QTS, which is awarded at the end of the initial teacher education period. These are part of a larger framework of standards which go through the various stages of teaching. They can be viewed on the Teacher Training Agency (TTA) website, which includes a range of support materials (TTA http://www.tta. gov.uk/induction).

Whether you go through a period of statutory induction or not it is essential to understand how to manage your professional development opportunities and to build on them throughout your career. Researchers and experienced mentors have stressed the importance of keeping a balance between professional development for our own growing skills and the assessment function of training programmes (Simco 1995).

This chapter introduces some basic notions relating to your professional development as an NQT and situates this development in the context of your teaching career. It explains how you can work with your induction tutor, or other school-based mentors, to support this development.

OBJECTIVES

By end of this chapter you should understand:

- the importance of the role of professional development and the place of the newly qualified period of training;
- how to work with your induction tutor or mentor to achieve your professional development priorities;
- the role of a Professional Development Portfolio in structuring your development;
- the benefits of reflection and evaluation in this developmental process.

YOUR PROFESSIONAL DEVELOPMENT

As a teacher you exercise your professional judgement many times throughout the school day. The teacher's job is multifaceted and embodies many skills, and a wide grasp of subject knowledge, knowledge about how to teach, and about the pupils. You are constantly learning, which is one of the reasons why many people stay in teaching. As a responsible professional you will keep these skills and knowledge up to date, and extend their range. So being in charge of your own professional development is itself an important skill, to enable you to grow and extend as a teacher. The process you begin at this point will benefit you throughout your career and start you off on the right path, in charge of your own progress. Understanding ways in which development can occur is especially important for you as an NQT, because a great deal of your learning occurs this year, building on what you have already achieved and consolidating and progressing throughout the year. It is advisable to be actively monitoring progress and steering it in a preferred direction.

You may find it helpful initially to read the section 'Transition from student to newly qualified teacher' in *Learning to Teach in the Secondary School*, 3rd edition, as a way of thinking through some issues of induction and support in your new post. It might be helpful to think about some of the phases you might go through during your first full year of teaching, and beyond. These might be:

- *Early idealism*: strong identification with pupils; idealism and the rejection of the image of the older cynical teacher.
- *Survival*: shock at the reality of the classroom environment – the complexity of the situation is overwhelming, and both individual pupils and many lessons are a blur. Resort to the quick fix and tips for teachers approach to development, which provides some respite from the constant demands on the teacher's knowledge, judgement and sympathy.
- *Recognising difficulties*: an awareness of the difficulties and their causes; an appreciation of the limitations of what teachers can do to alter situations; over-concern, but an understandable concern, about personal performance; the question uppermost in the teachers mind is 'Will I make it?'.
- *Reaching a plateau*: beginning to cope with the teaching situation and achieving some success; anxious to establish routines which work and a growing resistance to trying new things; success has been earned and the teacher does not wish to upset routines and behaviours which work; the focus is on successful management, less on pupil learning.
- *Moving on*: a recognition of the need to pay more attention to the quality of pupil learning – without support and intervention by successful, experienced teachers this process may not blossom. If unsupported there is a danger of 'burn out' by committed teachers trying to cope alone, or of the 'moving on' grinding to a halt.

(Adapted from Maynard and Furlong 1995: 12–13)

This support is vital and can be gained from experienced teachers in the school. You can also do a great deal to help yourself, and this chapter aims to give you some ideas in this direction.

WORKING WITH YOUR INDUCTION TUTOR OR MENTOR

One essential element of support will be your work with an experienced mentor. If you are working in one of the schools which follows the statutory induction regulations referred to above, an induction tutor supports and assesses your progress throughout the induction period. The precise recommendations are laid out in Circular 90/2000 (DfEE 2000) (available online at http://www.dfes.gov.uk/).

There are also books which can help both you and the school to understand your entitlement and responsibilities if you are undertaking statutory induction, (e.g. Bubb 2001 and Bleach 2000). We recommend that you gain a clear understanding of the whole process so as to achieve the maximum benefit from this crucial period. The Teachernet website has good links for useful information on induction (available online at http://www.teachernet. gov.uk/). This site is also useful for any new teacher going through a probationary period or just wanting tips and advice.

Briefly, statutory induction should comprise:

- a 10 per cent lighter teaching timetable than other teachers in the school;
- a job description that doesn't make unreasonable demands;
- meetings with your school 'induction tutor' (mentor), including half-termly reviews of progress;
- an individualised programme of support, monitoring and assessment;
- objectives, informed by strengths and areas for development identified in the Career Entry Development Profile, for you to meet the induction standards;
- at least one observation of your teaching each half term with oral and written feedback;
- an assessment meeting and report at the end of each term that is sent to the local education authority (LEA) which acts as the regulatory 'Appropriate Body'; procedures to air grievances at school and at Appropriate Body level.

You may also be able to draw on the following whole school support:

- a school induction programme in which you and other NQTs share experiences and/or receive in-service support;
- a self-help support system for NQTs in your school or in the local area – you may have to organise this yourself;
- an in-service programme for NQTs run by the LEA;
- in-service courses for NQTs run by the local higher education institution – some courses may be free if associated with initial teacher education partnership arrangements.

We use the title 'induction tutor' to refer to the formal role for support and assessment as outlined in Circular 90/2000 (DfES 2000). However, the need for an experienced guide or mentor to act as both support and assessor is crucial throughout your period as an NQT, whether or not you are undergoing a period of statutory induction. Precisely who this person is varies from school to school. The role may be taken by the officially designated induction tutor, or another member of staff, with the induction tutor being in charge of the formal aspects of monitoring overall provision and overseeing the assessment process.

It is very important that you sort out from the beginning of your NQT period who will take these various roles, if they are taken by more than person. What should be common to all the titles is the underlying process of mentoring. Your professional relationship with the primary mentor, whatever his or her title, is essential. One feature of that relationship is openness. As an NQT, you should examine your capacity to ask for, and your willingness to receive, advice. We suggest that you also think beyond the person designated as your primary mentor and think about how you can develop a network of support from within the school and from within your department, from peers across the school.

Previous NQTs have said that the whole school culture has a great impact on their development. Schools with successful induction practice had a shared understanding and ethos of a learning environment for all staff and pupils. Where schools were supportive, NQTs recognised the input of a variety of staff: for example, one secondary NQT talked about receiving 'invaluable support' from heads of year over behaviour issues. A primary NQT said 'the whole staff' helped her. Several NQTs explained how the staff as a whole, together with good LEA support, can make for a positive induction experience (Heilbronn et al. 2002: 383). These schools have a 'learning culture' and induction is an integral part of the wider professional development of all members of staff. Research continues on what constitutes an effective professional learning community (EPLC) and the relationship between the EPLC and the other areas of learning, e.g. work–based, informal and continuous professional development. McMahon *et al.* (2002) have pointed out that 'interest in the concept of a professional leaning community and its perceived importance stem from the belief that when teachers work collaboratively the quality of learning and teaching in the organisation improves'. Such a community has 'the capacity to sustain the learning of all professionals and other staff with the collective purpose of enhancing pupil learning' (McMahon *et al.* 2002).

It is worth remembering to draw on the expertise within the whole school and to seek out advice because ultimately your progress depends on your taking initiative for your own development. You have experienced the support of a mentor, or designated tutor, during your initial teacher education course. Clearly, as you are now a qualified teacher, this new relationship ought to be different as you take more responsibility for your own development and are more proactive in identifying and setting targets and drawing up agendas for meetings with your induction tutor/mentor. In the following comments we use the term 'mentor' to refer to the primary support and assessment role, with the understanding that this role is usually, although not always, taken by an induction tutor.

It is both your responsibility and that of your mentor to direct your attention to areas of strength and weakness and to ensure that progression in teaching takes place. Importantly, your mentor should ensure that you increase your understanding of pupil learning, which is at the heart of good teaching. Nevertheless, you should have a stronger and more active role in setting the agenda as the year progresses. In addition, as your concerns as a NQT move beyond subject work and look to wider school involvement, questions about your pastoral role and other professional skills and knowledge required by a teacher arise and should be examined and discussed (see also Chapter 4).

We turn now to ways in which you can work with your mentor. It is essential that this role is clearly defined. Inevitably, a mentor has more than one function, one of which is to assess your progress. Some roles of mentors are listed in Reflective Task 1.1. It is important that you establish quite early on what you can expect in terms of patterns of meetings, how frequently they can take place, at what time, where and for how long. The length of time of such meetings is less important than the focus and purpose of them.

Earlier in this chapter, the question of openness was mentioned. If possible, try to insist you meet in a *quiet place* in which free and open discussion can take place and, in addition, where you can be reasonably free of interruption. If you can set aside at least 30 minutes a week for such a meeting you should have time to talk through developmental issues, provided the purpose of the meeting is clear. You are likely to need more time at different periods. You need to set an *agenda* in consultation with your mentor and for both of you to know what each expects of the other. It may require you to bring material, for example related to your lessons, or an evaluation of a week's lessons with a class. On the other hand, your mentor may wish to report on lessons which she or he has observed and so a report is required in duplicate for discussion. Ideally, such a report should be given to you in advance. Other issues for discussion should be identified. Statutory induction procedures lay down what should happen in formal meetings for review and assessment and the content of the meetings (DfEE 2000). These procedures are important, but so are the ongoing mentor meetings, which should take place regularly.

At the end of the meeting, any agreed action should be recorded so that both you and your mentor know what needs to be done next. A set of notes arising from the meeting, comprising a short record of what was talked about, what was agreed and proposed action is helpful to you, both as a reminder and a record of events. In a formal induction programme this must be recorded and advice on how to do this can be found on the TTA website at the end of this chapter.

Reflective task 1.1
What is your mentor to you?

Identify words from the list below that:

1   represent the role you wish your mentor to take on;
2   do not describe the relationship you want with your mentor;
3   need discussion with your mentor;
4   are missing and you wish to raise with your mentor.

colleague	guide	appraiser
protector	motivator	teacher
consultant	assessor	listener
helper	diagnoser	trusted guide
reviewer	facilitator	counsellor
expert	challenger	critical friend

Discuss with your mentor the ways in which she can respond to your needs and promote your development. Remember, your mentor has a responsibility to you, to the school and to the profession.

During the early weeks and months in your first post, there are a number of issues that may be prominent; one such issue is behaviour management (Chapter 7). In such a case, you may wish to discuss the ways in which you deal with particular situations or individuals. Whereas your induction tutor/mentor may know very well the general context of the class you describe, you should come prepared to discuss the details of the problem (see Reflective Task 1.2).

Reflective task 1.2
Preparing for a meeting with your induction tutor/mentor

Identify a class with which you have particular issues, either in general management terms or with individuals. List briefly:

• the behaviours to which you object;
• the lesson plan, activities and demands on the pupils;
• any action you have taken and the results of that action;
• evaluations you have of lessons with this class made by you, a colleague or head of department;
• any factors in your teaching which may contribute to the situation;
• any special information you have about pupils in the class that could contribute to the events;
• action you propose to take which could be used as a basis for discussion.

LESSON OBSERVATION

For many NQTs issues to do with pupil learning and progression soon emerge. Indeed, if progress in teaching is to be achieved, it is on aspects of pupil learning that attention must soon focus. These concerns include assessment and recording, the appropriate use of language and ensuring access to the material in the lessons by most pupils. These issues may be met, in part, by a consideration of the teaching methods adopted and your willingness to try out and apply a range of methods. All or some of these concerns may be made the focus of a session with your induction tutor/mentor.

Solutions to these concerns may be identified by observation of your lessons to see how you are tackling them. Lesson observation is one of the key mechanisms though which a new teacher can learn to improve practice, and this includes both lessons where you observe experienced teachers and those where you are being observed. Recent research questioned a range of professionals, induction tutors, NQTs, headteachers and personnel in local authority professional development roles about what constituted effective induction practices. Most of the NQTs questioned found being observed and receiving feedback very useful for their professional development. One said: 'It's vital. It's so informative having someone watch you teach because you can't see everything and sometimes you don't see what you do well, as well as the things you need to develop.' Another said, 'I love showing my kids off as well … I choose my lowest sets … It raises their own self-esteem and it makes me feel really proud of them' (DfES 2002d: 94).

So a key role of your mentor is to monitor your teaching, partly through observing your lessons. You should agree in advance which lessons are observed. Bear in mind that your mentor is a busy person and timetable restrictions exclude some options. In addition, it helps both your development and your observer's task if you both agree in advance what is the focus of observation and agree how the observation will be recorded. The examples shown above in Reflective Tasks 1.1 and 1.2 indicate the type of shared context useful for discussion between you and your mentor. The data direct your discussions and provide you with a focus for professional development. You should seek ways to deepen the discussion by selective use of the current literature, e.g. education journals, the *Times Educational Supplement* and publications by your subject association, textbooks, etc. See, for example, 'Further Reading' at the end of this chapter.

PROFESSIONAL DEVELOPMENT PORTFOLIO

One very useful way to focus your development is to keep a professional development portfolio (PDP). You may already have a profile or a portfolio from your initial teacher education and this can form a good basis for further development in the NQT year. Towards the end of the year it can also document and support an increasing engagement with research and theory (see Chapter 6). The nature of schools and teachers is such that teachers engage in developmental work all the time. Some teachers are better than others at recognising their worth and presenting others with evidence. Everything teachers do in school is important and so is much of what is done out of school, since schools employ the whole person, e.g. your out-of-school activities and interests add to your repertoire of skills, on which you draw without any conscious planning. Having a specific place to file and demonstrate documents related to the totality of your own personal career makes you more reflective, and this in turn is a good thing. The opportunity to reflect on your development as a teacher is not a mere public relations tool for the career opportunities you may wish to map out, although career development is important. The major advantage of working with a portfolio is to support your work in schools.

Your PDP will be a structured collection of evidence of your work and critical reflections on that evidence. These two strands are both important. Collecting evidence is important at all stages of your professional life and of course if you are undergoing statutory induction you need to keep evidence to show that you have achieved the induction standards. Your PDP can be very useful, for example, if you are applying for a post of responsibility or moving schools, and for any process of review. It is a working document which needs to be constantly updated and revised.

The process of developing and updating your PDP has the following advantages. It:

- stimulates the collection of evidence about your teaching and research accomplishments and provides this evidence;
- promotes reflection about early teaching and other professional experiences;
- encourages discussion about teaching and professional activities with peers, department, year teams, key stage teams, etc.;
- stimulates thinking about a philosophy of teaching and a developmental or research agenda;
- assists in job applications;
- provides evidence of commitment to teaching, by articulating the principles and practice of teachers' work.

There is a strong underlying element of self-evaluation and reflection in the creation and upkeep of a PDP and much of the evidence you select for it is self-generated. If you are undergoing statutory induction in England and Wales you should document your progress against the induction standards. It therefore makes sense to incorporate references to them in the portfolio. Later in your career, when engaging in any form of professional review, it will prove extremely useful to have a wide range of evidence available, generated from yourself and others, without having to gather any of it especially for the purposes of the review. If updating and reassessing professional performance happens routinely at convenient intervals (possibly half-termly), the material in the PDP will have been selected within the context in which it arose and the statements in it will be relevant to the material illustrated. The task at review is then one of selection only. This is why it is important to use the portfolio as a working document and to keep updating it.

WHERE ARE YOU NOW?

If you are undertaking statutory induction you have reflected on where you are now, at the end of your initial teacher education, and have completed the first section of the Career Entry Development Profile (CEDP). It is published by the TTA, and information is available on the organisation's website (full details of the website and specific pages are printed at the end of this chapter).

The TTA website gives information on how the profile is designed, to give structured guidance at 'key milestones' in your professional development: towards the end of initial education and at the beginning and end of your induction period. The CEDP refers to these periods as 'Transition Points', and provides guidance to help teachers 'to make constructive connections between these points'. The CEDP is designed to be a flexible working document that can be used with other professional records. You take this record to your first post to consider alongside the Induction Standards, England and Wales, and the demands of your new post, in setting professional development objectives for your induction period. As soon as possible, you should share your CEDP with your induction tutor and your headteacher.

How will your PDP show your progress from your initial education year?

Teaching is a complex activity and classrooms are places where multiple interactions, interpretations and responses occur. The PDP is a vehicle for identifying and understanding key aspects of this activity. The portfolio should aim to capture significant aspects of teaching and learning in the NQT year and to record and analyse 'critical moments' in your development as a teacher. It should indicate your effectiveness as a teacher in the widest sense, in terms of pupil learning, thus providing evidence of professional teaching competence. This evidence includes:

1   the broadening and deepening of subject knowledge, by teaching new curriculum topics/areas, age groups or to meet particular pupil needs according to the phases taught;
2   pedagogic knowledge, exemplified by your development of resources or long-term planning, which show how you turn your subject knowledge into teaching and learning material, and into learning activities which can be assessed;
3   deeper understanding of pupils' learning, and how to recognise the complexities of pupil development in a variety of ways, by identifying aspects of their progress – you could draw on the wide body of research related to learning theory, some of which forms the basis of the English Key Stage 3 strategy (see Chapter 5).
4   evidence of a wider contribution to pupils' learning and development beyond the classroom;
5   engagement in research and scholarship (see Chapter 15);
6   evidence of meeting the induction standards in England and Wales – this includes the format required by the regulations, such as the CEDP and Developmental Record, which will form a part of your wider PDP.

What could go in the PDP?

The portfolio will contain items which you contribute and which come from other colleagues or sources. You could provide:

- an index and dividers, labelled and numbered, to make the portfolio easy to use;
- a reflective Teaching Statement;
- evidence of your wider teaching role, e.g. pastoral responsibilities, contact with parents, cross-curricular work, citizenship, etc.;
- your selection of further material which illustrates professional development,

including a copy of your CEP documentation if available, and a revised CV;
*   reports from the termly statutory induction assessment meetings if you are undertaking statutory induction in England and Wales.

Other staff could give you:

*   summaries of lessons they have observed;
*   statements from colleagues about activities such as pastoral work, team planning etc. in which you have been jointly engaged;
*   curriculum development and research reports where you have been involved;
*   pupil statements or evaluations which show their response to your teaching or other input and initiatives;
*   review statements by mentors;
*   videotapes and photographs of key teaching or other episodes;
*   evidence of attendance at induction meetings, content and participation; lectures/talks given to their groups of NQTs/teachers.

Reflection and evaluation

A process of review and reflection is essential to successful learning. This is based on the same principles which you apply to your own pupils' learning, when you make sure that they have time to absorb and consolidate their learning. David Kolb (1985) has identified a learning cycle, which is reproduced in Figure 1.1 (see also p. 246 of *Learning to Teach in the Secondary School*, 3rd edition, in which the topic is discussed)

A model of practice-based learning which fits with this learning cycle is that of the reflective practitioner: that is, one who undertakes 'reflection on action' (Schon 1995). One of the foundations of this learning is understanding the processes involved. This is apparent when considering pupil learning. An example might be the rationale for the good practice of sharing the learning objectives of each lesson with the pupils, which

Figure 1.1   Kolb's experiential learning circle (1985)

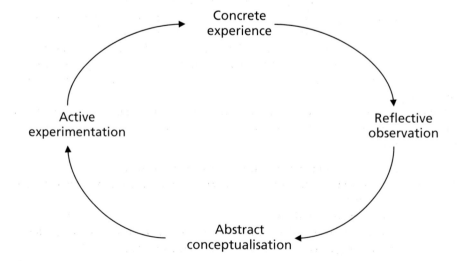

means telling pupils what they should be able to do or show to demonstrate their achievement (see also Chapter 8). The same process applies to your own professional development, as some writers have pointed out well (Joyce and Showers 1995). In terms of your NQT year, you should evaluate your work within your own learning cycle, which means that you start with your own teaching practice and with the help of your mentor reflect on that practice, in some of the ways suggested above. This process enables you to evaluate aspects of your practice, and this in turn forms the foundation of a new application. In other words, you teach a group again, or develop a topic, or try new behaviour management strategies. This new application stems from your guided and critical reflection on your own practice and in turn leads to further understandings and the development of your skills and knowledge about teaching and learning. (See also 'the active learning model' in *Learning to Teach in a Secondary School*, 3rd edition, p. 256.)

The reflective teaching statement

As part of the process of reflection and critical evaluation of your work you should be able to articulate your understanding of the role of the teacher and give a reflective account of it, which includes the professional values underlying it. Personal statements are increasingly required as part of job or promotion applications so it is useful to have one updated in the portfolio. In addition, the statement helps you to focus on your own strengths and developmental needs. We suggest that you revisit it each term to provide a focus for evaluation and reflection. If you decide to make changes the new statement will take the place of the former one and you can incorporate your development in such terms as 'during the term I developed from …'.

The statement explains how you have developed over the year and may refer to 'critical incidents' and evolving understandings of the role of the teacher, which form the basis of detailed analysis elsewhere in the portfolio. It should include how your views of the teacher's role have developed. You may give particular examples of how the teaching methods you typically use reflect that interpretation of your role as a teacher, and how your teaching methods have been modified in response to changes in pupils, course materials, curriculum changes and other factors such as your better understanding of pupils' needs.

After discussing the questions in Reflective Task 1.3 with your mentor or a colleague, try to write the reflective teaching statement and put it in your PDP.

Remember to revisit your reflective teaching statement and to amend it at intervals. It can be very useful as a baseline to view your own development. When you review the statement you could ask yourself what has changed and what has not and if you can see progress in your development.

If you are involved in statutory induction your reflective teaching statement could go in the PDP alongside your references and statements about the induction standards and you could include:

- specific objectives from review meetings which you have met;
- the termly statutory induction assessment objectives report, together with any supporting material;
- feedback/lesson observations;
- feedback on professional development activities e.g. in-service training (INSET) courses, planning meetings, observations of colleagues etc.;

Reflective task 1.3
Writing your reflective
teaching statement

It is a good idea to work with another teacher or with your mentor to discuss your statement, since the process of discussion creates meanings and shared understandings. As you revisit the statement at each key stage (possibly termly) you can reconsider some of the areas, so that by the end of the year you are able to show your own progress by assessing how far you have achieved the goals you set yourself at the beginning. Write down brief answers to the following questions:

1 *Your teaching goals:* What are your priorities at the beginning of the year?
2 *Your subject knowledge*: How do you intend to maintain, broaden or deepen it? It is useful to think in the short and medium term here.
3 *Your views on pupil motivation, pupil learning*: What is your understanding of its importance and how might you influence it?
4 *Your relationships with pupils* as groups and individually and with the wider school community: How do you view them? Why?
5 *Assessment*: What interests you in differing approaches to assessment?
6 *Your personal and professional values*: How do they relate to your sense of vocation as a teacher?
7 *Scholarly activity*: How have your understandings been informed by your readings, etc.?

- reports from colleagues and reflective responses to these;
- objectives for continuing professional development.

It is important to collect material for the PDP throughout your NQT year, as its great strength is the use you can make of it to structure your reflections on your own progress and development.

SUMMARY

The chapter asked you to consider phases and models of teacher development and identified the reflective practitioner model as one which offers you the opportunity to gain insights into your own teaching performance. In practice, of course, different teachers develop their teaching in different ways useful to themselves and, more importantly, in direct response to the needs of their pupils. The guidance and support of an experienced mentor are essential to your progress. Your commitment to reviewing and assessing your own progress at key intervals is also extremely important. Keeping a PDP and updating your reflective teaching statement can help you to do this effectively. Your NQT year is an important one in your teaching career and you will be making a difference to the learning of your pupils as well as contributing to your school. An induction teacher in the research quoted earlier said of her NQTs:

In the vast majority of cases, they're young people who are enthusiastic, enjoy their work, and you know I find it very refreshing and I learn from watching them. I think this is the thing that's perhaps surprising, an experienced teacher can go and watch an NQT and still pick up some tricks.

(Heilbronn *et al.* 2002: 381)

So bear in mind, while you are undergoing the steep learning curve of the first year of teaching, that your contribution can be a very valuable one to your school.

FURTHER READING

Bubb, S., Heilbronn, R., Jones, C., Totterdell, M., Bailey, M. (2002) *Improving Induction: Research-based Best Practice for Schools.* London and New York: RoutledgeFalmer. A book addressed to the school senior management team and induction tutors which outlines best practice for ensuring good quality training and professional development for NQTs undertaking induction. Based on DfES research (DfES 2002d).

Kelly, T. and Mayes, A. (1995) *Issues in Mentoring.* London: Routledge. This book is addressed to teachers, educators, student teachers and NQTs. It is a collection of short essays focusing on teacher development in initial teacher education, induction and staff development.

Watkins, C. and Whalley, C. (1993) *Mentoring Close Up: Resources for School-based Development.* Harlow: Longman. This collection of resources is designed to support teacher development in schools. It is of direct interest to mentors and NQTs, providing models of learning and development. It is a source of many and varied activities.

Professional development support for newly qualified teachers is available from the following sites:

Department for Education and Skills (DfES) http://www.dfes.gov.uk.

General Teaching Council (GTC) http://www.gtce.org.uk.

Teacher Training Agency (TTA) http://www.tta.gov.uk/induction.

Teachernet http://www.teachernet.gov.uk/professionaldevelopment/opportunities/nqt/induction/newinductionstandards.

2 Managing Yourself and your Workload

Susan Capel and Ahmad Al-Mohannadi

This chapter is not meant to scare you. However, teaching is a challenging profession and it is likely that you will feel stressed at some point – either during your newly qualified teacher (NQT) year or later in your career. You will not be alone, as many teachers experience stress at some point (see, for example, Burke *et al.*, 1996; Dunham, 1994; Gold and Roth, 1993; Hart and Hurd, 2000; Mills, 1995; Phillips, 1993; Schamer and Jackson, 1996). There are many causes of stress:

> Teachers complete paperwork, prepare for their classes, plan and prepare for future instruction, evaluate students, remain up-to-date in their teaching areas and maintain their instructional programmes. They regularly encounter both positive and negative interactions with students, colleagues, school administrators, support staff, parents and other community members.
>
> Adams, 2001: 223

One of the major stressors is workload and insufficient time in which to do everything that needs to be done.

A stressed teacher is unlikely to teach effectively and this can impact on pupils' learning. It is also worth remembering that pupils can be stressed too, e.g. when they are learning new or difficult material, and a stressed teacher may increase their stress, which may further impact on their learning. Therefore, it is important not to add to pupils' stress through your own. Although we do not address pupils' stress in this chapter, it should help you to recognise stress in pupils and enable you to help them manage that stress.

What is stress? Some stress is positive – we all need a certain amount of pressure to perform effectively – but too much or too little can result in negative effects. Today, reference to stress is generally negative, and when we talk about stress in teachers we are usually referring to too much pressure with which the teacher cannot cope effectively.

This chapter provides information about the causes, symptoms and ways of managing stress, which should allow you to develop mechanisms appropriate for you. It then considers in detail one cause of stress, that of not using your time effectively, and identifies some techniques to enable you to manage your time to best advantage, both at work and at home. It is important to be aware of stress and to take steps to reduce, alleviate and/or cope with it from the beginning of your career. Learning to manage your stress, your workload and your time early on will stand you in good stead throughout your career.

OBJECTIVES

By the end of this chapter you should understand:

- what causes stress;
- symptoms of stress and ways of managing it;
- reasons why you might not be managing your time effectively and how this can be improved.

STRESS

Who is likely to become stressed?

Whether or not you experience stress depends on a number of factors, including your past experiences, your perception of the current situation and your expectations. However, some groups of teachers are more likely to be stressed than others. For example, a study by Griffith *et al.* (1999) found that younger teachers were more likely to feel stressed, perhaps because at the beginning of their career they had not learned how to cope with working conditions. Woods (1989) suggested that there are four groups of teachers more vulnerable to experiencing stress:

- probationary and inexperienced teachers, for they have not yet learned how to cope with the dilemmas and contradictions [of teaching];
- teachers who lack knowledge and understanding ... of such things as pupils' culture ...;
- teachers who find it difficult ... to 'orchestrate' their teaching; and
- senior teachers, such as heads and deputies, who are in the position of greatest role conflict.

(Woods, 1989: 95)

Conscientious, enthusiastic, highly committed teachers are often idealistic and think they can 'change the world'. However, if teachers are unrealistic about what they can achieve, they may work very long hours and place unreasonable demands on themselves, trying to do as much as they can for the pupils. This could mean spending much free time at school trying to help individual pupils and taking on extra-curricular activities which may result in doing most of their planning, marking and other work at home in the evenings and at weekends. They may make a list of jobs to do before the next day but, not having set a time limit for each job, spend longer on each job than expected. They may not set a time for finishing work in the evening, irrespective of how much they have done, and continue to do 'just one more thing'. As a result, they often do not make time for themselves after they have completed the jobs on the list and, by the time they have worked through the list, they are so tired that they just fall into bed. They can get into a cycle of doing more and more work, as they repeat this pattern night after night. Consequently, they may be more prone to stress than teachers who are realistic about what they can and cannot achieve. These more realistic teachers appreciate that they cannot put everything right and cannot 'change the world'. Therefore, although they work hard, they set a time limit to the amount of work they do outside their directed time and take time off from work for themselves and their families.

Which of these teachers are you? Are you realistic about what you can achieve? As a conscientious, enthusiastic, highly committed NQT you are especially vulnerable to stress. You should be aware of the increased possibility of stress if you do not take time off work for yourself and your family (whilst, of course, continuing to work hard – we are not discouraging you from that). You therefore need to consider possible causes of stress for you.

Reflective task 2.1
Managing your stress

In this reflective task, complete each point as you read the relevant section of the chapter. You might also like to return to it when you are experiencing stress to help you to think through its cause and possible solutions.

- Are you realistic about what you can achieve as a teacher or do you expect to 'change the world'? What does being realistic mean to you?
- What, if any, are the causes of stress for you at the moment? (If they are new, what has changed to make this a cause of stress?)
- If you do feel some stress, what are the symptoms? Is this impacting on your teaching and/or your pupils' learning?

Discuss with your mentor and/or another person the causes of stress, what you can do to address these causes of stress and what strategies you can put in place to help you to manage your stress.

What causes stress?

Some causes of stress arise outside education and the job, e.g. at home or in the family. Other causes are integral to the education system, but outside the school and classroom, such as the pace of change in education, changing societal attitudes towards education and authority. Many teachers feel under great pressure because of constant changes and demands on their time and resources. Travers and Cooper (1996), for example, reported the five top sources of stress for teachers in England to be problematic changes: lack of support from central government; constant change within the profession; lack of information as to how changes are to be implemented; diminishing social respect for teaching; the move towards the National Curriculum. Another aspect of teaching which has been identified (e.g. Ferguson et al., 1999; Scanlon, 1999) as being stressful is Office for Standards in Education (OFSTED) inspection, with 'post-OFSTED blues' occurring immediately afterwards: with feelings of inspection, exhaustion, burnout, lack of motivation and depression.

Being part of an organisation, such as a school, may itself contribute to stress, especially if you perceive that parts of the organisation are not working effectively. Some aspects of the work environment are more likely than others to contribute to stress, e.g. poor work practices, lack of communication, having to work too long hours because of unrealistic demands of work or insufficient time to enable you to complete the tasks required (Hart *et al.*, 1995; Proctor, 1994; Tollan, 1990). As a result, you may feel confused or misunderstand what you have to do and, as a result, become frustrated and stressed. In a school without a supportive ethos, stress is generally seen to be the 'fault' of an incompetent teacher, whereas in a school with a co-operative, supportive environment, stress is generally seen as everyone's responsibility, and therefore a teacher can admit to having problems and other staff can offer support.

In addition, teaching itself is stressful and stress can result directly from your work in the classroom. Renshaw (1997) identified that teachers tend to work under constraints of mental and emotional demands. Working with individual pupils with different needs and demands is very intense and emotionally demanding and is therefore likely to be stressful. A fundamental skill for teachers is to be able to maintain control in their classes. Many teachers indicate their main cause of anxiety as being unable to maintain discipline, especially if they know there are disruptive pupils in their classes. Dealing with difficult pupils can result in conflict, causing the teacher to become frustrated, nervous, tense, anxious, angry or depressed, all of which can result in stress. For further information see Chapter 6 about improving the effectiveness of your teaching and Unit 3.3 in *Learning to Teach in the Secondary School*, 3rd edition, about managing classroom behaviour.

Factors identified as major causes of stress by several authors (including Brown and Ralph, 2002; Capel, 1992; D'Arcy, 1989; Kyriacou, 1989, 2001; Vandenberghe and Huberman, 1999) include:

- poor leadership; incompetent management and/or administration;
- poor communication, including lack of effective consultation and not being involved in decision-making about work you do;
- poor relationships, including weak interpersonal relationships with superiors; inadequate feedback from, or disagreement with, a supervisor; little support from, or poor relationships with, colleagues;
- feeling that other people direct your life (external locus of control), rather than feeling that you direct your own life (internal locus of control);
- a school climate which makes it difficult to admit to suffering from stress;
- poor working conditions; financial constraints; lack of educational resources; overcrowded classrooms;
- time pressure and workload, including the amount/demands of administrative work; lack of control over the pace of work;
- large classes; lack of time to spend with individual pupils;
- role conflict; role ambiguity (e.g. lack of clear objectives); role overload;
- inadequate training for the job;
- self-esteem and status; lack of recognition for extra work;
- personal perceptions and feelings, including coping with innovation and change;
- relationships with parents and the wider community; teacher-pupil relations;
- teaching pupils who are not motivated; pupils' poor attitude to work; discipline problems, resulting in constant monitoring of pupils' behaviour; physical and verbal abuse;
- being evaluated by others.

On the other hand, having too little to do, hence having too little pressure, can also be stressful, especially if the person feels that their skills and abilities are not being used fully or properly or they are stagnating (we are sure this latter situation does not apply to you as an NQT). However, in either case, performance at work is likely to suffer if a teacher is stressed.

The person–environment fit theory considers stress to be an interaction between the person and the environment. A mismatch between a teacher and school and/or job causes stress. A mismatch may be long term. For instance, if you find yourself in a job for which you are not qualified, because the job description at interview was different from that in practice (e.g. you are teaching outside your subject area), or if you do not agree with the way the school is organised or its ethos. One NQT reported how the working environment contributed to her stress. In her initial teacher education course she was placed in a school considered to be 'tough', but the management strategies in the school supported her in dealing with problems which arose and, consequently, she was not stressed. However, in her first teaching post she reported feeling that she was 'fighting a losing battle' as she was not supported in dealing with problems which arose. She left this post because of the school ethos and because her expectations were different from those of the management. Despite having much more work to do, she reports being much happier and less stressed in her second post.

On the other hand, a mismatch may occur as circumstances change within a school (e.g. a new headteacher, change of circumstances of the teacher), which may be long or short term. Alternatively, the mismatch may be transitory/temporary, e.g. you disagree or have had an argument with a colleague, are dealing with a difficult pupil or aggressive parent, or have to give an assembly for the first time. Although they were writing about teachers in universities, Blix *et al.* (1994) considered the ideal work situation to be one where there is a good fit between the needs of the person and the rewards available from the job.

Different factors can cause a mismatch for different people. The main sources of stress for any individual teacher are unique to that teacher and depend on the interaction between values, personality, skills and circumstances, and the environment. Also, the same teacher may respond to causes of stress and cope with stress differently at different times. Thus, the extent to which you experience stress depends on a number of factors. It is important that you identify whether you have a good fit with the environment in which you are working or whether there is a mismatch. If the situation causing you stress can be identified, it is possible for you to take action. Therefore, try to identify what is causing the mismatch and what action needs to be taken to achieve a good fit. This may mean changing the situation, anticipating problems to prevent them happening or learning to cope in a situation which cannot be changed.

How does your stress show itself?

Just as there are different causes of stress for different people so there are different symptoms. When you are stressed you are unlikely to cope effectively with yourself, your colleagues and your work. Your teaching and your pupils' learning may be adversely affected and there may be an impact on your life outside work, e.g. you may lack motivation to go out.

Many of the symptoms of stress are those which traditionally have prepared the body for the 'flight or fight' response associated with physical danger, e.g. increased heart rate, respiration and perspiration; increased adrenalin in the system; burning sugar more quickly to provide the energy needed to deal with the situation. These responses may not be appropriate in the classroom where you cannot take flight or fight. In such a situation, therefore, you cannot always release the tension created by stress and must learn to cope with it. This may lead to other unpleasant symptoms in the short term, which, if you do not deal with them, could lead to more serious consequences in the longer term. Thus, stress is potentially debilitating. Some of the other symptoms, identified by a number of authors, including Eskridge and Coker (1985); Farber (1984a) include:

- talking too much;
- losing interest in everyday activities or giving up your hobbies or not spending time with friends;
- always being exhausted;
- not being able to sleep or wanting to sleep too much;
- smoking, drinking or taking more medication than usual;
- having frequent headaches or colds;
- having problems with digestion;
- increased blood pressure or cholesterol levels;
- being depressed;
- mood swings;
- lowered tolerance for frustration;
- suspiciousness;
- paranoia;
- responding irrationally;
- frequently being impatient, getting angry, or short tempered or feeling increased irritability;
- often crying;
- loss of caring for others;
- feelings of helplessness;
- lack of control;
- greater professional risk taking;
- ineffective and inefficient in professional role.

It should be noted that the cause of many of these symptoms may be other than stress, so you should check whether there are other causes.

How your stress affects pupils

Your stress may be communicated to pupils both directly and indirectly, mainly through you showing anxiety and your teaching performance being negatively affected. When you are stressed your teaching is less effective: for example, your thinking may be confused; you may hesitate before making a decision; you may give hurried, hesitant or imprecise instructions; use inappropriate or ineffective teaching and management strategies; and be less flexible in your teaching. Your pupils may therefore be unsure about what they have to do, which may cause them stress and anxiety. Mancini *et al.* (1982) found that teachers who are stressed are less likely to praise pupils, are less ready to accept pupils' ideas and actions and interact less with pupils. Their pupils are actively engaged in class activities less often, accumulate less academic learning time and are therefore less successful and effective in what they are trying to achieve. These pupils may become disruptive. Therefore, the behaviour of teachers who are stressed tends to encourage behaviour from pupils which the teacher cannot manage and is trying to avoid. This further increases teacher stress, resulting in loss of confidence and lowered self-esteem, and negatively affecting teaching performance, creating a downward spiral from which it is difficult to escape. Thus, just when you need to be able to meet the demands placed on you, stress can reduce your ability to meet them effectively.

HOW CAN YOU COPE WITH YOUR STRESS?

If you can, it is better to prevent stress than to deal with its effects after the event. However, you are bound to feel stressed sometimes. It is therefore important that you recognise the symptoms of stress, which can enable you to take action early to relieve it. However, it is important also to realise that if you cannot deal with your stress alone there is help available, within the school and outside.

Effective classroom management techniques

Effective classroom management enables you to prevent some problems arising, thereby reducing one possible cause of stress. Specific techniques vary from teacher to teacher. You have learnt many 'tricks of the trade' as a student teacher to make the task more manageable, e.g. developing a routine for entry to and exit from the classroom. As you gain further experience of teaching you learn what to expect and should be able to organise yourself and manage your class more effectively. During your first year of teaching you should therefore concentrate on further refining your classroom management techniques (see Chapter 7).

Other techniques to help you cope with stress

Many techniques have been identified to help you prevent or alleviate stress. Some of these aim to reduce the cause of the stress, others to enable you to cope better. Some coping techniques identified frequently by various authors (e.g. Borg and Falzon, 1990; Cockburn, 1996; and in *Learning to Teach in the Secondary School*, 3rd edition) are listed below.

- *Generally keep your planning under control.* Plan ahead, prioritise and prepare for stressful situations when you are not under pressure, e.g. prepare lessons before the day on which you are teaching them.
- *Actively prepare for, rehearse and practise a problematic situation,* e.g. prepare a lesson more thoroughly than normal for a class which is causing you anxiety. Anticipate scenarios for difficulties which may arise and strategies for managing them. Rehearse and role play these to develop a repertoire of responses available at your fingertips and/or visualise what you can do to overcome the problem. This helps you to focus on the problem, and rehearse how you are going to cope.
- *Develop effective classroom management techniques,* e.g. establish routines so that you can do things automatically, particularly when you are tired (see Chapter 7).

- *Make time for your own reflection to enable you to evaluate what has happened.* Recognise your own limitations and try to develop your strengths as well as your weaknesses.
- *Deal with problems.* Face them and do not bury them. Start to think through strategies to 'move' the problem on. However, keep problems in proportion and do not fret and worry about them.
- *Avoid confrontations.* Keep your feelings under control.
- *Develop support systems to discuss problems and express feelings with others,* such as other NQTs, your mentor, other teachers, a partner or friend. You may link with other NQTs to provide mutual support, talk about your concerns, develop a shared understanding of a problem, and provide possible alternative solutions and practical help. Sharing your stress and its cause with your mentor may help to alleviate it. Having a strong support system in which positive self-esteem is reinforced is one way of helping you to adjust to the different roles you undertake as a teacher.
- *Identify where you can get help,* e.g. workshops on skills such as stress and time-management, communication, assertiveness or priority setting. If these and the regular feedback on your teaching and sources of support are not enough, there are further sources of help, for example, the teacher support line (see 'Further Reading' below).
- *Rest and relax.* Work will fill as much time as you can give to it. You therefore need to pace yourself sensibly and find time to do the things you enjoy (see below). Decide how best you can tackle your work to maintain a good work–life balance. This helps you to remain mentally and physically fit and prepared for work. You need time to switch off, to spend time with family and friends and enjoy your leisure time. Guard your time outside work for leisure and do not let work intrude. Planning your use of leisure time helps you to use this time effectively, otherwise it is easy to erode it. Although there are times when you feel you have too much to do to relax, as a general rule, it is important that you do NOT forget to take time for yourself when you get too busy or feel stressed. This is exactly the time when you need most to take some time for yourself. Release the tension – have a friend or family member you can laugh at it all with.

Techniques for good time management can also prevent or alleviate stress (see 'Managing your time' below). You may be able to identify other coping techniques. What works for one person may not work for another; therefore decide what is appropriate and put into

Reflective task 2.2
Visualisation of lessons

Prepare a lesson you are concerned about, e.g. with a class you have not yet taught or one with whom you have experienced difficulty because of a difficult pupil or group of pupils. Visualise yourself taking the lesson, e.g. starting it, presenting the material, organising the pupils for any practical activity, distributing any material or apparatus you need, managing the activity, etc. This visualisation does not have to be done during 'useful time', it can be done at any time, e.g. while walking to school. You may want to ask your mentor to observe the lesson. After you have taught the lesson evaluate it as usual and also discuss with your mentor how it went. Did your visualisation help in any way?

practice those strategies that work for you.

Although you can learn to manage stress you cannot totally overcome it. For example, you cannot overcome problems inherent in your work environment. You may be able to alter some causes of stress, such as inadequate communication between staff or uncertainty about school rules, but others are outside your control. Therefore, other people also have a responsibility to create a working environment in which causes of stress are reduced. If you experience problems with stress or identify ways in which the working environment can be improved to reduce stress, discuss them with your mentor. A number of authors, including Cartwright and Cooper (1997) and Rogers (1996), identify characteristics in the work environment that reduce stress. These include good communication between staff; a strong sense of collegiality; consultation to inform management decisions – with forward planning by management; consensus on key values and standards; whole-school policies in place and adhered to; clearly defined roles and expectations; positive feedback and praise; a good physical environment, with maintained buildings; a level of resources and facilities that supports teachers; support to help solve problems; minimal red tape and paperwork; skills matched to those required for extra duties; advice given on induction and career development. Therefore, it is important that you:

- *Try to influence the causes of stress over which you have some control, or which you may be able to alter.* For instance, if you are concerned about the behaviour of some pupils, look at how school rules are applied. Even though there are some factors which you may feel you have less control over and little power to alter directly, you can make sure that those with responsibility to do something are aware of the situation. Feeling that you are trying to do something may in itself help reduce stress.
- *Learn to accept what you cannot change* and learn how to cope with any resulting stress.

MANAGING YOUR TIME

The time demands of teaching

Lack of time or poor time management have been identified as a major cause of stress (e.g. Carter, 1987; Cox et al., 1989; Johnstone, 1993; Kyriacou, 1989; Trendall, 1989). For example, Abel and Sewell (1999) identified too much paperwork, lack of time to spend with individual pupils and demands on after-school time as major causes of stress for teachers. We cannot manufacture time, save it to use later or manage it. We can only manage ourselves in relation to time to enable us to use it effectively. In order to do this, it is therefore important that you 'learn how to save time and spend it wisely' (Adair, 1988: 1).

As you have probably found on your school experiences, effective teaching demands a great deal of time and energy inside and outside the classroom and beyond the school day. Many teachers do their planning, preparation and marking at home because they cannot find time at school. During the school day there is little time to relax. Even break and lunch time can often be disrupted and it may seem as if there is not enough time to do everything necessary to meet all the demands of teaching. This means that you must plan to use your time and energy effectively over a week, a term and the school year. Pacing yourself and your work is important, otherwise you may become stressed and your health and job performance may suffer.

We consider below several different aspects of time management.

How teachers spend their time

Although you may work roughly the same hours as people in other jobs, in teaching your work is undertaken in a more condensed time span and your workload is not spread evenly over the year (Marland, 1993). Most of the work demands have to be achieved quickly, e.g. dealing with a pupil's problems, marking work and feeding back to pupils. Pressures are different at different times during the school year, e.g. examination marking and writing reports in the summer term must be completed in a short timescale. Thus, much of your work cannot be put off until a less busy time of the year.

However, it is hard to specify exactly what any one teacher does and the possible range of tasks to be done makes it difficult to stop the job expanding. You may like to list here the range of tasks you do as a teacher and the rough amount of time you spend on each of these.

Reflective task 2.3
How much time do you spend on school-related activities per week?

List the range of tasks you do as a teacher, e.g. teaching, lesson planning, preparing materials, evaluating lessons, marking homework, taking extra-curricular activities. Estimate the amount of time you spend per week on each of these school-related activities. What activities do you spend most time on? How does it compare with how time is spent by another NQT that you know? Discuss the implications of your findings, e.g. is your time being used appropriately or do you spend longer on some jobs than you should and neglect others? Why is this and how could you use your time more effectively and economically?

Although this may seem to be a time-consuming task at a busy time, taking a small amount of time now should help you to save time later on.

Planning and preparation before you start a new job, new year or new term

It is generally agreed that the more time you spend planning and preparing, the less time it takes to do a task.

Every job takes an NQT longer than an experienced teacher because you do not know the procedures for doing things, nor necessarily who to ask for help and advice. Planning and preparation before you start in your new school, as well as before each new school year and each term, is important as it decreases the amount of work and hence demands on you during term time. For example, you plan how a topic should develop over time and you may want to prepare some of the resources you need to teach a scheme of work so that you get the topic off to a good start. However, do not try to do too much before you start to teach the topic, otherwise you may find yourself planning lessons twice or preparing different resources. For example, the worksheets you have prepared may not cater for the specific learning needs of a group of pupils or you may change your mind about what you are going to teach as you pick up new ideas, learn about the group or when you talk to more experienced teachers. Other teachers can share their resources with you, and you may have found or have used different resources and can share these with other teachers.

Although we advise planning ahead, do not spend all of your holiday preparing for the next year or term. Plan well so that you do your preparation at the end of the previous term or in the first or last few days of the holiday. Make sure that you keep your holiday time to relax.

How you can manage your time effectively

How do you deal with time demands during the school year? Do you use your school time well, making effective use of free periods? One NQT told us that noting in his diary what he wants to achieve in each of his free periods helps him to use them effectively. Many writers, e.g. Adair (1988), Fontana (1993) and Scott (1992), have identified techniques to help you manage time effectively, some of which are summarised below.

- *Do work that you need to think about at your best time of day.* Identify when you are at your best for working effectively, as you do jobs more quickly and efficiently than at other times. One NQT told us that she finds it difficult to work after she has eaten in the evening and therefore stays at work for an extra hour so that she does not have to take work home with her.
- *Plan for the short, medium and long term.* Plan and prioritise activities and use your time effectively to achieve your short-term objectives. At the same time plan to use time and energy on what you want to achieve in an academic year (medium term) and on how you want your career to develop over a period of time (long term).
- *Identify what you need to do, monitor your progress and measure whether you have achieved it.* For example, if you aim to mark 'x' number of books in 'y' minutes, you can measure whether each one takes this amount of time, or more or less time. Next time you can be more realistic about the time needed for marking.
- *Prioritise jobs that need to be done to achieve your objectives.* The best lists contain jobs organised by urgency and importance into high, medium and low priority. High-priority jobs should be done first. Think ahead and try to anticipate jobs which need to be done. Do not always do jobs when they become urgent, plan when to do them so that you take action at the right time rather than always trying to catch up. However, find a balance. Do not try to do a job too early, e.g. without having all the necessary information, as you may waste time having to repeat the job or revising what you have done.
- *Write a list of things to do* in a small notebook. Several lists on small pieces of paper may require you spending valuable time finding what is on each list, which defeats its time-saving purpose. If you do not achieve everything on the list in the timescale allowed, try to identify why, e.g. there was too much to do, you procrastinated over a particular job, a job was too difficult or you were constantly interrupted. Plan how to prevent this from happening again.
- *Do not overcommit yourself.* Identify what you do and do not need to do. If you are asked to do a job over and above your duties but already have too much to do, or do not have the expertise, say no straight away. Be firm and definite and do not let yourself be persuaded to change your mind.

- *Do not do more than one job at a time.* If you do too many jobs at once, you may not concentrate effectively on any of the jobs and waste time redoing them.
- *Set aside blocks of time and set a time limit for each job wherever possible.* You have probably established the amount of preparation required to plan effective lessons, although at times you may want to spend longer planning one particular lesson, e.g. for a difficult class with whom the last lesson did not go well, or if you are less familiar with the material. It is more efficient to block out a period of uninterrupted time to concentrate on completing a demanding job, otherwise you waste time picking up from where you left off each time you restart. Also, do not spend longer on a job than you intended, than is valuable or proportionate to its importance, e.g. with practice you can develop a good lesson plan fairly quickly, but you can waste a lot of time if you try to get it perfect. Therefore, learn when to stop working on something.
- *Be efficient with paperwork.* Do not let paperwork eat into your block of time for demanding tasks. Do routine paperwork in short blocks of time when you cannot undertake a demanding task. Be systematic in dealing with paper. Keep your desk tidy, otherwise you create additional work and waste time looking for a piece of paper or information. If possible only handle a piece of paper once, e.g. respond to a simple memo or request as soon as you read it rather than holding it to reply later. Develop a good filing system in which you file a piece of paper away as soon as you have finished with it.
- *Do something you have to do straight away (as soon as you have all the information you need) or put it out of your mind.* It is especially important to get jobs which you do not like doing out of the way quickly otherwise you may put off doing them until they become urgent and important. Big or unpleasant jobs are best broken down into several smaller ones so that you can gradually do each part in turn until you finish the job.
- *Do not dwell on an unpleasant incident.* Worrying about something you cannot change wastes time and creates stress. Try to think about it only long enough to follow it up, to clear up any misunderstanding and to learn from it, to avoid the same thing happening or to handle a similar incident better in future.
- *Do not be afraid to ask for help or guidance when you need it.* You can waste a great deal of time trying to solve problems on your own.
- *Do not stay up late every night, or get up early every morning, preparing work for school.* Allow yourself a wind-down period before you go to sleep. Find out how much sleep you need so that you have enough energy to meet the demands of teaching. Do not try to survive on less sleep in order to get work done and do not go to bed worrying about work. If you are rested you are better able to cope with the demands of the day.
- *Plan for your own leisure time* (see above).

We recognise that it is easy to advise you to 'do these things' but not easy to actually carry them out. However, it is worth working at them so that you gradually become better at them and can make them work for you.

> **Reflective task 2.4**
> **Prioritising jobs to be done**
>
> Make a list of jobs that you have to do. Score each job on two scales, one scale for urgency and one for importance, with each scored 1–5, with 1 being the most urgent or important and 5 the least urgent or important. Combine the two scores and re-order your list to put the most urgent and important jobs as highest priority, at the top of the list. Does the list surprise you? Why are the jobs in this order? Look at this information alongside the information you gathered for Reflective Task 2.3 above and compare your priorities with what you did during the week. Did you spend the appropriate amount of time achieving your priorities? Did you waste time on jobs that were not a priority? How can you spend time more effectively? Record your notes in your portfolio and check on these every so often.

SUMMARY

Your first year of teaching can be a 'baptism of fire'. You develop many techniques to increase your effectiveness as a teacher. These in themselves should reduce stress associated with teaching. However, they cannot eliminate all stress in teaching and it is likely that you will feel stressed at some point in your teaching career. You must take responsibility for managing yourself, your work and therefore your time and stress. However, your school should also help you and other sources of help are also available. This chapter has considered causes and symptoms of stress and techniques you can use to manage it. Particular attention has been paid to techniques which will enable you to manage your time more effectively. If you do not manage stress and time well, you may develop ineffective ways of working. If, on the other hand, you can use this information to manage your stress and time effectively, you should be able to develop effective ways of working and have a sound basis for an effective and rewarding teaching career.

FURTHER READING

Help in managing stress is available from the teacher support line (telephone the support line at 08000 562 561 or look online at http://www.teachersupport.info), a national counselling service for support and advice for all teachers in England and Wales.

See also http://www.teachernet.gov.uk/professionaldevelopment/opportunities/nqt/ stress/

Stress

Education Service Advisory Committee (1998) *Managing Work-Related Stress: A Guide for Managers and Teachers in the Schools*, 2nd edition. London: HMSO.

Kyriacou, C. (2000) *Stress-Busting for Teachers*. Cheltenham: Stanley Thornes.

Kyriacou, C. (2001) 'Teacher stress: directions for future research', in *Educational Review*, 53 (1): 27–35.

Wilson, V. and Hall, J. (2002) 'Running twice as fast? A review of the research literature on teachers' stress' in *Scottish Educational Review*, 34 (2): 175–87.

These latter two articles review the major research findings on teacher stress and suggest directions for future research.

Time management

Brown, M. and Ralph, S. (1998) *Time Management for Teachers*. Plymouth: Northcote House.

3 Working as Part of a Team

Kelly Ashford and Susan Capel

As a newly qualified teacher (NQT) you spend a great deal of time working with groups of pupils in the classroom, but you also spend time working with colleagues in a number of teams/groups. Historically, the culture of schools was one of professional individualism (Metcalf, 1998) but as the importance of effective teamwork has been recognised in whole-school development, there is greater emphasis on academic and pastoral teams. In the early 1990s the lack of teamwork in schools in England and its impact on their performance was highlighted in an OFSTED report:

> At present the performance of most institutions and services is patchy and poorly co-ordinated. Either some aspects have been developed and others ignored, or success has depended on individuals' strengths rather than on shared purposes and concerted teamwork. Often, policies and projects are not sustained long enough to make an impact.
>
> (OFSTED, 1993: 43)

During the following five years, and in response to the criticisms outlined in the above report, progressive improvements in the quality of teamwork and leadership took place:

> There have been significant improvements in the quality of leadership and management … Where leadership is good, the head teacher gets the best out of staff by establishing clear priorities, developing effective teamwork amongst senior staff and motivating and enabling teachers to teach well.
>
> (Her Majesty's Chief Inspector of Schools, 2000: 46)

How well teams of staff work together has a direct influence on how effectively the school functions. A productive team utilises the skills and abilities of all members of staff and can often achieve more than the sum of the individuals working alone (Zander, 1982). The experience of working in formal teams and informal groups has benefits for you as an NQT: it should help you learn what is expected of you as a teacher in your school and how you can contribute to the school. Working in a team widens the scope of your professional development and provides a different kind of support and experience from that given by your mentor or other colleagues on a one-to-one basis.

A team has been defined as:

> ... a collection of two or more individuals who possess a common identity, have common goals and objectives, share a common fate, exhibit structured patterns of interaction and modes of communication, hold common perceptions about the group structure, are personally and instrumentally independent, reciprocate interpersonal attraction and consider themselves to be a group.
>
> (Carron and Hausenblaus, 1998: 13)

In summary, it can be deduced that in a school context, teams involve interactions between a number of teachers who join together for the purpose of achieving a common goal, e.g. developing a behaviour management strategy. They have a structured communication and meeting system, and develop a good working environment in which each member's contribution is valued.

This chapter is designed to support you in functioning effectively as a member of different teams in your school. It begins by looking at how a school might be structured and how the whole school team might be grouped into academic and pastoral teams, as well as other teams that might be important. Also within this section we highlight structural issues that are important in terms of decision making and power, which reflect the influence of teams.

The chapter continues by considering some of the formal teams in which you work in your school. It also considers how you fit into the whole staff team – including the informal interactions which are important in your being accepted as a member of staff. The chapter concludes by looking at the functioning of teams.

As an NQT you already possess many skills and abilities to contribute to the various teams in which you work. This chapter is designed to build on your previous experiences of teamwork, no matter how small or large, and support you in achieving an understanding of how you can function effectively as a member of different teams in your school. This chapter also provides knowledge and understanding to enable you to provide appropriate learning opportunities to enable pupils to develop teamwork skills.

OBJECTIVES

By the end of this chapter you should understand:

- how schools might be structured and how staff might be grouped into teams;
- how the structure influences decision making in school;
- how you can fit into staff teams and become an established member of staff;
- how the academic and pastoral teams in which you are working function;
- the relationship between individual and team productivity;
- how effective teams function and how you can enhance your effectiveness as a member of different teams in your school;
- what qualities contribute to a successful leader;
- the importance of leadership to the performance of teams and the school.

THE STRUCTURE OF SCHOOLS AND DECISION MAKING

Within the school environment there are numerous teams, each with their own roles and responsibilities. While the responsibilities may be divided differently from those that you have come across on school experience during your initial teacher education course, commonalities exist between all of them, and the overall hierarchical structure of schools is usually similar (see Figure 3.1). As an NQT your predominant focus is likely to be within academic and pastoral teams. Understanding how decisions are made and communicated throughout the school is essential. Specifically, you need to understand your role within these teams, the decisions that they make and your relationship with other teams, as you are accountable for carrying through decisions made and, in time, will become fully involved in influencing decision making.

In addition to the teams identified in Figure 3.1, there are also ad hoc teams in schools, e.g. an assessment and examinations team. Some of these teams may be created to do a specific job and therefore are temporary in nature, i.e. they are brought together and disbanded as the need arises. You may be asked to be a member of one of these groups.

Senior Management Team. While every secondary school has a senior management team, its name may be different: it is sometimes called the Senior Team, or Management Team. The team includes the head and deputy heads as well as other senior staff. Generally, the team meets to make decisions about the management of the school. Minutes from these meetings are usually published in the school bulletin or posted on staff noticeboards.

Academic Structures: Departments and Faculties. The curriculum within secondary schools is often organised into subjects; these are usually based on departments and are under the leadership of a department head. Occasionally, members of staff may take additional responsibility within the department, e.g. organising a key stage. In some schools, departments may be grouped into faculties under a faculty head. Departments or faculties are responsible

Figure 3.1   Example of the structure of a school.
Source: Adapted from Leask *et al.*, 1997

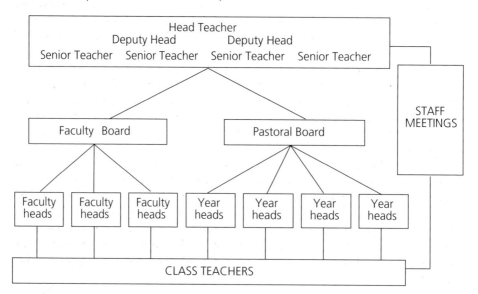

for delivering the academic programme within their area. Curriculum decisions may be made at a meeting of heads of department or faculties, sometimes called a curriculum board meeting. You can expect to be part of these teams and the head of the department or faculty is usually the person to whom you are immediately responsible.

Pastoral Structure. The pastoral system looks after the welfare, behaviour and personal and social development of pupils. This is usually organised in the form of a year or house system. Year heads, or house heads where they exist, take responsibility for the welfare and development of pupils in their year/house. Additionally, each pupil belongs to a registration group and each group has a tutor responsible for registration and welfare. You are likely to be one of these tutors. Chapter 4 provides more information on the pastoral system.

Reflective task 3.1
The structure of your school

By looking at your school and department handbook reflect upon the structure of your school. Is it the same as the one above? If not how does it differ? Does it have departments; if so, how do these fit into the structure? Find out how these work in practice, e.g. do staff know what is happening? Are there regular meetings? How is information shared between them? Is the structure represented diagrammatically like the one above? If not, try drawing one yourself. Also, familiarise yourself with the school's policies and see how these are reflected in your department policies.

As you can see, school structures are hierarchical and vertical in nature. Hierarchically, the head has day-to-day management responsibility. You are therefore responsible to the head through your head of department. Thus, decisions flow down to you. However, in effective schools, communication is such that views of individual members of staff are taken into account. Additionally, you work vertically across academic and pastoral teams. You have an important role to play in both and a valuable contribution to make. As a member of a subject team as well as a tutor you can monitor both academic progression and personal and social development of individual pupils.

However, how the formal school structure works in practice affects where decisions are made and who has power. For example, there may be a member of staff who has been in the school for a long time and has considerable influence on decision making. Thus it is important to not only learn about the formal structure, but also who else may make decisions and where power lies. This may influence the behaviour of other staff and therefore influence your behaviour.

Finally, you should be aware of, and be sensitive to, any changes in the school that may influence staff room interactions, e.g. if there is a new head or deputy head, this can influence relationships among staff as new relationships are developed, or inter-departmental rivalry may escalate as money becomes tight and all departments are trying to secure it for their own resources. You should keep in mind that everyone is working towards the same end and all are facing the same difficulties. You should not, therefore, be drawn into any action that you may regret or which may affect your relationship with colleagues in other departments.

WORKING IN TEAMS

The team of staff in your school

As a team of teachers, the members of staff within your school strive towards enabling pupils to achieve their best. Your acceptance into this team is very important, as it brings support, guidance and respect from other members of staff during your first year of teaching. As you adjust to becoming a full member of the staff team, you learn about and adapt to the structure in your school, and continue to develop as a teacher. You also recognise that you are a member of both formal (subject, department or pastoral) and informal (e.g. social) teams. Developing and enhancing good working relationships, both within your department and the staff room, can help to produce a good atmosphere in the school, motivate staff in a positive way and help to build strong effective working relationships and teams.

Formal staff teams

As a member of the staff team you work in formal teams ranging from the whole school staff team to smaller teams, e.g. your academic, pastoral, extra curricular and vocational responsibilities require you to work with a variety of different people in a number of teams. In undertaking your responsibilities you work closely with teachers in your department as well as other teachers who teach your pupils and, in some situations, your head of department, head of year, and professionals from outside the school who are working with pupils in your class (see Chapter 4 for further information about these).

As an NQT the majority of your work is likely to be in your subject department. You undertake a role within the department beyond teaching your classes, which often requires you to work closely with other members of staff and attend departmental meetings. As highlighted below one of the roles of an effective team is to support its members. Your initial port of call is your mentor (see Chapter 5 for further information about the mentoring process); however, you can expect to be supported by other department members in your work, both formally and informally. This could be in terms of, for example, team teaching, observing or being observed in lessons and discussing your progress or any concerns you may have. Do not be afraid to seek help and advice from other members of the department, but remember in return you are also expected to support your colleagues.

In order for you to become an accepted and functional member of formal teams your initial interactions with other team members are extremely important. Find out how or more importantly why things are done the way they are before offering opinions and making suggestions. Any scepticism about practice is best kept to yourself while the fuller picture emerges. Although you want to show commitment, enthusiasm and professionalism by taking on responsibilities, you do not want to take on a workload that you cannot cope with. Try to strike a balance. Evaluate and control the commitments you take on so you can also address your personal needs without conflict. One way in which NQTs can do this is only to undertake short-term commitments or a specific job, where the demands are clear. It is best to avoid open-ended commitments outside the remit of your main job, until you are sure you can do that effectively. Always keep in mind that first of all you must teach effectively. Other members of staff support you in this, but they expect you to take control of teaching and be effective in that role. This must be your first priority.

Attending meetings

'Meetings are one of the most common ways in which groups of teachers work together formally. You attend a wide range of meetings. Your performance at and contribution to such meetings in your first few months in school is important, as this is another means by which other staff form opinions of you. Although your previous experience is very beneficial to you here you should be sensitive to the context of your new school and to how you can best make an effective contribution at meetings.

In order to make an effective contribution at meetings, and also make the meeting effective for the other members, you should be prepared for them. You must read papers circulated before a meeting. If you need further information or clarification about points you do not understand, it may be helpful to do this informally before the meeting rather than at the meeting itself. Once you have an understanding of the context and purpose of the meetings you attend you may wish to put an item on the agenda. You should check how you do this, as the mechanisms in your school may be different to those you have experienced previously. Also be aware that the mechanisms may vary for different types of meetings. Therefore, find out who sets the agenda, the deadline for agenda items to be submitted and whether or not you are sent a note asking for agenda items. You may also want to check with other staff beforehand that the item is appropriate for the meeting and what reaction you are likely to receive. It usually helps to get support for your agenda item and for you from colleagues prior to the meeting.

Informal staff groups

A good way to establish relationships and become an accepted member of staff is in the staff room.

Most staff rooms are friendly places; members of staff are welcoming towards NQTs and accept them as colleagues. However, some NQTs find acceptance less easy because of the way they interact with staff members, e.g. they do not follow the 'code of practice' or etiquette, or they may voice their opinions loudly when it would have been better to air them in a departmental meeting. Do not expect to make an impression immediately in the staff room: if you do, it is probably a bad one. Start by being friendly and approachable, talk to other teachers about rules, pupils and other school matters. You will find that you begin to mix and eventually as you learn about the school and individuals you are able to join in with social chats with confidence.

You will find that different groups of staff have different routines: some may meet together informally at break and lunchtime while others mix with different people. As an NQT you normally find yourself joining existing groups of staff, which typically works well, and you are made to feel welcome and accepted. However, there may be times when you feel isolated or rejected if you feel a clique has developed and you are obviously not welcome. Until you have a chance to assess fully the interactions that take place in the staffroom it is probably best if you mix with a variety of groups and people. This helps you to establish where you fit best and with whom you feel most comfortable. This also gives members of staff time to develop their knowledge about and trust in you, although this also partly comes through your quality of work. Do not repeat information that you find out about other teachers; this is a very quick way of destroying the trust and relationships you have worked so hard to gain.

There are often many opportunities for mixing with staff in informal situations, particularly at staff social events. These provide opportunities for you to become involved in the life of the school and are a good way of learning more about the school, your colleagues, your department and the teams in which you are working. It also provides information about your present work situation, relevant background about school or departmental policies and about the politics of the team.

MAKING TEAMS EFFECTIVE

What makes teams effective or ineffective?

As a team is forming, its members immediately begin to interact. As an NQT, you and other new members of staff join existing teams, e.g. your subject team, thus causing a change of membership within these teams. This affects the dynamics and functioning of the team. In order to operate effectively the team has to learn about the attributes and strengths of the new members, so that they can be used effectively. Thus, there is a certain amount of reforming of the team that takes place. This is important in order to develop and maintain the structure and effectiveness of the team (see the section on 'Information on the productivity of teams' below). Each team may operate quite differently for many reasons and in this sense they are all different. However, they are all similar too, since the groups remain united in the pursuit of an underlying common purpose (Carron, 1982) – to contribute effectively to the school.

Teams in which a variety of different roles and responsibilities are adopted and fulfilled have generally been found to be effective. Many authors have defined roles that should be undertaken by team members to enable a team to function effectively (e.g. Belbin, 1981; Posthuma, 1999). Posthuma (1999) divided these roles into three general categories:

1   group task roles, which help the group to carry out and meet the goals of the team;
2   group building and maintenance roles, which are directed towards helping the team function and work well together;
3   individual roles which fulfil team members' individual needs and are not necessarily good for the group, as they can often disrupt progress.

For a team to be balanced and function effectively the roles within categories 1 and 2 need to be filled. Thus, members of small teams may need to undertake more than one role. Although you and other team members have preferred roles, you need to be flexible and able to take on different roles and responsibilities as required by the team. If you are interested in finding out more about this, or about the characteristics and qualities of the different roles, refer to Belbin's or Posthuma's books in 'Further Reading' at the end of this chapter.

As can be seen from the description of 'individual roles', you should recognise that people do not always work for the good of the team. Typically, when teams come together they interact for some common publicly stated purpose. This could be to work on a problem and come to a decision in order to meet the team's goals and objectives (Posthuma, 1999). However, sometimes team members have other goals in mind that they hope to achieve for themselves. These private, covert goals are often referred to as 'hidden agendas'. In the worst scenario, the team members may try, deliberately or otherwise, to prevent a team achieving its purpose. There may be a variety of reasons for this: they may have their own objectives and purposes which are different from the formal objectives or purposes of the team and/or

Figure 3.2   Information on the productivity of teams

PRODUCTIVITY OF TEAMS

Lewin (1951) proposed that two principle processes are associated with group involvement: cohesion (activity associated with the formation, development and maintenance of the group) and locomotion (activity related to the output and achievement of the group objectives). Although these processes are different, they are interrelated, suggesting that the more cohesive a team becomes the more effective it is in relation to performance (Carron and Chelladurai, 1981). The following equation proposed by Steiner (1972) displays the relationship between individual and team performance:

Actual productivity = Potential productivity–Losses due to faulty process

Potential productivity refers to a team's best possible performance based on the relevant resources of the individuals within the team, for example, a team containing members with a broad range of skills, abilities and experience, who complete the roles assigned to them effectively, would be considered to possess excellent group resources.

Steiner (1972) proposed that individual ability is one of the most important resources in a team. He also proposed that actual productivity (the actual performance attained by the group) will be lower than the potential productivity (the potential performance that could be attained using relevant resources) due to faulty processes within the interaction of group members. Faulty processes can be attributed to two general categories: co-ordination losses and motivational losses.

Co-ordination losses. These may arise if ineffective strategies or a breakdown in communication occurs and may lead to a decrease in team effectiveness. Shared facilities such as a staff room or departmental office can contribute a great deal to team identity and cohesiveness. Team members who are located near to each other tend to interact more frequently and engage in informal discussion related to their team's objectives, therefore creating a productive and effective team. In contrast, team members who are divided by location and who rarely meet, other than at designated meeting times, may find difficulties in operating as a cohesive unit compared to teams in close proximity, resulting in co-ordination losses unless additional effort in developing effective working relationships is invested.

Motivational losses. If an individual or the team feels that their contributions are not being acknowledged or the team feels that it is not achieving its aims and objectives, motivation may decrease. Only when a team uses its available resources to meet task demands effectively, does its actual productivity approach its potential. Therefore, it is important that coordination and motivation losses are kept to a minimum. As a member of a team you may want to think about how you can contribute to preventing coordination and motivation losses.

other team members, or they may be following their own individual agendas and promoting their own interests at the expense of the group. These can result in negative interactions with team members and the disruption of the team. Sometimes a team member may try to influence you unduly to support the achievement of his or her own ends, which, if you allow it to happen, can be detrimental to the team, your acceptance by the rest of the team or to your being an effective member.

It is not always easy to see when people have hidden agendas. Signs or behaviours employed by members of the team in order to impede its work could include:

- personal attacks, complaining
- failing to listen to others' point of view
- interruption, talking over people
- failing to recognise alternative points of view
- raising irrelevant or unhelpful points
- ambivalence of opinion or commitment
- avoiding a particular issue
- scattered, fragmented work procedures
- trying to return to an issue on which a decision has been made
- withdrawal/failing to participate

(Tyson, 1989 cited in Posthuma, 1999: 62).

It is important to be aware of any such behaviour in the teams in which you are working. It also helps for you to reflect on your own behaviour and to understand what motivates you and what you are enthusiastic about, so that you can see more clearly why others behave in a particular way.

Reflective task 3.2
Observing teams

Identify a team within your school that you have joined. Observe the structure of the team, how you fit in, and what place it has in the overall structure of the school. Now, think about a team in which you have previously been a member. Consider the similarities and differences between the two teams, e.g. membership, tasks and roles undertaken by various members. Also consider whether and how you worked differently in each of these teams for any reason, e.g. the different personalities of team members, the difference in tasks or your different role in the team. In light of this information, discuss with your mentor how you can increase your effectiveness within the teams in which you work.

Repeat this task in a few months' time and compare how the team has changed from your initial observations: for example, has the structure changed? Have your roles changed?

Leading a team effectively

Generally, you find that effective, productive teams have an effective leader. All teachers have leadership roles. The roles that teachers undertake can, to some degree, depend on their experience, e.g. more experienced teachers may chair meetings or be involved in a management role. As an NQT you also have a leadership role to fulfil: e.g. there may be support teachers working within your classroom who require you to inform them of the curriculum content, aims of the lesson and how they can help effectively. You may have a particular skill or area of expertise that you may wish or be expected to develop through extra-curricular activities, e.g. a sport, putting on a dance, drama or music production – or you may wish to plan a trip or visit for a group of pupils which would require you to lead the planning and organisation as well as a team of staff and pupils during the activity itself. Depending on the task and the needs of the situation a number of leaders may be required, with different people leading at different times to ensure that everything runs smoothly and safely.

As an NQT you may already have a wealth of experience as a leader. This enables you to make a significant contribution to leadership roles within the school, providing you take account of the context in which you are working. Whether you have a lot, or very limited, experiences of leadership, the final section of the chapter is designed for you to reflect on what effective leadership is, and some of the qualities an effective leader may possess. It helps you to develop a greater understanding of leadership and allows you to develop your leadership skills. There are a number of key areas that a leader must take responsibility for in order for their team to function effectively; however, responsibility can be shared with other members of the team depending on the circumstances.

Leadership responsibility includes:

- *Establishment of clear aims and objectives.*
- *Setting priorities* – short-, medium-, and long-term goals with realistic time frames can make a seemingly endless task manageable.
- *Helicopter vision* – the ability to understand how the team fits into the wider picture and how it contributes to the school. Establishing links with other teams provides a connection between whole-school strategies and the work of smaller teams.
- *Coordination* – this is very important for team effectiveness, especially since many individuals are members of multiple teams, each of which exerts its own pressures. If people understand their responsibilities, know what they have to do and how their contribution benefits the team it helps to motivate them.
- *Communication* – effective communication also leads to greater team effectiveness; it allows the distribution of knowledge, fosters understanding and can lead to effective decision-making.
- *Evaluation, monitoring and support* – teams require evaluation and feedback on all aspects of their work, and where necessary support and guidance. This helps to reinforce aims and objectives, can increase productivity, and can help individuals develop their knowledge, skills, insights and attitudes.
- *Delegation* – distribution and delegation of tasks enables the team to utilise everybody's efforts and talents in achieving the team's goals.
- *Motivation* – fostering the will to work and succeed through careful consideration of individuals personal needs.

(Adapted from Metcalf, 1998 and Waterhouse, 1983)

There is no set of core attributes for successful leadership. However, successful leaders appear to have many qualities in common. The following attributes are a combination of what Posthuma (1999) and Parcells and Coplon (1995) believe to be qualities of a successful leader:

- objectivity
- accountability
- flexibility
- preparedness
- loyalty and respect
- resourcefulness
- confidence
- patience
- enthusiasm.

As effective teams have effective leaders, so successful schools have effective leadership to support effective teamwork.

SUMMARY

A school is a complex organisation made up of numerous teams and therefore it is not easy to recognise what makes it function effectively or not. However, effective teamwork and effective leadership within a school have been identified as major contributors to this. It is therefore important to be aware of, and understand, as much as you can about the structure and decision-making processes within your school and what is making your school and teams within it function effectively or not.

Staff in a school should be working to achieve the same outcomes, but working together to achieve these outcomes is not easy. As an NQT you work with many different people as a member of a number of teams. The effectiveness of a team depends largely on how well its members relate to and communicate with each other, which is to a large extent based on trust.

Such trust takes time to develop, and as you 'prove yourself' and develop effective working relationships with colleagues you see it grow. Remember, this process begins as soon as you start in a post; therefore, the first impression you make and how this impression develops over time is vital.

Once established in your teaching role you may want to think about developing your leadership skills in order to prepare for the next stage of your career. If you want to develop as a teacher and become, for example, a head of department, year or house, or move into another senior management role, you need effective leadership skills. The role of a leader in a team is, however, very complex. There is no set of rules that you can follow to become an effective leader. In order to develop your leadership skills you may want to read some texts that deal with this aspect of teamwork. There are many that have been written for educational purposes and others that have addressed the issue within organisations as a whole. Several of these are included in 'Further Reading' below.

ACKNOWLEDGEMENT

We would like to acknowledge Marilyn Leask, Joan Stephenson and Ian Terrell from whose work in the first edition of this book (1997), the section of the chapter entitled 'The structure of schools and decision making' was taken.

FURTHER READING

Belbin, R.M. (1981) *Management Teams: Why They Succeed or Fail*. Oxford: Butterworth-Heinemann Ltd. This book considers in detail key roles to be performed by members of teams in order for them to be effective. It then examines the influence of a number of different factors on team effectiveness. The book also contains a self-perception inventory to enable you to match your personality to particular team roles.

Bowring-Carr, C. and West-Burnham, J. (1997) *Managing Quality in Schools: A Training Manual*. Harlow: Longman Information and Reference. This workbook is designed to help make schools more effective. It identifies principles and practices which inform the reader of actions to support the development of quality management processes and techniques. It includes chapters on teams and leadership in schools.

Handy, C. (1993) *Understanding Organisations*, 4th edition. London: Penguin Business. Although this book is aimed mainly at business organisations the chapters on the working of groups and leadership should provide a sound understanding of how groups work and effective leadership, which can be applied in a school situation.

Posthuma, B.W. (1999) *Small Groups in Counselling and Therapy: Process and Leadership*. London: Allyn and Bacon. This book is aimed primarily at establishing effective counselling groups. However, the topics which it considers, e.g. group development, leadership attributes and leadership techniques, can easily be applied to the school context.

Rowland, V. and Birkett, K. (1992) *Personal Effectiveness for Teachers*. Hemel Hempstead: Simon and Schuster Education. This book addressees various topics which help you to improve your effectiveness. It includes a chapter on teamwork and a chapter on chairing work meetings, which should be useful to you in your professional development to enable you to be an effective member of teams in which you work in school.

Part II

Establishing Your Teaching Role

4 The Pastoral Role

Tutoring and Personal, Social and Health Education

Ruth Heilbronn

YOUR PASTORAL ROLE

All adults working with children have a responsibility for their pastoral care, which means ensuring their well-being for the time they are with you. Your pupils' emotional state and sense of self esteem will influence the way in which they respond in class, and the learning and progress they achieve. You will need to be aware of the possible causes for their variable behaviour and responses, to understand how to take account of them and to intervene within the context of the school.

Pastoral care

Pastoral care is a very broad and diffuse area of education. It encompasses all the provision made to support pupils in their personal and social development. You have a duty of pastoral care, as a subject specialist teacher, to the pupils in your class. You may also be a tutor to a form group. Here you have specific responsibilities, defined by the school, involving interactions with pupils, parents, other colleagues and outside agencies. It is important to be prepared for this aspect of your work and to build on any experiences and training you have already undertaken in your initial teacher education. Pastoral care has always been an important element in teaching and teachers have traditionally been held in high regard as transmitters and upholders of social and personal values. Indeed, the challenges and rewards in becoming a supportive, trusted figure in the lives of young people, perhaps especially where few such figures exist, continue to draw significant numbers of people into the teaching profession.

The pastoral curriculum

As well as the specialist subjects which are taught in the secondary school there are other aspects which relate to pupils' well-being and broader development. This is widely known as 'the pastoral curriculum'. Some areas of the pastoral curriculum have a natural place in subject areas, such as reinforcement of all the school values and ethos: i.e. your classroom exists within the school community and the behaviour and expectations of the pupils are framed by that wider community. An example of a pastoral dimension within a subject area is the widespread use of group work. Apart from the subject-specific objective of the exercise at any one time, the pupils experience the value of working with others. This is also a 'key skill' of the English national curriculum (see Chapter 11). Similarly, when values are expressed and reinforced, pupils' welfare and the well-being of the whole school community are reiterated. As a subject teacher you deal with such areas on a daily basis, and this is discussed more fully in Chapter 12. If you are a form tutor as well as a subject teacher you may teach specific aspects of the pastoral curriculum, under a name such as Personal and Social Education (PSE). Health Education is often added (PSHE), and it sometimes encompasses Citizenship Education too (PSHCE) (see Chapter 12).

This chapter will provide you with an overview of these three aspects of pastoral care in school. It begins with a short introduction to the various ways in which schools are organised to cater for their pastoral role, which is generally known as the pastoral system. It is vital to understand how this functions in your school and what the lines of communication are when you need support with a pupil, or to pass on important information, regarding the pupils' behaviour or work. Information on the school referral system is included in this section on the school pastoral system.

There then follows a discussion on pastoral care in general, what it is and how it has been addressed in schools, according to recent research. This section includes information which relates to you as a subject teacher, since it gives an overview of pastoral care that underpins all work in school. The chapter continues with a section on the function of the form tutor, detailing the specific responsibilities that are attached to this role, and leads to sections that give advice and information relevant to all adults working in school, which are therefore important to your work both as a subject teacher and a form tutor, if you are one. These are:

- communicating with parents;
- the legal requirement for registration of pupils;
- working with other professionals who are involved in the welfare and education of pupils at school.

The chapter ends with a section on PSHE, incorporating information on the English national curriculum guidelines (Department for Education and Employment [DfEE]/ Qualifications and Curriculum Authority [QCA] 1999: 188–95). This section outlines how specific guidelines have been published to try to ensure consistency in an area of the curriculum which has been recognised as less rigorously conceived than other curriculum areas in most schools.

OBJECTIVES

At the end of this chapter you should:

- have built on your understanding of the nature of pastoral care and your contribution as a teacher (both as a form tutor and subject teacher);
- understand how pastoral and referral systems can be organised;
- be aware of the role of parents and of appropriate communication with parents;
- be aware of the roles of other professionals working with you in a wider educational context;
- understand what skills, knowledge and understanding underpin an effective personal and social education curriculum.

THE STRUCTURE OF THE PASTORAL SYSTEM IN SCHOOLS

Many schools have taken steps to break down the so-called pastoral–academic divide, the division of responsibilities between the care, welfare and behaviour of pupils and their academic progression. In some schools, departments and faculties take responsibility for both the academic progression and the personal and social development of each individual pupil. In others, the pastoral team is responsible for academic monitoring as well as pastoral care (see Marland and Rogers 1997). This can certainly have the advantage of providing a holistic view of the schooling process for the pupil, in which achievement is the focus, and care and control are seen in the context of the pupils' education.

In most schools, tutor/form groups are organised within a larger grouping, such as a year or a house system. Both systems have their advantages and each school chooses a form of organisation which suits its aims and its practical situation. Very briefly, the advantage of a year system is that the pupils have common concerns, which the head of year and form tutors can address across the whole group, through assemblies, for example. One such concern might be settling in at the beginning of the first year of transfer from primary school, or making curriculum option choices some time towards the end of Key Stage 3. One simple advantage of a house system is that pupils can relate to others across the whole age range of the school, which is not otherwise easy in a large secondary school. This may give younger pupils, for example, a chance to work with older pupils on specific house activities. Brothers and sisters can share the same experience of a house identity and loyalty.

The school referral system

Each school has a system for referring pastoral issues to a teacher with overall responsibility in this area. In some schools this is the head of year or head of house. You must know the names of the relevant people in your school to whom difficult and delicate issues must be referred. Certain cases, such as suspected or disclosed neglect or abuse, come under the Children Act, which came into force in England and Wales in 1991 and with some differences in Northern Ireland in 1996. In Scotland the relevant act is the Children (Scotland) Act 1995. Each school must have a named child protection officer, to whom referral must be made. If your school has not made the procedures for referral clear you need to ensure that you find them out. Under the Children Act teachers have a 'duty of care' towards the pupils. This means that you have to have the pupil's welfare uppermost in your mind. In cases of child abuse, for example, you must inform the designated teacher. If such a situation does arise it is vital that you make detailed notes of any disclosure. This means that if a pupil says that he or she wants to tell you something only if you promise not to tell anybody else, you have to be honest and tell the pupil that as you do not know what he or she is going to tell you, you cannot promise that you will not tell anybody.

It is important for teachers to be sympathetic and good listeners but it is also important to understand the limits of teachers' roles and to know when pupils bring issues to you which require more help than you can give. It is crucial to know who is trained and authorised in school to give this further help, and what systems exist for dealing with individual pupils. In cases where pupils tell you about confidential issues, always remember to let them know that you may have to seek advice or that you may need to arrange for the pupil to go to see someone else. In some cases that person may be a trained counsellor.

Reflective task 4.1
Dealing with confidential issues

Find out what you do in the following situations and discuss with your mentor the implications of the procedures. Do you agree with them?

- How do you document your meetings with pupils on confidential matters and where are these notes kept?
- How do you discuss the issue of confidentiality with pupils and how do you explain to them if you have to pass on something they have told you in confidence?

PASTORAL CARE

What does the term 'pastoral care' mean in practice? A recent research review attempted to define this broad and diffuse area. Written by Ron Best and undertaken by the British Educational Research Association (BERA), it distinguishes between the transmission of knowledge, as conceived in curriculum subjects, and the idea of 'the initiation of the individual into a selection of concepts, facts, skills and attitudes which have to do with a world outside and separate from the learner' (Best 2002: 4). The review identified five 'pastoral tasks' that schools routinely undertake as a defining framework for the study.

- *Proactive pastoral casework* undertaken on a one-to-one basis in response to the needs of children with problems of a social, emotional, physical, behavioural, moral or spiritual nature.
- *Proactive, preventive pastoral care*, often in the form of presentations or activities undertaken in tutor or form periods and assemblies, which anticipate 'critical incidents' in children's lives and are aimed at pre-empting the need for reactive casework.

- *Developmental pastoral curricula*, aimed at promoting the personal, social, moral, spiritual and cultural development and well-being of children through distinctive programmes of PSE, tutorial work and cross-curricular activities.
- *The promotion and maintenance of an orderly and supportive environment* by building a community within the school, through extracurricular activities, the 'hidden curriculum' of supportive systems and positive relations between all members, and the promotion of a pervasive ethos of mutual care and concern.
- *The management and administration of pastoral care* in the form of planning, motivating, resourcing, monitoring, supporting, evaluating, encouraging and otherwise facilitating all of the above.

(BERA 2002: 4)

Most new teachers will have had more experience of pastoral work in schools than was true in the 1980s and 1990s, when criticisms of this aspect of initial and induction training were made. Michael Marland, who has consistently sought to raise the status of pastoral care, and pastoral care education for teachers, wrote in 1989 that the profession was untrained for its central, daily tutoring task (Marland, 1989). Her Majesty's Inspectors (HMI 1993) drew attention to inadequate induction for newly qualified teachers into this area of work, in their report *The New Teacher in School*. In another piece of research some new teachers confirmed that they lacked confidence in their role as pastoral teachers because of weakness in their initial teacher education. They cited several reasons:

- lack of clarity of the role compared with their role as subject teacher;
- different approaches to teaching, different pedagogy required for the role;
- lack of support and guidance provided by teaching practice schools during the training year;
- having to work with difficult or inadequate (often centrally produced) material;
- time constraints on preparation;
- lack of enthusiasm amongst pupils;
- limitations of university-based elements of the course in relation to teaching the pastoral curriculum.

(adapted from Calvert and Henderson 1994)

The situation is still patchy and it is true to say that while being a form tutor can give teachers significant professional satisfaction, and also significantly promote the achievement and development of pupils, this does not happen in all schools. Where form tutoring works well the whole school will be involved and the pastoral and academic systems work together to support pupil achievement. In some schools, however, form tutoring is disconnected from other aspects of teachers' work (Watkins 1992). A good pastoral support system can help to develop pupils' motivation and confidence, which in turn can support their achievement.

All teachers have a role in pupils' pastoral care, as the pupils' emotional state influences how secure and safe they feel in the learning situation, which impacts on their motivation and hence on their achievement. In this sense pastoral care is a fundamental requirement of schools and a fundamental duty of all teachers and those with responsibilities for children. In addition to this crucial responsibility there is a specific pastoral curriculum. Identification of some of the issues which pupils have found problematic at times in their school experience underlies the content of most schools' pastoral curriculum, which, as was stated earlier, is usually, although not always, a specific subject called PSHE or some variant of this title. A number of studies have formed the evidence base of the identification of those pupil concerns in school. These concerns have included moving schools, especially transfer from primary to secondary school; anxiety about achievement and about relationships; bereavement and loss; bullying; health; money and family disagreements (BERA 2002: 9–12). The issue of self-esteem strongly underlies these anxieties. The pastoral curriculum has therefore developed as a response to these pupil needs. It is generally taught by a form tutor, although some rare schools have a dedicated department, with specialist teachers.

Skills for pastoral care

You may want to develop your knowledge and understanding of pastoral care during your induction year, or later in your career, in which case some specialised training for the skills needed for pastoral casework is recommended. An example of a school which prioritised casework is one where over 10 per cent of the school roll had refugee or asylum seeker status. Some were unaccompanied children and as such had need for specialist support and help. All the heads of year and several other teachers received specialist training for the specific case work undertaken in the school (Heilbronn and Jones 1997).

Useful information on counselling can be found on the dedicated web pages of the TeacherNet website (this site is referred to at the end of the chapter, but the specific pages relevant here are http://www.teachernet.gov.uk/professionaldevelopment/opportunities/nqt/Pupil_counselling/).

THE ROLE OF THE FORM TUTOR

The first and most obvious role of the form tutor is to be a support for pupils, both pastorally and academically. However, tutors also receive notification of pupils' misbehaviour and in most schools are expected to intervene, reinforce school rules, support other members of staff and uphold school policies. Some early writers on pastoral care have said that form tutors have been the primary means of controlling pupils' behaviour rather than pastoral carers and that the control aspect has been the primary function in many schools (Best *et al.* 1977). Recent studies have also shown that 'a good deal of casework either focuses on, or is triggered by, behaviour that is defined as unacceptable, deviant, or (more generously) "challenging"' (BERA 2002: 28). However, this emphasis varies from school to school and it is worth your thinking about the balance between support and discipline for pupils in your school.

As a form tutor, you need to know how the school policies and practices work in all the areas in which you deal with your form tutor group. Often you communicate directly with another member of staff to sort out a complaint about pupil behaviour, for example, or to follow up on an issue relating to the pupils' work. Communication with parents will also form part of your role. Usually these communications are straightforward, if time-consuming. Some other areas of your work might be:

- referring pupils to the head of year or house or another senior member of staff where appropriate, for example over behaviour, or underachievement, or personal matters;

**Reflective task 4.2
A form tutor's approach to
pastoral care situations**

As a form tutor what would you do in the following cases? Give reasons
for your decisions and then check with your mentor how the school
pastoral care system would deal with these issues. Is the system in your
school proactive or reactive?

1   A child comes to you and says that she is hungry because she hasn't
     eaten any breakfast and you have noticed other signs of possible
     neglect.
2   You notice a pupil bullying other pupils.
3   A child in your class always sits on his own and seems to have no
     social relations or friendships with his peers.

- dealing with formal registration requirements and following up absences;
- working with outside agencies, i.e. with the educational social worker (ESW) and
  the educational psychologist (EP).

Later sections of this chapter go into these areas in more detail.

COMMUNICATING WITH PARENTS

A crucial part of your pastoral role, both as a subject teacher and a form tutor, is your
communication with parents. The term 'parents' is used here to include guardians. The first
essential is to be informed about an individual pupil's home care circumstances and to
whom your communication should be addressed. There may be special circumstances which
you need to take into account before and when communicating with the pupils' parents.
Establishing relationships with parents is extremely important and you can affect the parent–
school relationship from the start. We suggest that you ask your mentor or a colleague for
advice. Most parents respond positively to someone who cares about pupils as individuals,
works hard and is a good professional teacher. In this regard, what your pupils say about
your lessons is important, as are the tasks you set them to do at home. Your attitudes to these
and your performance in marking them are influential in forming parents' opinions of you.
Homework can be one of the most effective ways of actively involving parents in your
work.

   Report writing is another essential area of communication between school and home
and it is essential to follow school procedures and communicate clearly according to school
reporting policy. Similarly, parents' evenings and review meetings are an essential forum for
communicating information about individual pupils' attainment and progress, which is what
most parents wish to know. If you have not already done so in your initial teacher education
you should sit in on a parents' evening with your mentor or an experienced colleague to
see how the relationships are nurtured and how such information is conveyed. At best these
meetings can be a valuable way of deepening your relationship with the individual pupil,

through gaining a stronger home–school bond, so it is important to be well prepared and to convey accurate information about the pupil, framed positively to enable progress to be made. The discussions should never become negative or argumentative. This is not always easy, particularly with a 'difficult' or an underachieving pupil. Such skills do develop with time.

Most parents are naturally protective of their children and this can result in you receiving a complaint of some kind. If this happens, take time to write down an account of what happened, first from your view point and then from theirs. Reflect on any misunderstandings and make a list of points which could have alleviated the differences. Refer to the relevant responsible teacher, such as a head of year/house, or the head of department/faculty, and discuss this aspect of your work and your experiences with your mentor as a learning experience for future dealings with parents.

To end this section it is worth noting that schools spend a great deal of time supporting parents. In 1999 a project called Parentaid, run by the Community Education Development Centre, undertook some research in schools in Northamptonshire and the West Midlands. Sam Spittle, national coordinator of the Home Office-funded programme, explains:

> It was staggering. We found that schools were second only to GPs' [general practitioners'] surgeries in time spent dealing with families in crisis. As you might expect, primary schools were worst affected, but staff in secondary schools also felt that parents' evenings and other events were often hijacked by parents' own problems.
>
> (Quoted from the TeacherNet website, page reference at
> http://www.teachernet.gov.uk/professionaldevelopment/
> opportunities/nqt/parents/)

The research also found that teachers felt they did not know where to refer parents for help, and that some heads were spending as much as 50 per cent of their time dealing with family problems that were not related to education at all. Each school was dealing with an average of 13 family problems a week. The extent of the problem becomes clearer when you realise that a local education authority (LEA) with 100 schools may have around 1,300 families to help in a single week. To find out more about Parentaid, look on the website (see 'Further Reading' below).

REGISTRATION

As a form tutor, you may wonder why so much emphasis is placed upon the routines regarding the completion of the attendance register. Pupil attendance and rates of truancy have been highlighted over the past 20 years as indicators of school effectiveness (Rutter *et al.* 1979; DES 1989). This relationship is now taken very seriously. For example, behaviour and education support teams (BESTs) have been operating in a number of LEAs since January 2003. They are multi-agency teams that work with children aged 5–18 and their families and schools, intervening early to prevent and address emotional and behavioural issues. They work in targeted primary and secondary schools, and in the community, alongside a range of other support structures and services, usually as part of a wider Behaviour Improvement Programme.

The Department for Education and Skills (DfES) has stated that the aim of a BEST is to promote emotional well-being, positive behaviour and school attendance, and help in the identification and support of those with, or at risk of developing, emotional and behavioural problems. By April 2004, more than a third of the LEAs in England will have BESTs working in some of their schools.

As a form tutor you will be expected to keep the register of pupils' attendance and to follow up any unauthorised absences with parents, with the support of the relevant responsible senior member of staff, and on the basis of the school policies and procedures. Your mentor should enable you to understand precisely how you should achieve this function. Also very useful to you in this connection will be the dedicated website on attendance run by the DfES (http://www.dfes.gov.uk/schoolattendance/goodpractice/index.cfm). The site has very good links to policies and to good practice in this area and is worth referring to for guidance on the duties of registration and to learn about the issues concerning attendance, your duties as a form tutor, and the roles of the school, LEAs and parents.

Truancy receives a focus in many legislation and guidance documents, not least in the Anti-Social Behaviour Bill that began its passage through Parliament on 27 March 2003. Truancy has such a high profile because of its impact on pupils' education and because of concern that young people may commit crime when they are not in school. A Youth Justice MORI survey of young people in 2002 shows that those who play truant are more likely to offend than those that do not, with two-thirds of truants having offended versus less than a third of those who have not played truant (source: http://www.dfes.gov.uk/school attendance/truancysweeps/index.cfm; accessed 15.09.03) Controversy surrounds recent parental prosecutions for their children's unauthorised absences. The Anti-Social Behaviour Bill is intended to enable LEAs and police officers to issue fixed penalty notices to parents for failure to ensure their child's regular attendance at school. Headteachers will also be able to use this power if they decide it is appropriate. The Bill will also include legislation to give LEAs and schools the statutory right to ask parents to sign parenting contracts committing them to attend parenting classes. The DfES is also looking at ways of making Home-School Agreements, which spell out the responsibilities of the school and what it expects of pupils, more effective (http://www.dfes.gov.uk).

WORKING WITH OTHER PROFESSIONALS

As a form tutor or a subject teacher you are unable to deal with all pupil problems that are brought to you, nor should you attempt to do so. In addition to the head of year/house, the head of department and, of course, your mentor within school there are many teachers with specific responsibilities who support you: the special educational needs co-ordinator (SENCO), the designated member of staff with responsibility for child protection and the teachers with responsibility for careers, examinations and work experience, all of whom are experienced and a potential source of support for you.

However, there may be times in your career when you find that a member of your form tutor group should be referred to a professional colleague working outside school. Two of the most likely external professional colleagues are the education social worker (ESW) and the educational psychologist (EP). In the past, and still current in some LEAs, the ESW was known as the education welfare officer. More information on these roles is given in the sections that follow.

The educational social worker

As a form tutor responsible for pupil registration you may well work with the ESW Service, a department within the LEA which monitors pupil attendance in relation to the policies in force. Attendance Regulations require schools to publish their attendance figures and such information is requested by OFSTED inspectors, who are obliged to comment in their inspection report on any year group with less than 90 per cent attendance during a specified period.

A number of regulations form the legal basis of pupil registration, including the 1996 Education Act and the Amendment Regulations published in 1995, 1997 and 2001. These can be viewed through the links on the DfES website page mentioned above. They also refer back to Section 36 of the Education Act (1944) in which parents and carers are required to 'secure efficient full-time education, whether in school or otherwise'.

To ensure that schools and parents fulfil their responsibilities relating to attendance, pupils arriving 10 minutes after the register is closed should receive a late mark, while any pupil arriving more than 30 minutes late should be recorded as an unauthorised absence. A pupil whose attendance falls below 80 per cent over a two-month period must be referred to the ESW and the parents informed. Find out the procedure in your own school for following up on pupil absences as this varies from school to school. You should always alert your head of year/house if there are any concerns. The legislation currently requires that the LEA perform an annual register check for each school in its authority. While the exact detail of his or her work may vary slightly in different LEAs, the ESW is likely to be involved in at least the following activities:

- attending meetings in schools to discuss individual cases;
- home visits;
- liaising with other appropriate agencies (e.g. Social Services);
- attending court as a witness in case of continued poor attendance and lack of co-operation from parents/carers;
- issuing Child Employment Work Permits and Entertainment Licences.

To learn more about the working practices of the ESW attached to your school it might be useful for you to obtain further details from the LEA and even to arrange to meet him or her during a visit to you school.

The educational psychologist

EPs are concerned with children's learning and development, and work mainly in schools, with teachers and parents. EPs have a degree in psychology and professional training in educational psychology. They are also qualified teachers who have taught for at least two years. They carry out a wide range of tasks with the aim of enhancing children's learning and they offer psychological support and advice to enable teachers to help children more effectively.

As teachers they are aware of the range of social and curriculum factors which affect teaching and learning, and they specialise in difficulties children may experience between early childhood and late adolescence, including developmental difficulties, learning difficulties, emotional and behavioural problems, physical disabilities, speech and language delay, and vision and hearing problems. They work closely with the LEA to help meet the educational needs of these children. The psychologists contribute to the assessment of children's educational needs and advise teachers, schools, parents and the LEA how these can best be met. In general, for pupils in the state sector the child's school will refer a pupil to an LEA EP following consultation with a pupil's parents.

An EP might therefore work with pupils in your class if they have been assessed as having a variety of learning needs, which may include:

- emotional and/or behavioural difficulties;
- general learning difficulties compared to pupils of their age or specific difficulties with reading or writing, such as dyslexia;
- psychological problems, relating to hearing or sight impairment.

EPs are responsible for carrying out assessments related to the Code of Practice for Special Educational Needs (see *Learning to Teach in the Secondary School*, 3rd edition: 218–33).

PERSONAL, SOCIAL AND HEALTH EDUCATION CURRICULUM

You may also teach a specific pastoral curriculum, particularly if you are a form tutor. In most schools form tutors are given a scheme of work to cover, which is either drawn up by the head of year, or house, with a team of tutors, or another group set up in the school to oversee the pastoral curriculum. In some schools, rarely, form tutors draw up their own schemes. As described above, the pastoral curriculum may consist of PSE, PSHE, or even PSHCE. Guidance for what the subject could fruitfully encompass can be found in the National Curriculum published by the DfEE and the Qualifications and Curriculum Authority in the section entitled 'Framework for Personal Social and Health Education at Key Stages 3 and 4' (DfEE/QCA 1999: 188–95. This can be found at The National Curriculum Online, available at http://www.nc.uk.net/index.html).

The guidelines for PSHE which appear in the National Curriculum were intended to standardise the delivery of PSHE across England and to make it appear more like the other curriculum subjects, with a breakdown of the underlying rationale for the curriculum, and requisite rigorous terminology. However, two critical elements are missing if the guidelines intended PSHE to be given comparable status with other school subjects in the minds of pupils and teachers. First PSHE is not intended to culminate in any recognised exam, and secondly no specialist training of teachers is required to teach it.

Since it is not a statutory National Curriculum subject in England, schools are not obliged to follow these curriculum guidelines and, as it does not culminate in any recognised accreditation, there is no agreed form of assessment for PSHE. This tends to devalue it as a subject for some schools and pupils. As a form tutor you may be expected to interpret the PSHE guidelines and, whether your school follows them or not, it is important to know what they contain.

The guidance outlines the knowledge, skills and understanding which pupils could be expected to develop at Key Stage 3 and Key Stage 4, under three headings:

1   Developing confidence and responsibility and making the most of their abilities;

2   Developing a healthier, safer lifestyle;

3   Developing good relationships and respecting the differences between people.

(DfEE/QCA 1999: 189–90)

The guidelines also include Breadth of Opportunities statements which suggest that PSHE is not in fact to be thought of as a discrete subject like the others but more like the 'cross-curricular themes' which the National Curriculum intended schools to deliver across different subject areas. These were Education for Citizenship, Education for Industrial and Economic Understanding, Health Education and Environmental Education (Department for Education and Science, 1987). The Breadth of Opportunities statements show how PSHE knowledge, skills and understanding are meant to be gained outside defined PSHE lessons, for example through extra-curricular activities.

During Key Stage 4, for example, pupils should be taught the knowledge, skills and understanding through opportunities to:

a)   Take responsibility (for example, by representing the school to visitors and at outside events).

b)   Feel positive about themselves (for example, by gaining recognition for the role they play in school life, such as organising activities for younger pupils or working in a resource centre).

c)   Participate (for example, in an initiative to improve their local community; in challenging activities involving physical performance, public performance or organised events outside the school).

d)   Make real choices and decisions (for example, about their priorities, plans and use of time; about their choices post-16, with regular review and support).

d)   Meet and work with people (for example, through activities such as work experience and industry days).

e)   Develop relationships (for example, by discussing relationships in single and mixed sex groups).

f)   Consider social and moral dilemmas (for example, young parenthood, genetic engineering, attitudes to the law).

g)   Find information and provide advice (for example, by providing peer support services to other pupils).

h)   Prepare for change (for example, in relation to progression to further education and training).

(DfEE/QCA 1999: 193–4)

Schools are meant to design their PSHE programmes to ensure the development and assessment of pupils' progress and your school may have guidance from other professionals, in the field of health for example. Useful guidance at every level is given on the Teachernet website at http://www.teachernet.gov.uk/pshe/, where you can also access an example of a scheme of work for PSHE which incorporates the guidelines. This further guidance is relevant also to Scotland, Wales and Northern Ireland, which all have related guidelines and defined skills, knowledge and understanding in the area. Also, from September 2003, a new General Certificate in Education (GCSE) Learning for Life and Work was being piloted in some Northern Ireland schools, based around the learning outcomes for proposed statutory core components at Key Stage 4, which are intended to cover the topics of Local and Global Citizenship, PSHE and Education for Employability.

The Teachernet website also publishes good practice from schools and links to further documents, such as official reports and policy documents. In addition, the site outlines professional development opportunities and offers a diagram showing the different topics which are encompassed by the term PSHE. Each area can be investigated in detail, through links on the titles. The diagram can be seen in Figure 4.1.

It is important to understand how progression may be built into a PSHE syllabus, relating to what is appropriate for pupils at various stages of their development. Taking one extremely pertinent topic as an example, the DfES has reminded teachers that:

> It is a common mistake to tell too much too soon about various topics, not only drugs, at lower levels of the school. Yet, while departments are well disciplined at breaking down subjects to appropriate levels of attainment and awareness, PSHE issues tend to be delivered 'with a trowel' if we are not careful. Not only should we engage the children where they are, but deeper levels of knowledge and insight can be held over to higher years, when they will have developed more as individuals, with their own opinions, too.
>
> From 'Teachers' Notes' to accompany the *KS4 Scheme of Work*, published on the TeacherNet website (URL below)

SUMMARY

All teachers engage in pastoral care, whatever subject is taught, and the effectiveness of the school pastoral system influences every aspect of school life. Good pastoral systems in a school are essential to the development of pupils' self-esteem and hence motivation and achievement. As a teacher and form tutor it is important to know how the school pastoral system works and how the various strands of personal, social and health education are managed in your school. There are sources of information available through the websites

Figure 4.1   Topics generally included in a PSHE programme in the UK
Source: Teachernet (available online at http://www.teachernet.gov.uk/pshe/)

**Reflective task 4.3
Interpreting PSHE curriculum
guidelines**

- read the Key Stage 4 Breadth of Opportunity statements above;
- obtain a copy of the National Curriculum guidelines for PSHE (DfEE/ QCA 1999), which can be downloaded from the National Curriculum Online website, address given above;
- choose one of the seven PSHE strands which interests you, from Figure 4.1.

Now reflect on the following questions, note your answers, discuss with your mentor or another colleague and/or write up your notes:

1   How far does your school encourage pupils to take these opportunities?
2   What qualities do you think these opportunities might help to develop in pupils?
3   How far should the school provide the scope for these developmental opportunities, in your opinion?

and publications mentioned in this chapter. Further, you can and should draw on the support and expertise of other professionals, both inside and outside school, to develop skills in dealing with some of the major issues which affect pupils' welfare.

One of the most important aspects of teaching as a profession is fulfilling the pastoral role, whether as a form tutor or a subject specialist teacher. In doing so you are demonstrating your own positive values and showing respect and consideration for your pupils' development. This can be very demanding; it is also extremely rewarding. There can also be career development opportunities, and you could move through the pastoral system and develop as a deputy head of house or year and then a head of house or year. This in turn can lead to the position of deputy headteacher (pastoral) and to headteacher.

FURTHER READING

Best, R., Lang, P., Lodge, C. and Watkins, C. (1995) *Pastoral Care and PSE*. London: Cassell/ NAPCE. This book provides a very good overview of contemporary issues in pastoral care.

National Association of Pastoral Care in Education (NAPCE). This organisation was founded in 1982 to establish links between all those who have an interest in pastoral care and personal-social education. It publishes the journal *Pastoral Care in Education* and a variety of books, resource packs and response documents. Address NAPCE Base, c/o Education Department, University of Warwick, Coventry, CV4 7AL. Website: http://www.napce. org.uk.

TeacherNet, available online at http://www.teachernet.gov.uk/pshe. There is a dedicated PSHE area with some particularly useful links, developed by the DfES.

Lifebytes, available online at http://www.lifebytes.gov.uk – for Key Stage 3 resources.

Mind, Body & Soul, available online at http://www.mindbodysoul.gov.uk – for Key Stage 4 resources.

Parentaid website at www.durhameaz.org.uk/parentaid/.

5 Developing Teaching and Learning Strategies

Diana Burton

To be effective in helping their pupils achieve their full learning potential, an understanding of how learning happens for individuals is vital (Burton, 2001). Through your practice in the classroom, your reading and reflection on the ideas of others and your discussion with other teachers, you have developed a range of knowledge about learning and the differences between the approaches, motivation and competences of your pupils. This chapter explores briefly some of the research that has been undertaken to reveal more about human learning with particular reference to school-age children. For a more in-depth overview of learning theories please refer to Bartlett *et al.* (2001), Chapters 4 and 5.

Theoretical perspectives which currently influence our understanding of how learning happens tend to be those that have some direct influence on pedagogic strategy, such as notions of metacognition, which describes how learners understand and control their learning strategies, social constructivist emphases on social interaction and scaffolded support for learning, and, although old, some of Piaget's ideas about learning readiness and active learning, which also endure. Work on learning styles, thinking skills, different manifestations of intelligence and research into brain chemistry are also of increasing interest to teachers who are engaged in best practice action research or are striving to accelerate learning.

OBJECTIVES

By the end of this unit you should have developed further your understanding of:

- some of the current ideas about how pupils learn;
- the implications for your pedagogic strategies;
- your own approach to learning.

HOW DOES TEACHING INTERACT WITH LEARNING?

Teachers make hundreds of sophisticated judgements every week about how to engage, motivate and challenge groups of pupils and how to respond to individual pupils' learning difficulties and achievements. Your decisions rest heavily on your internalised knowledge of a complex range of factors. These factors include knowledge about individual pupils, the aims of the teaching, the nature of the subject matter, the pupils' motivational levels, your preferred teaching style, your beliefs about intelligence or 'ability', your engagement with learning theory and your reflections on cognition in practice. What is certain is that teaching and learning co-exist in a dynamic interplay of teacher–pupil interactions, some of which are preplanned but many of which are unpredictable and exciting. Thus teaching and learning are organic and no two learning episodes are the same. To equip yourselves for this demanding and stimulating daily endeavour you need time at the end of the day and between lessons to reflect on why certain interventions you made in pupils' learning were effective whilst others were less so. In order to structure your reflections you could take sections of this chapter and apply the questions they pose to particular lessons or groups you have taught. To get you thinking about ways of analysing the impact of teaching on learning, try Reflective Task 5.1.

Reflective task 5.1
Predicting learning outcomes
and teacher interventions

Choose four pupils in one of your teaching groups who each present with different learning challenges. Draw up a table similar to Table 5.1 and record the learning outcomes you predict for each pupil within each of the three aspects of learning identified. Next, insert the teacher interventions you anticipate making as a consequence of these outcomes. An example from English has been provided to guide you.

Table 5.1   Recording the learning outcomes for selected pupils

Pupil	Thinking skills	Interpersonal skills	Motor skills	Teacher intervention
E.g. Sarah	Contributes enthusiastically to small group discussion about Lady Macbeth's culpability.	Interrupts Mark when he is sharing his ideas.	Records outcomes poorly into exercise book.	Ask S to rehearse and respond to Mark's ideas. Suggest S practices handwriting at home by writing down words of favourite CD track.
Pupil 2				

PERSPECTIVES ON LEARNING

Learning to think – thinking to learn

Guy Claxton, who has for many years been studying how people learn, believes that a teacher's job is to build pupils' learning power, to help them learn to learn. He defines this power as comprising the four 'R's (Claxton, 2002: 17):

- *resilience*: the ability to concentrate fully and avoid distractions;
- *resourcefulness*: being able to draw on a wide range of learning methods and strategies;
- *reflectiveness*: thinking strategically about one's own learning, drawing lessons from experience and adapting approaches as a result;
- *reciprocity*: being able to work profitably alone and with others.

Claxton recommends that teachers' time would be most profitably spent helping pupils to develop these four competences.

Whilst it is probably true that we could define Claxton's four aspects of 'learning power' in a number of ways, and that the alliterative use of 'R' is simply a device to help us remember them, the advice he offers teachers and learners is accessible and sensible for developing long-term learning strategies. Claxton describes the teacher's role in relation to building learner power again using a four-fold model (Claxton, 2002: 69). Teachers need to:

- *explain* what learning power is to pupils so that they are thinking about how they learn and can learn better;
- *commentate* on pupils' development of learning power informally and formally;
- *orchestrate* activities and environments which develop the four 'R's;
- *model* effective learning by externalising their own thinking about problems or talking about their own learning histories.

Much of this is what good teachers are already doing.

Claxton's approach sits within the school of thought that believes that *metacognitive* learning, knowing what you know and how you came to think about or know it, is essential to properly equip people for a lifetime of learning. Another major proponent of this process approach is Philip Adey, who researches thinking skills in pupils (Adey and Shayer, 1994: 67–72). Pupils who understand and can control their own learning strategies, such as techniques for remembering or ways of presenting information when thinking, experience significant benefits in their learning.

Learning to know – knowing to learn

It is almost universally accepted that in teaching we start from where the pupils are in terms of their prior learning. Reviewing research into the role that prior knowledge plays in learning, Dochy *et al.* (2002) conclude that it is the single most powerful predictor of future learning. As Philip Adey has said:

> If you talk to an expert about a field in which you're equally knowledgeable, lots of learning takes place. So knowing lots already actually promotes the process of learning. This works with five-year-olds who know about dinosaurs just as much as it works with professors who know an enormous amount about nuclear physics.
> (Adey, 2002: 50)

Reflective task 5.2
Thinking about thinking

Working in pairs, ask your pupils to try to explain to each other how they tackled a piece of work: for instance, how they approached the structuring of a particular argument within an essay, how they went about designing a product or learned a mathematical equation.

They may need a lot of help with this if it is new to them; you may need to feed in questions or comments such as 'Do all the points in an argument appear at once in your thinking?' 'How do you sort them?' 'Did you think about the whole product first and rough that out or did you tackle it in steps?' 'How do you think about an equation? Do you see it in your mind as two separate things?'

It is very important to allow your pupils time to talk with one another and not to give up if they find it too novel a task. See Adey et al. (2001) and Adhami et al. (1998) in 'Further Reading'.

Enabling each individual to retrieve this knowledge is what presents teachers with a challenge as pupils experience the same learning event differently and have their own distinct attitudes towards, and methods of processing, prior knowledge. The processing of knowledge has been a fundamental focus of study for psychologists, with Piaget (1932, 1954) arguing that learners generate new understandings through an active exploration of the world. Information-processing theories treat knowledge development as a systematic process of sensing stimuli, working on it in the short-term operational memory and storing it as abstractions of experience in the long-term memory (Atkinson and Shriffin, 1968). Researchers in the Vygotskyan tradition stress the importance of socially constructing knowledge through interactions with others (Brown, 1994; Rogoff, 1998). These perspectives on learning are discussed in more detail elsewhere (Burton, 2001). Reflective task 5.2 invites you to review your lesson planning against these ideas.

If we take the view that brains are similar to computers in terms of their processing approach, in that 'brains and computers embody intelligence for some of the same reasons' (Pinker, 1998: 26), it is easy to see why the better the teacher explains a topic, the easier it is for pupils to understand, commit to memory and remember later. If it is structured systematically, breaking down the ideas in a task or concept in a meaningful rather than haphazard way, pupils are better able to work with the material and store it logically in the long-term memory. Since it is often helpful to learn generalities by examining specifics, it is also helpful if teachers provide concrete examples to illustrate an idea. It is also vital, of course, to link back to what pupils may already know about the topic.

Using formative, in-class assessment, teachers can examine the progress of individuals in order to determine when to increase the intellectual demand on them. Many pupils (and some teachers!) become comfortable with work that they can always complete and do well in but all learners need the challenge of difficulty and some even need the possibility of failure in order to make cognitive progress. The influential American psychologist, Bruner (1966), argued that difficult ideas should be seen as a challenge and, if properly presented, can be learned by most pupils. Adey (2002) agrees, arguing that holding fixed views of intelligence is what stultifies this approach. If teachers adopt the view that intelligence is not fixed but can be developed, this liberates learners and requires teachers to make learning

Reflective task 5.3
Knowledge storage and retrieval

How systematic is your organisation of learning material? Take a lesson plan and evaluate it using the following questions:

- Is the lesson's central idea introduced in general, broad-brush terms so that pupils get a feel for what they are exploring?
- Do you probe pupils' previous understandings (in pairs and groups as well as whole class)?
- Have you thought through the structure of the concepts so that you can present them to pupils in a logical format? This applies equally to skills and knowledge learning. For example:
  - o   in a physical education lesson you may practice discrete tennis skills before building up to a full game;
  - o   in a mathematics lesson you teach about triangles and angles as constituent elements of Pythagorus' theorem;
  - o   in history you may approach the study of imperialism through related concepts of power, economic growth, racial tension and so on.
- Do you scaffold pupil's learning by helping them record new ideas against key words or headings? See the section 'Learning to talk – talking to learn' below where scaffolding is discussed; and unit 5.1 in *Learning to Teach in the Secondary School*, 3rd edition, under the sub-heading 'Bruner'.
- Do you summarise at the end of the lesson what has been learned?

challenging yet achievable. The more recent finding that the brain has enormous potential 'to grow', in the sense that the more it is exercised the greater the number of neural connections are made between the brain cells (Greenfield, 1997), provides some neurological support for this argument.

Building on an idea of Piaget's about creating 'cognitive conflict', Adey links Vygotsky's emphasis on social interaction to the intellectual challenge that is required to promote learning. If children develop 'argumentation skills' through their exploration of subject-specific concepts and propositions with other pupils and teachers, they are able to extend their understanding. These skills are also then available to them in different contexts: at home, in the playground and so on. Adey's evidence suggests that the transferability of such skills has positive effects on General Certificate in Education (GCSE) results in general (Monk and Osborne, 2000: 169).

Learning to talk – talking to learn

The status of talk in the classroom and its centrality to learning is a key theme of current pedagogical training. The ideas of Russian psychologist Lev Vygotsky and those of Jerome Bruner in the USA have increasingly influenced educators in recent years, although Vygotsky's work dates from between the 1920s and 1930s having been suppressed in Soviet Russia until the 1970s.

For Vygotsky (1978), psychological activity has socio-cultural characteristics from the very beginning of development. Thus children will learn new concepts from a range of different stimuli as they interact with one another and with adults, implying a problem-solving approach for pupils and a facilitator role for the teacher. Whereas Piaget considered language a tool of thought in the child's developing mind, Vygotsky held that language was generated from the need to communicate and was central to the development of thinking. Vygotsky believed that adults' communicative interventions with learners could reduce a pupil's 'zone of proximal development' – the gap between the current level of learning and the level the child could be functioning at with adult or peer support. 'What a child can do today in co-operation, tomorrow he will be able to do on his own' (Vygotsky, 1962: 67).

More recently, the American adult educator, Jack Mezirov (2000), has also emphasised the central role that communicative learning plays in developing and refining 'meaning schemes'.

The utility of group work to teachers assuming a Vygotskyan or social constructivist approach to teaching and learning is well known and long established. Research into peer tutoring, various forms of group and pair work and in-class setting has revealed advantages in promoting argument and sharing complex ideas (Brown, 1994; Gillies and Ashman, 2003; Kutnick and Manson, 2000; Rogoff, 1998). Wigfield et al. (1998), reviewing students' motivation for learning, emphasised the importance of learning as an inherently social activity. Learners gain emotional strength and enhanced self-esteem from the affirmation they receive in 'safe' learning groups and are more likely to ask for help from teachers if they are experiencing problems (Sharp et al., 2002).

Fazey and Marton (2002) explain that one of the reasons why helping children to talk about their learning is so productive is that individual learners tend to assume that the reality which they experience is the reality that others experience too. Greenfield (1997) has shown how even the perceptions and interpretations of the same experiences by identical twins lead to unique sets of memories. Fazey and Marton (2000) found that, in introducing 'variation' in the form of the views of others, experiments show children develop a greater capacity for learning from new experiences. See Reflective task 5.4.

Bruner (1983) highlighted the importance of structured intervention within communicative learning models. The teacher's job is to guide pupils' discovery of new principles through the input of focused questions or stimulus materials at appropriate points – this is known as 'scaffolding'. In a recent study of the use of metaphors with 10 year olds in science learning, Cameron (2002) found that mediation of the interpretation of the metaphors by the teacher maximised the use of the strategy. For a fuller discussion of scaffolding, see Urquhart, 2002.

Accelerated learning approaches

In recent years educational consultants and trainers have popularised certain research findings by extrapolating from them the implications for learning and teaching. Thus, there is now a plethora of training courses and publications for teachers on 'accelerated learning' (AL) and 'neuro-linguistic programming' (NLP).

AL may be described as an umbrella term for a series of practical approaches to learning developed from study of a range of research disciplines, including: the study of aspects of brain function, theories of human attention and motivation, the psychology of optimal performance and intelligence theory (Smith, 2003). AL draws on recent advances in how the brain works – research into the effect of environmental factors on learning, such as

Reflective task 5.4
Talk, talk and more talk!

How much talking do you do? In the classroom, at home, in the staffroom, in the corridors? Instructional/questioning? To the girls/to the boys? Inquisitive/inquisitorial? Challenging/endorsing?

How much talking do your pupils do? Teacher contrived/pupil-led? On-task/off-task? Constructing new relationships between ideas/reproducing or reading text?

We could go on with these juxtapositions; use these or think of others that are of greater significance in your teaching, and organise some observation of other teachers' classrooms. Be brave and wear a dictaphone all lesson so that everything is recorded. Alternatively, set up a camera in your classroom, but remember, for ethical reasons, to warn others about it and to seek the head's and parents' permission to visually record pupils.

What may be easier is to ask a teaching assistant or trainee teacher to complete an observation schedule for you on, e.g. the amount of instructional as opposed to questioning talk you use or the amount of teacher talk as opposed to pupil talk that occurs (you may be surprised).

drinking water regularly or listening to music whilst working. It stresses the preparation of learners for lifelong learning and promotes metacognitive training or learning to learn (discussed earlier). This knowledge is drawn on eclectically to devise more efficient ways of learning, e.g. the Accelerated Learning Institute (ALI, 2003) advocates the use of games and activities, motion and music, relaxation, role play, colour and mind maps in order to maximise learning. The central ideas of accelerated learning are that individuals have preferred learning or thinking styles, multifunctional intelligences, the potential to exploit their emotional intelligence better and the need for a variety of stimuli and experience.

Learning styles

In emphasising the different learning styles that learners may have, accelerated learning practitioners tend to use the VAK construct, i.e. the *visual, auditory* or *kinaesthetic* learning styles. There is a great deal of research into learning styles and strategies which has developed many different ways of measuring and defining the differences in how people approach their learning; see Burton, 2001 for a brief synopsis or Riding and Rayner, 1998 for a thorough overview of the research to date. Dryden and Vos (2001) explain that the VAK idea is that some learners are strongly visual, learning best by 'seeing' pictures, videos or graphics. Others benefit from hearing information and may learn best while listening to music, while many people are kinaesthetic learners who learn best through physical movement and activity.

Neuro-linguistic programming

Whilst individuals may well exhibit natural preferences between the learning styles described above, there are tasks which lend themselves more to one or other of these 'modalities', and most learners need to use all at some time or another. Good teachers incorporate all three styles within their classroom activities. Researchers into NLP believe that most learning is subconscious and that teachers need to consciously orchestrate subconscious learning in their classrooms. This includes placing 'peripherals', such as posters, paintings and graphics, around a classroom to emphasise main points on any subject; and then to organise games so that students sit in different positions during the day in order to absorb key information subconsciously from the 'peripherals'. Accelerated learning techniques incorporate these NLP ideas.

Multi-functional intelligence theory

Sternberg (1985) proposed a model of intelligence, which he termed 'triarchic', comprising three major aspects which interact with one another: analytical, creative and practical thinking. Analytical or *componential* intelligence is what is normally measured on intelligence quotient (IQ) and achievement tests: that is, planning, organising and remembering facts then applying them to new situations. Creative or *experiential* intelligence is the ability to see new connections between things and to develop original ideas. Practical or *contextual* intelligence is the ability to read situations and people and manipulate them to best advantage. According to Sternberg, neither experiential nor practical intelligence are measured in IQ tests and yet it is these very abilities that often help learners to make progress.

Howard Gardner (1983, 1993a and 1993b) has developed the theory of multiple intelligences, arguing that there are eight distinct intelligences which exist independently of one another: linguistic, spatial, logical–mathematical, musical, bodily-kinaesthetic, interpersonal, intrapersonal and naturalist; see also Unit 4.3 in *Learning to Teach in the Secondary School*, 3rd edition. Gardner explains that individuals have different entry points to learning depending on the strength of their various intelligences. Gardner's work has become very popular in educational circles, possibly because it offers a dynamic view of intelligence to counter the long-held view of intelligence as unitary and fairly stable, and it encourages a focus on developing particular individual capabilities to their highest potential.

Emotional intelligence theory

Salovey and Mayer (1990) developed the construct of 'emotional intelligence', which has been further elucidated by Goleman (1996). An individual's emotional state and ability to deal with their feelings can impact on their educational performance. Educators have perhaps only paid lip service to this 'affective' domain of experience with their main focus being on the 'cognitive' domain. It is now receiving more attention as a result of Goleman's popular work. He has related the ability to control impulses, motivate oneself and regulate moods to improved thinking and learning.

Brain gym

A major determinant of how well pupils learn is how good is their attention to the task or stimulus. Gaining and maintaining attention is vital for learning penetration. A popular approach to ensuring pupils are ready to attend well to their work is that of 'brain gym': short, sharp exercises designed to improve concentration, alertness and hand-eye coordination. Primary teachers plan them to occur several times during the day and at secondary level they are commonly used at the beginning of lessons to help pupils focus. They can also act as a way to break up long learning tasks to energise pupils when concentration or motivation begins to flag or with learners whose attention span is limited. Many children find it difficult to sit still for a long time and find excuses to get out of their seats. As teachers you are probably more mobile than your pupils so you don't experience what is actually quite an unnatural immobility. Legitimating some movement at regular intervals in lessons may serve to reduce the level of off-task behaviour.

Brain gym sessions usually last for three or four minutes and may be linked to work that is being taught, e.g. practising tables with quick-fire questions or a game to help learn the periodic table in chemistry. More usually, though, they take the form of physical movement exercises, e.g. pupils making shapes with their bodies, or trying to rub their tummies while tapping their heads (see Table 5.2).[1]

Brain gym exercises were originally developed in the 1960s by American researcher Paul Dennison, who was dyslexic. He was intrigued by the connection between physical activity and learning ability. Some centres for the treatment of dyslexia have developed quite complex schemes of physical activity for individual children. These schemes are said

Table 5.2   Brain breaks (Smith, 2003)

Try these 'Brain Breaks' form the ALITE website
• With your forefinger and thumb of each hand pinched together, extend your hand out in front of your face and trace large circles in the same direction. Keep your lips and teeth together. Now trace the circles in the other direction. Now try with one hand going clockwise and the other anti-clockwise. Swap again.
• With your writing hand hold an imaginary pencil in front of your face and write the key words from your lesson in the air. Say the letters of the word as you write. When you have finished try and write them backwards. For fun, write the keywords in the air, but with your nose! Watch your neighbour and try and guess what the word is. Now try it with your ear!
• Hold your ear and slowly roll your earl lobes between finger and thumb. Do it nice and slowly and all the way round your ear. How does it feel?
• Do finger aerobics! With a partner sit alongside each other or either side of your desk. You partner should place both hands flat on the desk and so should you. Take turns to lift different fingers without taking any fingers off the desk
. Do it together and in sequence. Start with simple lifts with each finger in turn, then taps, then bends, then big stretches. Now one of you be the aerobics instructor and the other has to do exactly the exercise the instructor demonstrates!
• Use finger sums by showing your partner a number sum with your fingers and then seeing if your partner can get the correct answer. Remember crossed hands mean add, one hand across your face means take away, hands in a diagonal is multiply and a hand across your face with a dot above and below is

to improve the condition through the strengthening of neural connections. The exercises stimulate neurological pathways, helping both sides of the brain to work together. The right hemisphere controls the body's left side and is responsible for the emotions and creativity. The left hemisphere controls the right side of the body: academic functions, language, etc. In school learning we tend to emphasise the use of the left brain. Chowcat (2002) points out that left and right brain functions complement each other and most activity requires regular and complicated interaction between the two sides. Given the current emphasis on creativity in education, Chowcat argues that the need to maximise the brain's interactive potential is vital.

Accelerated learning proponents contend that we need to develop both sides of the brain so that we learn to use emotion and creativity productively rather than allowing it to obscure our understanding at times of stress. Mind mapping is becoming an increasingly popular technique for learners to organise their thoughts. It encourages both sides of the brain to be used more fully and in harmony, facilitating problem-solving and the development of creative ideas. If teachers and pupils also verbalise the process afterwards the learning is enhanced and retained better. Pole-bridging, describing to themselves why they are doing something, is also advocated as a way of pupils consolidating their learning as it happens.

Smith (2003) claims that, when properly motivated and appropriately taught, all learners can reach a level of achievement which may currently appear beyond them. He advocates that teachers should use an accelerated learning cycle:

- be relentlessly positive and scaffold all learning challenges;
- give an overview of what's to be done first;
- connect to previous learning and current understanding;
- embed questions and essential vocabulary early;
- provide variety in input (*visual, auditory, kinaesthetic*);
- structure lots of learner questions and language exchange;
- review throughout individually and collectively;
- preview what's next as you end.

This kind of guidance is not really new – note, for instance, the resonance with the previous sections of this chapter – however, many teachers have found the accelerated learning approach fresh and inspirational as it offers practical ideas in accessible ways.

SUMMARY

Teaching and learning today is not only much better informed by research into ways pupils learn but also by the developing understanding of how the brain may function. Professional development courses for teachers draw on this research, emphasising the need to accommodate a range of learning styles, to facilitate talk and group work, and to develop pupils' awareness of their approaches to learning. Teachers are encouraged to undertake small-scale research into their practice and many have chosen to investigate the extent to which contemporary learning theories can extend pupil learning and achievement. Another important factor contributing to improved teaching and learning is the growth of information technology and the use of computers in education. This change is not just about different ways of teaching and learning through the use of computers but is informed too by the associated development of artificial intelligence. Continuing professional

Reflective task 5.5
Accelerating your learning

Visit some of the websites to learn more about accelerated learning. There are tasks and tests for you to do which are a fun way of finding out more about your own learning styles, multiple intelligences and approaches to learning. These sites also provide helpful ideas and resources for educators. Here are some to get you started:
Accelerated Learning Institute (2003)
   http://www.accelerated-learning.com/
Accelerated Learning in Training and Education (2003)
   http://www.alite.co.uk/
Accelerated Learning (2003)
   http://www.accelerated-learning-uk.co.uk/
Accelerated Learning Network (2003)
   http://www.acceleratedlearningnetwork.com/

development now requires teachers to be aware of developments such as these and to look to ways in which they can supplement the teacher's traditional skills.

NOTE

1   For more information on brain gym exercises send a large self-addressed envelope and two stamps to Educational Kinesiology Foundation, 12 Golden Rise, London NW4 2HR.

FURTHER READING

Adey, P., Shayer, M. and Yates, C. (2001) *Thinking Science* and Adhami, M., Johnson, D.C. and Shayer, M. (1998) *Thinking Mathematics*. For further reading and ideas on metacognitive training.

Jarvis, P., Holford, J. and Griffin, C. (2003) *The Theory and Practice of Learning*, 2nd edition. London: Kogan Page. Gives brief overviews of main psychological theories and their implications for learning in the current educational context.

Smith, A. and Call, N. (2002) *The ALPs Approach*. London: ALITE. Practical accelerated learning approaches.

Whitebread, D. (ed.) (2000) *The Psychology of Teaching and Learning in the Primary School*. London and New York: RoutledgeFalmer. Very useful text drawing on up-to-date psychological research, which is as relevant to secondary as to primary teaching.

6 Improving the Effectiveness of your Teaching

Tony Turner

By the end of your initial teacher education course you had a fair idea what 'being effective' in your classroom meant. In your new school the pupils, the teaching programme and the resources are probably different from those in your school experience schools. So what does being effective mean in these new circumstances? This chapter asks you to reflect on the effectiveness of your practice in your new post. You should relate your progress to any statutory requirements for the completion of your first year of teaching (see Chapter 1).

In this chapter we raise some issues which you would have addressed in your initial teacher education course; you may need to review that material at points in the following discussions. In places we refer you specifically to the generic book is this series *Learning to Teach in the Secondary School: A Companion to School Experience* (Capel, Leask and Turner, 2001). You may find one or more units in that book helpful, in particular Unit 2.2, 'Lesson planning'; Unit 3.3, 'Managing classroom behaviour'; Unit 4.1, 'Differentiation' and Chapter 5, 'Helping pupils to learn'.

OBJECTIVES

By the end of this chapter you should be able to:

- identify criteria to review the effectiveness of your teaching;
- provide an evidence base for your lesson planning and for your own progress;
- identify ways to promote learning appropriate to a wide range of pupils;
- further your understanding of continuity and progression in learning;
- relate the effectiveness of your teaching to any statutory requirements for the completion of your first year of teaching.

WHERE AM I NOW?

Background and context

A recent report on secondary education in England shows steady improvements in both the quality of education and the standards achieved by pupils. Improvements in teaching have gone hand in hand with rising standards in pupils' attainment at all levels of education, including improvements in those aspects of schooling less easily measured (Office for Standards in Education [OFSTED], 2001). However, some pupils' progress slowed after their transfer from primary school. This concern was sufficiently strong for the problem to be addressed by the Department for Education and Skills (DfES) through the Key Stage 3 (KS3) Strategy; see DfES website (2001b) and Chapter 8.

An evaluation of the KS3 Strategy identified many important features of good teaching across several subjects (OFSTED, 2003). These features include:

- clear lesson objectives (learning outcomes), which were explained to, or shared with, pupils (OFSTED, 2003: paras 29, 65, 98) – some teachers gave models of what was required of pupils in their lesson and, where successful, a clear distinction was made between learning outcomes and the activity used to meet them;
- the use of a variety of activities in a lesson, or over several lessons, each with a clear purpose;
- the greater involvement of pupils in their own learning, such as small-group collaborative activities, interactive teacher-class engagement, pupils explaining strategies to the rest of the class, use of white boards by pupils to display responses;
- the importance of pacing lessons to ensure, e.g. that an end-of-lesson review of learning took place.

By contrast, the use of formative assessment techniques to assess progress and learning was described as weak (OFSTED, 2003: 3). Very little was said in that report concerning pupils' prior knowledge or the value of starting teaching from what the pupils know and can do already.

These general comments can be amplified by referring to inspection reports for your school carried out by central and local government (or, for fee paying schools, by the Independent Schools Inspectorate (address at end of chapter). Many whole-school inspection reports from OFSTED are posted on the internet (http://www.ofsted.gov.uk), as are many on subject teaching (http://www.archive.official-documents.co.uk). Reflective Task 6.1 invites you to explore this documentation.

LEARNING FROM YOUR OWN TEACHING

Some guidance has been given above about what is viewed as good teaching. But what counts is the learning that takes place in your classroom and the effect of your teaching on pupil progress. To find out about that you need to evaluate your teaching and your pupils' learning, i.e. act as a reflective practitioner. As well as reading reviews of teaching, such as those cited above, you need to be aware of the ways pupil learn (see Chapter 5 in this book).

In *Learning to Teach in the Secondary School*, 3rd edition, Unit 5.1 we introduced a learning model for use by teachers to help evaluate their teaching. You should review that model

Reflective task 6.1
What counts as good or bad
teaching in your subject?

Read the summary of a recent national inspection report on the teaching of your subject. Identify and list three criteria of importance to you by which the teaching of your subject at Key Stages 3 and 4 is judged. Describe some features of good teaching associated with those criteria. For each chosen criterion, write a short comment as it relates to your own development, using the following headings:

- its importance in the teaching of your subject;
- the local circumstances which support or inhibit your ability to include the good feature in your teaching;
- goals for your own teaching.

Share your report with your mentor and discuss any implications it has for addressing these factors in your own teaching. File your report and record of discussions in your professional development portfolio.

before proceeding. In this model, the terms 'Do, Review, Learn and Apply' are used, by which we mean:

DO   Your teaching – lessons or series of lessons taught on a topic.

REVIEW   List the successes and weaknesses of your teaching. From your evaluations of lessons check:
- whether pupils have learned what you intended;
- the evidence on which you make these judgements.

LEARN   Clarify what you have learned from the review and what questions remain. Identify the:
- problems you can solve;
- changes that need to be made to improve pupil learning;
- problems that you alone cannot solve.

APPLY   What practical steps can you take now to make the improvements needed? Return to the beginning of the cycle.

This model of learning is used throughout the next section, 'Moving forward'.

Moving forward: what are your lessons like?

Here are three possible scenarios:

1   you might feel that your classes are difficult to manage, that many pupils with behaviour problems dominate your lesson;
2   you have got through the day without much hassle, survived but have little idea how much the pupils have learned;
3   your pupils usually appear interested and enthusiastic in your lessons and complete most of the work set.

Other descriptions might apply but no one description is likely to apply to all your classes. Broad generalisations about your teaching or about the way pupils learn have a place but may not be appropriate in developing further your teaching or pupils' learning in a particular context. We suggest, therefore, that you focus on one class you teach regularly and identify the particular features of teaching and learning, both the successes and setbacks. Use Figure 6.1 to help you focus on 'where you are'.

The flow chart in Figure 6.1 identifies five scenarios which might apply to your teaching of a class, and the accompanying notes may help you make further progress with that class. Each diamond decision box has a question asking you to identify some characteristics of your teaching of the class. Each rectangular action box makes suggestions about what to do next; this box contains a number which corresponds to a numbered paragraph in the text

Figure 6.1   Flow chart: monitoring your teaching

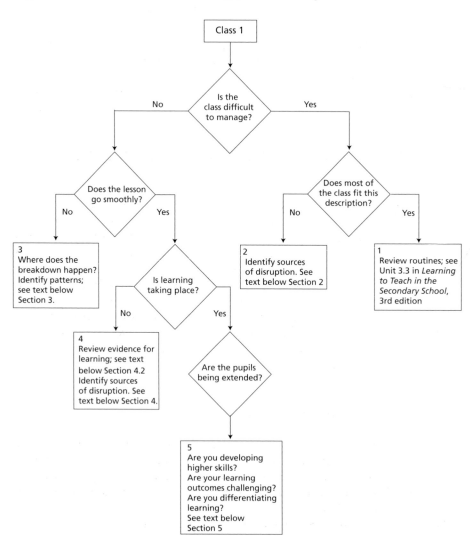

Reflective task 6.2
Where are you with your class, managing behaviour or managing learning

Select a class you are teaching. Read through:

1   the guidance about Figure 6.1 above;
2   the flow chart.

Use Figure 6.1 to identify the situation which best matches your progress and relationship with your chosen class; the numbered notes that follow assist identification.
   Summarise your findings in your diary or professional development portfolio.

below, amplifying the heading in the box, and refers you to further discussion about issues of management, teaching and learning which might be relevant to your situation. Use Figure 6.1 to help you with Reflective task 6.2.

The rest of this chapter, 'Ways forward', contains more detailed discussion of each numbered section, which provides insight and advice on ways to develop your teaching.

WAYS FORWARD: TEACHING STRATEGIES AND PROMOTING LEARNING

1 Routines for effective class management (Figure 6.1, 1)

The problem concerns establishing effective class management. If the problem is one of general class management, maintaining effective control, establishing ground rules, having in place routines of agreed procedures, etc. we suggest you refer to Unit 3.3 'Managing classroom behaviour' in *Learning to Teach in the Secondary School*, 3rd edition. Further discussion of behaviour management is in Chapter 7 of this book.

Little learning can take place until effective management is established. One factor to review is your lesson planning, because inappropriate choice of material or activities may contribute to management problems. A fuller discussion of the origins and management of unwanted behaviours is in Chapter 7.

2 Sources of disruption (Figure 6.1, 2)

This section addresses those circumstances in which the majority of pupils are reasonably well behaved but lessons are marked by interruptions from a minority of pupils. Identify those pupils responsible for the disruption and devise a short-term strategy for dealing with the situation while reviewing the longer-term strategy for the class; get to know better the individual pupils and their needs.

The behaviour of disruptive pupils may have a number of effects, such as to:

- disrupt the class;
- reduce the quality of learning environment for most pupils;
- interfere with the work of some pupils;
- take up a disproportionate amount of the teacher's time;
- lead to escalating confrontation;
- attract frequent punitive action from you;
- elevate themselves to popularity in the eyes of peers.

Some difficult pupils cause trouble elsewhere in the school and you are probably not alone in experiencing difficulties. Recognition of this situation is a source of comfort as well as help. Support groups within, or outside, the school are an effective way of sharing such problems and getting advice. We turn first to consider possible causes of misbehaviour and, later, a way of dealing with it.

Causes of misbehaviour are various, peculiar to the individual pupil and often need a unique solution. Misbehaviour can be the result of setting inappropriate work, such as tasks that are too easy or a repetition of work from earlier lessons, leading to boredom; equally work that is to hard leads to frustration and the pupil may not be able to contribute to class discussion.

The problem may lie within the pupil, such as poor self-esteem arising from a history of failure; alternatively the pupil may not receive the support from home that encourages intellectual activity. A similar attitude can arise if the pupil sees a lack of employment ahead and generates a 'so what' attitude.

Unacceptable behaviour can arise from emotional disturbances leading to, for example, an inability to work with peers. Other factors that contribute to unwanted behaviour can derive from school itself, such as a poor pastoral structure and an inability to diagnose and meet the pupil's needs; or the pupil disliking the teacher. Peer pressure such as poor role models or bullying can put pressure on a pupil and generate unacceptable behaviours. For further discussion see Kyriacou (1991: 92 and 1998: 88–92).

If you are to help individual pupils who cause you problems you could collect information about them before deciding on strategies to help them. This information may help you identify possible causes of pupil underperformance and help focus on setting appropriate work for them. Understanding the origins of unacceptable behaviour is central to identifying solutions: see Chapter 7.

A pupil profile

Table 6.1 identifies the sort of information you could collect and provides a basis for a record card. This information can be obtained from the school office, the head of year or from the form tutor; the information is sensitive and your records must be secure. Keep a personal record of any incidents related to the pupil, documenting what happened, when, to whom and stating any action you may have taken. Keeping such records helps you build a picture of the pupil, placing you in a better position to plan work and respond more confidently to his needs.

The information you have collected may establish:

- that the pupil is a problem for many teachers – if pupils misbehave only in your class then clearly you should consider why that should be, but this state of affairs is unlikely;

Table 6.1 Inventory for constructing a pupil record

Make a record card, giving name of pupil, the Year and class. Identify relevant background information, such as transfer from another school, or English as second language. The school will have confidential information about the family background, which might be important. Keep a note of your sources and date your records. You may wish to generate a blank form to collect this information.

Questions	*Evidence*
Academic record	• National Curriculum Level in your subject and core subjects?
Q Is the pupil performing to expectations or not?	• What is the rate of progress through the levels?
	• Comments/report from previous year
Q What evidence accounts for any shortcomings?	• Primary school transfer statement, including level statements
	• Results of assessment on entering school, e.g. of language, numeracy and non verbal reasoning scores and their interpretation
	• Linguistic skills, e.g. reading age, E2L; E2L support?
Academic or behavioural support	
Q Is there a record of learning difficulties (cognitive) or behavioural, emotional and social development (EBD) difficulties?	• Has in-class support teacher?
	• How frequent is the support?
Q Is there support for these difficulties?	• Other support from SEN department, e.g. withdrawal for speech therapy
Q Why does the pupil need support?	• Support from offsite centre
	• Needs support but does not get it
	• Recommended for statementing
	• Has a statement under the Code of Practice
	• Has pupil an Individual Education Plan?
Attendance and lateness	
Q Is attendance a problem?	• This year
	• Previous years
	• Reasons for absence; see personal file and letters from parents
	• Is lateness an issue?
	• Reasons for late arrival; personal file and letters.
Q Has the school followed this up and with what result?	• Actions
Q What role and stance have the parents taken on these issues?	• Response of parents and pupil
Detention	
Q Is the pupil in detention frequently?	• Is there a record?
Q Is there a common pattern for the detentions?	• Frequency, recent or irregular
	• Is there a pattern, e.g. day of week, subject link?
Q What role and stance have the parents taken on this issue?	• Response of parents
	• Response of pupil
Q Is the detention having a good or bad effect?	• On behaviour or on performance in class?
Health Record	
Q Does the pupil's health record provide reasons for poor performance or behaviour?	• Record of poor health, e.g. asthma, emotional upsets?
	• Has the pupil been referred to a specialist?
Q Does attendance record link with health record?	
Q Has any disability been identified?	• e.g. hearing disability, impaired vision, spectacles, dyslexia, glue ear, EBD?
Q Has any action been recommended?	• For example is the pupil prescribed spectacles? Does the pupil wear them? Should the pupil be seated near the front of the class?

- the existence of cognitive learning problems or emotional and behavioural difficulties (EBD);
- action taken by other staff, including those from the special educational needs (SEN) department;
- whether action has been taken by senior staff, i.e. it is a whole-school problem;
- whether parents have been involved and in what way.

An inquiry such as this may reveal not only information about your pupil but also the action taken by others in meeting the difficulties. As a result you may find strategies you can adopt to improve the behaviour and learning of your pupil. The following checklist may alert you to further ideas.

- Is the work you set sufficiently differentiated? Is the pupil capable of carrying out the tasks you set and are the tasks appropriate to his attainment level ? See Section 5 below, and Kerry (1999).
- Is the material presented at an appropriate language level? Reading material should be at or below the reading age of the pupil unless the purpose is to extend the language of the pupil. Tests to check the reading levels of material are available, referred to as 'readability formulae' (Sutton, 1981: 115; Chris and Keith Johnson website (www.timetable.com/reading.html)). Consult your SEN co-ordinator for help in preparing or rewriting your material. A discussion on 'Language and learning' appears in Chapter 9.
- Is your choice of learning tasks predictable or do you present tasks in different ways over a period of time, such over a whole topic? For example, a diet of worksheets can be boring. Not only does varying the way you present learning tasks increase motivation, it caters too for different learning styles. See Unit 5.1 'Ways pupils learn' in *Learning to Teach in the Secondary School*, 3rd edition.

It is important to gather evidence and reflect on it before making changes.

A learning contract

Sometimes drawing up a contract between you and the pupil can provide a framework in which the pupil can move forward. A contract can operate for one lesson or a series of lessons and should focus on the behaviours you wish to encourage, on increasing the quality of work produced by the pupil, or both. Many schools use this approach and sample contracts may help you draft one for your needs. Your mentor or head of department can advise you further; see also Gillborn *et al.* (1993: 54). The contract should state the consequences of not meeting its terms. The effort and progress of a pupil, however small, needs recognition and encouragement.

To monitor such pupils, ensure that the rest of the class can get on with their work. You should establish:

- that classroom rules are in place;
- ways of monitoring the class, bearing in mind that you may have several pupils in the problem category (see 'Monitoring techniques' below);
- alternative work for pupils who cannot cope with the set work;
- additional activities for those who finish their work early;

- arrangements for pupils who break their contract, e.g. working by themselves, being sent to another teacher (by agreement) or using the school support system.

Monitoring techniques

These skills are often part of the repertoire of the experienced teacher, acquired by experience and honed by practice. They include keeping an eye on the class by frequent scanning, moving quickly to pupils who need help, or making eye contact to effect control and avoiding interrupting a lesson. Circulating about the room and using all the space helps maintain a presence among the pupils, at the same time giving support and praise, nipping problems in the bud and ensuring pupils are on task. Space can be used to distance pupils from each other, as needed.

Movement and contact enables you to check progress by questioning pupils and ensuring that the majority of pupils get a word from you in the lesson, hopefully of encouragement and assurance. For a fuller discussion of monitoring skills see, for example, Kyriacou, 1991: 89–90.

Long-term strategies

For some pupils, only amelioration of the worst symptoms of poor behaviour is possible in the short term. The solution to some pupils' problems lies outside your classroom and you may need to refer a pupil to the head of year. Long-term strategies depend on a number of factors including the information gleaned as part of the short-term approach. Some pupils need help through a whole-school approach, often including diagnosis of the problem by other professionals and outside assistance.

Persistent unacceptable behaviour is difficult to tackle alone, especially if the causes lie outside the school. Nevertheless, the long-term goal of the teacher should be to establish a firm, caring relationship with these pupils. School may be the only place where there is a firm, fair and friendly framework to nurture acceptable behaviours and this framework can be welcomed by many pupils, even if they challenge it (Upton and Cooper, 1990). It is important to recognise that you cannot single-handedly solve all problems. Most teachers need help and assistance in some circumstances throughout their career. For further discussion on behaviour management see Chapter 7; case studies of behaviour management can be found on the Department for Education and Training (DfEE) website (see 'Further reading' below for details).

3 Developing lesson continuity and sustaining learning (Figure 6.1, 3)

We have in mind here a lesson that starts well but deteriorates part of the way through, with restless behaviour, lack of application and some pupils being an unnecessary handful. Ends of lessons get untidy, with work incomplete, homework lost in a hasty attempt to round off the lesson. You have difficulty sustaining learning through to the end of the lesson and enjoyment is suffering. Your following lesson has to rescue the previous one, with consequent loss of time, reduced motivation and poor understanding. Discussion with other teachers suggests that this class is not generally regarded as difficult but generally your lessons with them do not go smoothly and little learning takes place despite many pupils being on task.

One response to these circumstances is that aspects of lesson planning may need attention. The following questions may help review your planning and identify ways forward:

- Is there a scheme of work (SoW) in your department and are you using it? Does the SoW have advice about planning lessons?
- Does your lesson planning take account of prior learning? What do your pupils know about the topic, e.g. from previous teaching?
- What steps can you take to elicit this prior knowledge?
- Are you identifying learning outcomes for your lesson expressed in terms of what pupils are expected to know, understand or be able to do?
- Are your activities chosen to realise your learning outcomes?
- Do you share your learning outcomes with your class and explain what pupils have to do to achieve them? That is, what they have to write, read, listen to, present, etc.? Successful learning often occurs when pupils understand what they are expected to do, recognise that it is achievable and have some say over the way they approach and execute the task. See features of good teaching described in the section 'Where am I now?' at the beginning of this chapter.
- Do your lessons have clear stages of development: that is, have a clear start, consolidation and end? Look back to advice about this feature of lesson planning given to you in your initial teacher education course. There should be a clear transition from one stage to the next which pupils recognise. A stage in a lesson usually means the development of the main activity or the introduction of a new activity. Mediating the stages of a lesson is important and pupils need help; for example, how do you support those who have not finished the first stage but are asked to move on? Another issue is putting in place activities for those who have completed the work early and are waiting to move on. Changing focus and pace of lesson midway through a lesson can be motivating for some but can confuse others if not managed effectively.
- Is the pace and focus of the lesson suitable? Have pupils got enough to do for the whole lesson or are they rushing to finish the work you have set? Are many pupils left behind or are pupils sitting about and not getting much done?
- Are the learning outcomes realistic and in the grasp of most of your class, i.e. is the work set at a suitable cognitive level? Or is the work too challenging?
- Do your activities *frequently* demand low-level skills, such as copying notes or diagrams, colouring in pictures or just following instructions? In this case does the work lack challenge?

In addition to the suggestions made above, look again at Section 2 where we referred, firstly, to the advantage of differentiating the work you set and, secondly, to the value of employing a range of strategies over a series of lessons.

4 Is learning taking place? Review the evidence for learning (Figure 6.1, 4)

We consider now classes in which behavioural and organisational problems are more secure and focus on the effectiveness of your teaching and the quality of learning. Box 4 in Figure

6.1 describes a situation where the class is not difficult to manage and the lesson has gone smoothly.

A mark of effective teaching is a lesson that provides motivation and interest to the pupils through a choice of activities, leading to better learning. You need to review the evidence for learning by asking yourself questions such as:

* What assessment strategies do I have in place?
* Are assessment strategies built into my lesson plan?
* Have I shared the assessment findings with my pupils?
* Does the information from my assessment feed into planning future lessons?

There are a number of ways in which you find out if learning has taken place. Most classroom assessment is frequent and informal and designed to improve learning, i.e. it is formative assessment. Identifying assessment opportunities are vital to both you and the learner because they provide evidence for learning and enable you to identify further learning activities. Recently, the Chief Inspector of Schools in England wrote:

> ... teachers need to be aware of how much pupils know and can do and to use this information to plan challenging lessons and to make clear to pupils what they need to do to improve. This continues to be the weakest aspect of teaching and was unsatisfactory in one in six schools receiving a full inspection. In the three in ten schools where this was good, teachers used well-constructed questions to assess pupils' understanding, particularly at the end of lessons. Marking was regular, focused, consistent and gave clear messages to pupils. The information from assessment was used to adjust appropriately the pace and content of the lessons.
>
> (OFSTED, 2001: para. 77)

Homework provides opportunities for formative assessment. The same Inspector noted that where the use of homework was poor it was 'either limited in the challenge it provided or not consistently set and marked' (para. 79). A further report on an aspect of secondary education two years later noted little change in the use of assessment for promoting learning (OFSTED, 2003: paras 3, 9, 72).

The thrust of these reports draws attention to the most obvious of teacher skills, which is the ways in which you monitor and measure the progress in learning of your pupils. This can be achieved by identifying assessment strategies and opportunities in your lesson planning. Assessment opportunities include:

* joining small group discussions as pupils plan an activity;
* checking pupils' understanding as they work on a task, by questioning, by asking for explanations of process, concept or procedures;
* probing further to take successful pupils beyond the immediate task;
* challenging unexpected findings, unconventional approaches or wrong results;
* encouraging pupils to explain ideas to others, in a group or to the whole class;
* checking pupils' books as they carry out class exercises;
* marking set work.

These opportunities provide benefits to you and your pupils. Feedback can be given to pupils about their progress and identify successful learning. Misconceptions can be corrected. It provides the opportunity to give encouragement, to acknowledge success and support pupils who face difficulties, boosting motivation. Equally important is the opportunity to clarify learning outcomes with pupils so that they know what a successful learning outcome looks like.

These experiences help you monitor the effects of your teaching and suggest, for example, what to focus on in a plenary session at the end of the lesson. The information gained helps direct future planning and allows identification of successful activities for future reference.

The recognition of achievement, progress and effort is an important factor for many pupils, sustaining motivation and promoting self-confidence. Such information about your pupils and the impact of your teaching comes as well from extra-classroom activities. These activities include checking and marking books and setting and marking homework, to which we now turn.

Checking and marking books

Most schools have a marking policy to which you must conform and often distinguish between effort and content, awarding a grade for each. However, is the purpose of marking to check understanding and direct future teaching or is it to have a set of marks for end-of-term reports? It is important to record marks as evidence of both effort, in completing the work, and achievement but equally important is the feedback it gives you about your pupils' progress.

The way you set work is important. For pupils to do their best they need to know the criteria for a satisfactory piece of work, including:

- the learning outcomes expected;
- what they need to do to achieve them;
- how the work is to be marked;
- how marks are gained or lost.

When you mark books you need to refer to the marking criteria you have shared with your pupils. Pick out what pupils have done well. As well as correcting errors and omissions pupils need to know what marks have been awarded for and what they need to do in the future to improve their mark. A written comment is needed to convey this information in addition to a final mark. Note those features that need to be considered when planning the next lesson.

What sort of work do you set? Some tasks offer little challenge, such as transferring notes from the board to exercise books, completing unfinished class work, copying a diagram or following a worksheet. Activities such as these often engender poor motivation and may demand low-level skills. Sometimes such tasks are necessary but you need to ask yourself, 'What is being assessed?' when you mark such work.

More challenging and motivating activities which contribute to learning may include:

- completing class work that demands that the pupils add something of their own;
- requiring pupils to make notes to a specification;
- transforming rough notes into a report or summary;
- inviting an investigation;
- planning an activity/inquiry or course of action;
- making use of the environment;
- creating a diagram from a description or *vice versa*.

Examples such as these demand higher-order skills and thinking and the learning outcomes you identify for the task should be a guide to your marking; see also, e.g. DART activities (Unit 5.2, *Learning to Teach in the Secondary School*, 3rd edition).

Setting and marking homework

Homework, it can be argued, is an imposition on the pupil's time so it must fit clearly into your scheme of work, be valued by your marking and whenever possible used in subsequent lessons. Homework can:

- consolidate learning;
- extend understanding, including contexts beyond the classroom;
- provide the opportunity for quiet, private study to promote interest and intrinsic motivation;
- promote study skills;
- shift responsibility for learning towards the learner.

Homework set casually, or as a kneejerk response to a whole-school policy, tells pupils that it is not important. This can lead to rushed, untidy or wrong work, or neat but mechanically executed material to which little thought has been given. Setting homework is part of your lesson planning.

The purpose of homework must be clear to pupils, should interest them and extend their knowledge and understanding. Homework tasks need:

- instructions about what to do;
- advice about what a completed task looks like and the form of record expected;
- understanding of how it is to be made use of;
- statement of the criteria for assessment;
- where appropriate, their significance for grading;
- who to hand it to, when and where.

Writing and reading tasks are popular as homework. Turning rough class notes into a coherent account of an event can be a positive learning task but should not be merely an exercise in good handwriting. An instruction such as 'Write up a summary of our discussion in the back of your notebooks and hand it in on ...' can come as a surprise to pupils who hear it for the first time just before the bell. Advance notice about this homework task allows notes to be made during the discussion and you can guide them as the lesson unfolds.

Asking pupils to do nothing more than read a section from a book may not encourage learning, e.g. 'Read through pages 25–30 and make notes on the ...' is too open-ended. There are times when reading is set for enjoyment and to encourage reading habits. On the other hand, you may want the pupils to engage deeply with the text but they need to know what they are expected to gain from reading. Advice is needed about ways to go about the reading, such as identifying key words or ideas; or making a summarising table; or reformulating the material, drawing a diagram or flow chart, etc. Ask pupils to make a summary of an event or process and to report back to the class next day.

Homework can make use of the home, family or friends or the wider environment. For example, you might ask pupils to:

Reflective task 6.3
Setting and assessing
homework

Identify ways in which the following homework task could be improved:
Use your history books or other sources to identify the causes of the
Second World War. Make notes in the back of your exercise book.
You might identify:

- ways to sharpen the task's focus;
- ways to limit the task.
- criteria you would use to assess the task;
- what you would tell your pupils about gaining good marks.

Alternatively, identify a piece of homework set within your own subject
SoW and comment on that.

- Collect oral history from parents, grandparents or other adults: for example, how homes were heated when they were children and how this affected the way they lived.
- Monitor a newspaper for a week on a particular story, such as, for example, reports about doctors, hospitals, nurses or health. Write a one-page summary identifying three key issues occupying the press, their main points and why they seem important.

Begin a collection of useful homework and file it in your professional development portfolio.

5 Extending pupils: learning outcomes, progression and differentiation (Figure 6.1, 5)

In this section, we are assuming that your class is under control, a pleasure to teach and without management difficulties. The question being addressed is: 'Are your pupils being extended intellectually or are they coasting?' This question embraces, too, another question: 'Is your choice of activities sufficiently varied to address different pupil learning styles?' See Chapter 5 in this volume. A starting point is to review the aims of the lesson by asking yourself questions such as:

- Are your aims translated into learning outcomes?
- Do you share learning outcomes with your pupils?
- Do your activities address your choice of learning outcomes?
- How well do you know your pupils and their needs?
- Are your pupils developing higher-order thinking skills?
- Are your pupils being asked to take more responsibility for their learning?
- Are you teaching pupils study skills?

Many of these questions were identified in the government report mentioned at the beginning of this chapter (OFSTED 2003). In any given class it is likely that some pupils have grasped the main ideas of the lesson and need further development while others are working at the main idea. In practice there will be a spectrum of progress, and immediately the need for differentiated work arises. It would be foolish to imagine that you can make a bespoke curriculum for every pupil in your class. You need to be alert to ideas which may be helpful to a number of pupils in your class, albeit at different times, and to set differentiated work for pupils as the situation arises (see Kerry 1999). We address here extending pupils learning by developing higher skills.

By now you should have shifted your focus from the management of behaviour to the management of learning. This shift in approach requires you to adjust the learning outcomes for your lessons as suggested by the seven questions listed above (see Figure 6.2).

Figure 6.2 Shifting the focus of your teaching

In Section 4 we addressed ways in which you can informally assess pupils and this approach remains important as you seek to develop higher skills with your pupils.

LEARNING OUTCOMES

Learning outcomes, often referred to as lesson objectives, have been discussed and developed in your initial teacher education course. We suggest that you refer to those notes.

Whereas learning outcomes can be written in terms of 'to know', 'to recall' or 'to understand', we suggest here that progression in learning should embrace higher-level skills and achievements. What are these higher skills? We address them under the headings cognitive, process, attitudinal and social skills.

Cognitive skills include recall of knowledge and procedure. Clearly pupils need to understand what is recalled. Evidence for comprehension of knowledge may arise when pupils are asked to explain something, or to apply that knowledge. Higher-level skills include the processes of application of knowledge and the analysis and synthesis of data and ideas. You may ask pupils to apply their knowledge to a taught situation or to a novel situation; applying knowledge in a new situation has a higher intellectual demand than rehearsing those ideas previously taught.

Higher-level skills also include activities such as interpreting information, evaluating the ideas of another person; indulging in thinking about abstract ideas and their application to everyday situations and evaluating the work of others. All these skills demand an element of knowing, the ability to recall information and to use it imaginatively. Higher skills need to be taught.

Process skills are concerned with the procedures of inquiry, or study, or the means of achieving a given end. They include skills such as to knowing how to use a library index, to interrogate a data base, to design or follow a pattern for making clothes or to carry out a distillation. Process skills need to be taught and practised. They do not come naturally any more than do cognitive skills. Process skills require both thinking skills and the ability to carry out the task, and require the co-ordination of hand and brain to achieve an action.

Attitudinal skills include a number of features, including perseverance and a willingness to tackle difficult tasks with enthusiasm and humour. Another aspect of this positive attitude is that learning is fun and worthwhile in its own right. The ability to work with others and be responsive to their needs and ideas are important skills and attitudes to promote. Such skills may be fostered in daily classroom life or through activities such as discussion, simulations and visits as well as planning and executing tasks.

Classrooms promote *social attitudes*. The way pupils perceive men and women's role in society can be influenced by schools, as can pupils' response to people of beliefs, cultures and ethnicity different to themselves. School can help pupils respect people different from them in some way. Social attitudes incorporate a positive view of society and a willingness and need to contribute to the greater well-being of people. Another important role for schools is the promotion of the need for conservation of our environment. Your choice of working relationships, of resources and your own attitude are all vital ingredients in planning lessons which promote such positive attitudes and have links to the wider school curriculum.

Higher-level skills must consciously be built into your lesson plans and be recognised in the aims and learning outcomes for your lesson. Learning outcomes might be, for example, that pupils should be able to:

- identify the key features of ...;
- construct their own description of ...;
- draft a procedure for carrying out ...;
- construct a model of ... using ...;
- plan a visit to ...;
- take part in a debate about ...;
- summarise the outcome of a debate;
- prepare a poster on ... and give a 3-minute report to the class;
- work with others to ...

These objectives emphasise pupil action in terms of thinking and doing and often mean the pupil takes an active part in constructing meaning or understanding. Pupils are not simply told. Alternatively, action may require the pupil to develop ways of inquiry, such as the interrogation of a text book, the devising of a procedure to investigate a phenomenon, or to plan an activity alone or with others.

How frequently are your objectives for your pupils conceived in these terms? You may wish to consider if the tasks and activities you select give enough opportunity for your pupils to think and work at these higher levels. Planning work to develop higher-level skills is necessary for most pupils and provides further opportunities to provide differentiated work in your lesson planning.

THINKING STYLES

In planning lessons we have drawn attention to the need to attend to the present performance of pupils in order to help plan future teaching. However, implicit in this chapter has been the thought that pupils are different in the way they respond to tasks and in the way they learn. You may wish to consider the notion that some pupils may think in an analytical manner, while others may be imaginative thinkers (see Unit 5.1 in *Learning to Teach in the Secondary School*, 3rd edition).

Each type of thinker sees things differently and imagines the world in different ways. Some pupils may be described as *convergent thinkers*, others as *divergent*. The convergent thinker focuses on the sure, the safe and the known and is less likely to speculate. The divergent thinker is more likely to be imaginative and to think, 'What if?' These viewpoints are sometimes expressed through the terms *serialist thinker* and *holistic thinker*. The latter likes to see the whole picture in order to generate understanding. The serialist thinker needs to approach things stepwise, to understand each step of the way, finally putting the bits together to make the whole. Both types of learners may get to the same end point but by different routes and, from time to time, your pupils may need different types of learning material and tasks to reflect these differences.

There is evidence that intelligence cannot be represented by a single measured factor but that, by contrast, there are a number of discrete intelligence factors, independent of each other but interactive (Gardner, 1993b). It is mainly the logico-mathematical and the linguistic intelligence factors that are valued and assessed by Western society through its educational assessment procedures. The consideration of learning theories such as those mentioned above is a further step in your own development as a teacher. For further discussion about ways of learning and intelligence, see Chapter 5 in this volume and Adey and Shayer, 1994.

SUMMARY

Developing your skills as a teacher is an active process and one that needs to be worked at. We have emphasised the importance of developing your teaching on a basis of evidence. The person best placed to provide and identify that evidence is yourself. By providing a framework for identifying your progress with a class we hope that you will be able to focus on evaluating and analysing what goes on in your classroom. In your first year you have the support of a mentor to provide feedback from observation of your lessons, the experience to help analyse your progress and a sounding board for your ideas. The purpose of the activities suggested in this chapter is to develop your teaching by reflection on practice, to enhance pupil learning and help them enjoy a sense of achievement.

FURTHER READING

Department for Education and Skills (DfES) (2003c) *Improving Behaviour in Schools* website: http://www.dfes.gov.uk/ibis/case_studies/case_studies.cfm.

Gillborn, D., Nixon, J. and Rudduck, J. (1993) *Dimensions of Discipline: Rethinking Practice in Secondary Schools*. London: HMSO for the Department for Education. An important book for those who need support and advice about managing classrooms and individual pupils. It is addressed to school managers, teachers and newly qualified teachers.

Entwistle, N. (1988) *Styles of Learning and Teaching*. London: David Fulton. A book for those who wish to think more deeply about the task of teaching and learning. It is a valuable guide to reflection on how to think about optimising conditions for teaching thinking. It is not about tips for teachers.

OFSTED (2001) *The Annual Report of the Chief Inspector of Schools, 1999–2000*. London: OFSTED. Available online at http://*www.ofsted.gov.uk*. We suggest you read the section which appraises the quality of teaching (paras 72–9) and discusses the value of selected teaching strategies.

7 Challenging Behaviour in the Classroom

Learning to Cope

Philip Garner

In order that children learn *at least* at an age-appropriate level a class teacher needs to recognise that certain 'behaviours' are essential in establishing the conditions which promote engagement with the curriculum task set. So it isn't really surprising that emphasis for 'order' and 'discipline' has been a feature of many commentaries on the state of schools during the last 20 years or so (Young, 1997). At times there has been sensationalist coverage in the media on the failure of a school, or an individual teacher, to 'manage' pupils who challenge the system on account of their behaviour (Clark, 1998). Moreover, behaviour in schools carries with it a high dividend for politicians, so emotive is the level of feeling about the learning of others being disrupted. Ask any parent to explain what in their view makes a 'good' school and they will invariably include 'good discipline' as one of their top distinguishing characteristics.

From an official perspective, too, there has been recognition that dealing with behaviours that challenge is a pivotal strategy in establishing the conditions where purposeful learning can take place (Department for Education and Employment [DfEE], 1999a). This focus can be traced back many years, and clearly signals the importance of effective classroom management in the repertoire of required teacher-skills. Over 15 years ago the Elton Report, whilst acknowledging that there were no simple remedies to certain complex problem behaviours, nevertheless sought to raise awareness of a set of core skills in classroom management. The Report concluded that 'teachers' group management skills are probably the single most important factor in achieving good standards of classroom behaviour' and that 'those skills can be taught and learned' (Department of Education and Science [DES], 1989: 69).

Recognition of the latter by newly qualified teachers (NQTs) is vital. For a long time it has been a subject of debate as to whether the ability to manage the learning and social behaviour of a large group of lively young people in a single room is a skill which some teachers are simply born with. In reality, though, most new teachers face a period in which they must come to terms with the various challenges presented by their pupils. Echoing this dilemma, Smith and Laslett questioned whether there was '… some special personal magic which enables some teachers to quieten excitement merely by arriving at the scene, quell misbehaviour with a glance, make classrooms bustle with activity and hum with cheerful industry?' (Smith and Laslett, 1993: 3).

You should take heart from Smith and Laslett's response to their own question. It is a response that permeates the entire content of this chapter: 'learning behaviours' can be readily recognised and applied by newcomers to the profession. Moreover, the development of a learning classroom (for the term 'classroom' is meaningless if it is characterised by disorganisation, lack of focus and direction) is a key element in raising achievement levels of pupils. The Teacher Training Agency (TTA) refers to the establishment of a 'purposeful learning environment' and of the development of 'environments that assist pupils' learning' (Department for Education and Skills [DfES]/TTA, 2002).

Looking at the standards set out by the TTA for managing behaviour in greater detail, the Agency requires that the acquisition of Qualified Teacher Status (QTS) is dependent upon a student teacher demonstrating 'high expectations of pupil behaviour'. It goes on to state that students must '… establish a clear framework for classroom discipline to anticipate and manage pupils' behaviour constructively, and promote self-control and independence' (DfES/TTA 2002, S3.3.9: 12).

What will be apparent to those beginning a career in teaching is that the core principles of behaviour management, encapsulated within the TTA standard S.3.3.9 above, are mainly a refinement and a reinforcement of the sensible guidance offered in the companion volume to this book (*Learning to Teach in the Secondary School*, 3rd edition). The basic strategies, rehearsed in this companion volume, are further reinforced by the DfES (DfES, 2003e). The latter guidance comprises comprehensive auditing materials regarding behaviour; in particular, you are directed towards those annexes dealing with rewards and sanctions and classroom behaviour (http://www.standards.dfes.gov.uk/keystage3). The purpose of this chapter, accordingly, is to amplify and extend these core principles by inviting reflection on some of the social processes and inter-relationships which underpin the way in which children and teachers operate in the classroom.

OBJECTIVES

By the end of this chapter you should be able to:

- identify approaches to managing challenging behaviours presented by some of your pupils;
- be aware of ways to organise appropriate learning environments in which challenging behaviours can be best managed;
- identify features of some specific behaviours which challenge and ways to manage them;
- discuss research and related evidence which assists in understanding and improving behaviour management.

STRUCTURE OF THE CHAPTER

The chapter is divided into three parts, which seek to promote critical reflection as new teachers develop skills in respect of this standard. It should be recognised at the outset, however, that the chapter does not seek to reiterate the full repertoire of behaviour management skills. Comprehensive guidance on these can be readily found elsewhere, and some can be found in the bibliography (see, for example, Department for Education [DfE], 1994b; Blandford, 1998; Gray, 2002, Ayers *et al.*, 2000; McSherry, 2001, amongst others).

In each section a number of basic principles regarding pupil behaviour are examined. Attention to these, alongside the scrutiny of practice-related research evidence and the guidance of more experienced colleagues, will do much to enhance skills in managing a diverse range of behaviours.

The first part of the chapter examines the meaning of the term 'challenging behaviour', alongside a brief review of the main approaches that have commonly been utilised in their management. The next section suggests that proactive management of the classroom is a pivotal insulator against misbehaviour. Here some of the conditions which you must strive for to create a learning classroom will be briefly surveyed. A key element of this is your skill in group management whilst taking account of the diversity of learner needs. The third section of the chapter concentrates on individual behaviours which challenge, and offers some examples of strategies which teachers have found to be successful in their management.

Much of what is contained in this chapter is based on existing or emerging research evidence of strategies that work in the classroom. In lots of ways, too, they will strike chords with what have come to be regarded as the 'folk wisdom' of the staff room. The evidence base, drawn from our knowledge of theories of how children behave, is a powerful and persuasive one. This has been the focus of recent developments in initial teacher training (ITT), notably the establishment of a 'professional resource network for initial teacher training which deals with behaviour management' (TTA, 2004). The core premise of this activity is an understanding of five underpinning principles, adapted from the work of Bronfenbrenner (1979):

- Behaviour does not occur in isolation – it is the product of external and internal factors.
- Behaviour needs to be viewed in the context of individual development and social interaction.
- A teacher can understand the meaning of the behaviour of an individual pupil, and respond more effectively to it, if she has greater knowledge of the theories under-pinning development and cognition.
- Behaviours relating to social interaction can be better understood, and responded to, by a teacher if she has greater knowledge of behavioural, social and affective theories of development and cognition.
- Positive relationships enable learning.

Each of these principles is referred to at various points in the body of the present chapter.

Reflective task 7.1
Explaining pupil behaviour

What are your initial views about each of the principles which Bronfenbrenner argues are at the root of all behaviour? Can you identify any sources of tension between them and the way in which you interpret pupil behaviour?

CHALLENGING BEHAVIOUR: DEFINITIONS AND APPROACHES

When teachers talk about a pupil's 'behaviour' it is usually the case that they are referring to their inappropriate behaviour. Used in this way the term is a metaphor for all manner of colourful language: anti-social, disruptive, naughty, acting out, maladjusted, un-biddable, problem, confrontational, off-task, unwanted and so on. What really is missing is a prefix, so that we come to recognise that what we are really referring to is misbehaviour – those actions and activities which interfere with children learning and teachers teaching.

Reflective task 7.2
Describing pupil behaviours

Write down all of the terms/expression that you know which you/ colleagues use to describe children and their behaviour. Do they describe precise, observable behaviour? To what extent might they be susceptible to personal interpretation?

The Elton Report (DES, 1989) refers to misbehaviour as behaviour which 'causes concern to teachers'. Elsewhere the term 'emotional and behavioural difficulties' (EBD) has been used as a catch-all expression. It describes all those behaviours which comprise a continuum from 'normal though unacceptable' through to mental illness (DfE, 1994a). Currently this term has been expanded as 'SEBD', with the incorporation of social difficulties into the spectrum. But all teachers quite rightly ask for more specificity than this – such general terms have to be illustrated by particular pupil actions that are observable and measurable, in order that teacher intervention might follow.

One way of illustrating the types of behaviour that teachers have long regarded as unsatisfactory, in that they are generally disruptive and get in the way of their teaching, is to make further reference to the Elton Report (DES, 1989). In a helpful set of research data the study provides a summary of those pupil behaviours which a large sample of teachers (Key Stage 3 and Key Stage 4) encountered most frequently in their classrooms. These are summarised in Figure 7.1. What these data tell us is that it is mainly 'low-level' disturbance which constitutes the most problematic occurrences for teachers. Such disruption is principally characterised by talking out of turn, hindering other pupils, 'calculated idleness' and unwanted movement around the class. All of these, when they present as chronic features of a classroom, are likely to have a long-term negative impact on both the pupils' levels of achievement and their socially acceptable behaviour.

Figure 7.1   Frequency of problem behaviours (1 = most common) reported by secondary teachers (after the Elton Report, DES,1989)

1	Talking out of turn
2	Calculated idleness or work avoidance
3	Hindering other pupils
4	Arriving late to school/lesson
5	Unwanted non-verbal noises
6	Persistent infringement of class rules
7	Getting out of seat without permission
8	Verbal abuse of other pupils
9	General rowdiness or 'mucking about'
10	Cheeky remarks or impertinence to teacher
11	Physical aggression to other pupils
12	Verbal abuse to teacher
13	Physical destructiveness
14	Physical aggression to teacher

A more recent attempt to provide a tangible set of behaviours can be taken from a study conducted by Qualifications and Curriculum Authority (QCA, 2001). This identified 15 behaviours groupings by which a pupil's emotional and behavioural development might be assessed. These were divided into 'learning behaviours', 'conduct behaviours' and 'emotional behaviours'. Each of these groupings is sub-divided into sets of criteria, depicting desirable and undesirable behaviours (see Figure 7.2). A number of conclusions can be drawn from these lists, as well as a set of parallels with the earlier Elton Report. Not least amongst them is the underpinning theme which links social behaviours to learning behaviours in producing what pupils and teachers alike recognise as 'good' behaviour.

The task of identifying or defining 'misbehaviour' is an important one if a teacher is going to develop strategies to deal with them. There is a need, at the outset, to describe exactly what any unwanted behaviour actually comprises. Telling another teacher that 'Salim behaved really badly before playtime' tells a colleague little of value. Indeed, the lack of precision might well lead to Salim acquiring an unwanted label which would become an almost permanent negative descriptor. So it is essential, for both you and your pupils, that precise, objective language is used in any description of behaviour. The description needs to be of the behaviour, not the pupil. Moreover, you need to constantly remember the 'hidden "E" in EBD': as a professional group we invariably focus on 'acting out' (conduct), as opposed in 'acting in' (emotions) behaviour.

Reflective task 7.3
Which behaviours do you find the most difficult to manage?

Identify six pupil behaviours that you find most difficult to deal with. Compare this list with that of an NQT colleague or a more experienced teacher. Which of the QCA groupings in Figure 7.2 do your selections fit into?

Figure 7.2 Desirable and undesirable pupil behaviours

Desirable behaviour	Undesirable behaviour
L1. Attentive/Interested in Schoolwork • attentive to teacher, not easily distracted • interest in most schoolwork • starts promptly on set tasks/motivated • seems to enjoy school	• verbal off-task behaviours • does not finish work / gives up easily • constantly needs reminders • short attention span • negative approach to school
L2.Good Learning Organisation • competent in individual learning • tidy work at reasonable pace • can organise learning tasks	• forgetful, copies or rushes work • inaccurate, messy and slow work • fails to meet deadlines, not prepared
L3. Effective communicator • good communication skills (peers/ adults) • knows when it's appropriate to speak • uses non-verbal signals and voice range • communicates in 1:1 or group settings	• poor communication skills • inappropriate timing of communication • constantly talks • lack of use of non-verbal skills
L4. Works efficiently in a group • works collaboratively • turn-takes in communication/listens • takes responsibility within a group	• refuses to share • does not take turns
L5. Seeks help where necessary • seeks attention from teacher when required • works independently or in groups when not requiring help	• constantly seeking assistance • makes excessive and inappropriate demands • does not ask 'finding out' questions
C6. Behaves respectfully towards staff • co-operative and compliant • responds positively to instruction • does not aim verbal aggression at teacher • interacts politely with teacher • does not deliberately try to annoy or answer the teacher rudely	• responds negatively to instruction • talks back impertinently to teacher • aims verbal aggression, swears at teacher • deliberately interrupts to annoy
C7. Shows respect to other pupils • uses appropriate language; does not swear • treats others as equals • does not dominate, bully or intimidate	• verbal violence at other pupils • scornful, use of social aggression (e.g. 'pushing in') • teases and bullies • inappropriate sexual behaviour
C8. Seeks attention appropriately • does not attract inappropriate attention • does not play the fool or show off • no attention-seeking behaviour • does not verbally disrupt • does not physically disrupt	• hums, fidgets, disturbs others • throws things, climbs on things • calls out, eats, runs around the class • shouts and otherwise attention seeks • does dangerous things without thought
C9. Physically peaceable • does not show physical aggression • does not pick on others • is not cruel or spiteful • avoids getting into fights with others • does not have temper tantrums	• fights, aims physical violence at others • loses temper, throws things • bullies and intimidates physically • cruel / spiteful
C10. Respects property • takes care of own and others' property • does not engage in vandalism • does not steal	• poor respect for property • destroys own or others' things • steals things

continued ...

Figure 7.2 continued

Desirable behaviour	Undesirable behaviour
E11. Has empathy • is tolerant and considerate • tries to identify with feelings of others • tries to offer comfort • is not emotionally detached • does not laugh when others are upset	• intolerant • emotionally detached • selfish • no awareness of feelings of others
E12. Is socially aware • understands social interactions of self and peers • appropriate verbal/non-verbal contacts • not socially isolated • has peer-group friends; not a loner • doesn't frequently daydream • actively involved in classroom activity • not aloof, passive or withdrawn	• inactive, daydreams, stares into space • withdrawn or unresponsive •does not participate in class activity • few friends • not accepted or well-liked • shows bizarre behaviour • stares blankly, listless
E13. Is happy • smiles and laughs appropriately • should be able to have fun • generally cheerful; seldom upset • not discontented, sulky, morose	• depressed, unhappy or discontented • prone to emotional upset, tearful • infers suicide • serious, sad, self-harming
E14. Is confident • not anxious • unafraid to try new things • not self-conscious, doesn't feel inferior • willing to read aloud, answer questions in class • participates in group discussion	• anxious, tense, tearful • reticent, fears failure, feels inferior • lacks self-esteem, cautious, shy • does not take initiative
E15. Emotionally stable/self-controlled • no mood swings • good emotional resilience, recovers quickly from upset • manages own feelings • not easily flustered or frustrated • delays gratification	• inappropriate emotional reactions • does not recover quickly from upsets • does not express feelings • frequent mood changes; irritable • over-reacts; does not accept punishment or praise • does not delay gratification

Source: Adapted from QCA 2001.

Note

L, learning behaviour; C, conduct behaviour; E, emotional behaviour

During the course of your early career, several of these behaviours are likely to be encountered. The first question you may need to ask is, 'What do experienced teachers do when confronted with such pupils?' Generally speaking there are a small number of intervention models which are currently in common usage. Before briefly describing each of these it is worth adding a word of caution. Most teachers tend to use their personal judgement and intuition in responding to unwanted behaviour; in other words they will try for a 'best-fit' intervention, based on what they see as those elements of these models which, in their view, are appropriate and workable. So the key here seems to be the adoption of a 'pick-and-mix' approach to managing behaviour, so that the needs of the pupil and the teacher are catered for. A second proviso is that a classroom teacher needs to be aware of the broader 'behaviour ethos' within the whole school. And so individual actions need to be sympathetic to the spirit and aims of a whole-school behaviour policy.

Generally speaking the management of pupil behaviour is usually mapped against six broad conceptual models, informed by certain theoretical principles (Evidence for Policy and Practice Information [EPPI], to be published 2004). Each of these six models has its merits, and as has been pointed out in the preceding paragraph, there is a tendency for teachers to draw from each of these orientations. Recognition of their existence, and an understanding of them, will allow you to understand where a certain pupil behaviour is coming from and, because of this, enables you to arrive at an appropriate intervention (see Figure 7.3).

Figure 7.3 summarises both explanations and possible action and offers some clues as to what the underlying theories are, which can be drawn upon to justify or validate those actions. What is apparent, and confirmed by emerging research, is that teachers use an intervention model based in some part on their interpretation of the behaviour and the causal factors underpinning it (Garner and Gains, 1996).

Figure 7.3   Explanations of pupil behaviour
Source: Adapted from EPPI, 2003.

Frequent behaviour	Theory	Explanation	Action
Off task	Off task	Pupil gets more attention by being off-task	Reward on-task behaviour
Off task	Cognitive	Pupil thinks he can't do task	Encourage pupil to identify parts of task that he can do
Off task	Affective	Pupil fears failure	Build self-esteem (e.g. 'Circle Time')
Off task	Social/ Environmental	'He has a brother who is just the same'	Nurture group work/ work with parents/ family
Off task	Biological	Pupil has attention deficit hyperactive disorder (ADHD)	Refer for medical assessment
Off task	Developmental	Pupil not ready for independent work	Learning Support and set more appropriate learning target

**Reflective task 7.4
Identifying the cause of
unacceptable behaviour**

Discuss with a colleague the strengths and limitations of the models outlined in Figure 7.3. How applicable are they to a given pupil in your own classroom?

MEETING THE CHALLENGE IN THE CLASSROOM: PROACTIVE ENGAGEMENT

The first task of any teacher is to establish a positive learning environment. This is a key element in any approach to managing classroom behaviour. From the outset you need to ensure that a set of insulating conditions are established: these will go a long way to minimising problematic behaviour. Some writers on the topic have even stated that there are *deviance insulative* and *deviance provocative* teachers (Jordan, 1974). The former is able to prevent the development of long-term problem behaviour by ensuring that certain routines are followed. In Smith and Laslett's work (1993) the way in which this 'insulation' process is accounted for is straightforward. Teachers have to:

- get the pupils into the classroom;
- get on with the lesson which has been planned;
- get on with the pupils themselves; and finally
- get the pupils out of the classroom.

But whilst this four-stage process might sound relatively straightforward, each one of these phases requires thought and planning from the outset. If a teacher gets things 'right' the chances are that the classroom will be a place where all of the pupils come to recognise that purposeful learning takes place.

Entry and settling down

The key word here is routine. Pupils are creatures of habit; they like their teacher to adopt a set of sensible routines from the outset; and they like to know the framework and boundaries for their learning. This process will begin before they get inside their classroom. All the sensible advice states that the teacher must be in the classroom before the pupils; greeting pupils is very important. Studies have shown, for instance, that so-called disruptive pupils dislike being treated with disrespect – a friendly nod, a word of encouragement on entry to the room can prompt appropriate behaviour where otherwise it may not be forthcoming. Effective insulative teachers also make sure that they have a firm idea of how the class is to be seated – here again is a basic strategy to inhibit problem behaviour and promote learning (Hastings and Chantrey Wood, 2002). Such teachers are firm and directive, whilst ensuring that the pupils know why they are being seated in a particular place. A set of rules is an essential feature of learning classrooms – these need to be publicised and constantly reinforced. Good practice also suggests that the pupils are involved in this process. Again, research suggests that classrooms in which children take responsibility for behaviour are successful learning environments (Coulby and Coulby, 1995). It is worth remembering that you have to plan for learning behaviour as much as for actual curriculum content. All too frequently the basics of the 'social curriculum' of the classroom are left to just happen by chance. A failure to attend to learning behaviours is offering an open invitation to some pupils: you are indicating to them that you are not in control of the teaching space. Research studies also show that pupils who are inclined to misbehave prefer teachers who convey a strong message that they are 'in charge' (Davies, 1996).

It is worth pointing out, however, that compliance, pro-social behaviour and positive approaches to learning do not happen overnight. One of the frequently expressed concerns of new teachers is that they feel that their pupils are failing to respond to classroom protocols. Some pupils, they believe, do not want to accept the rules and procedures commensurate with effective learning. It is at this stage that you have to bear in mind two important issues. Firstly, that behaviour does change, but that it will be a slower process for some children. The key, therefore, is to persevere, keep your nerve and maintain (though monitor and review) established routines at all costs. The second issue is that you should make full use of the resources at your disposal in helping to develop classroom management skills. Close liaison with an induction mentor, making full use of training opportunities and, importantly, observing more experienced teachers in their dealings with pupils are three strategies which need to become second nature.

Teaching the lesson

The National Standards for QTS are perhaps a useful basis to explore the key pedagogical issues that help teachers to secure pro-social behaviour and advance the learning of all pupils. Teachers are required to address what are regarded as the three principles of inclusion: setting suitable learning challenges, responding to pupils' diverse needs and overcoming potential barriers to learning (TTA, 2002: 26). Consideration of these issues is, in fact, at the heart of many chapters in the present volume. But they have especial relevance to pupils whom, for whatever reason, present the teacher with unwanted problem-behaviour.

Circular 9/94, which addressed pupil behaviour and discipline, confirmed a long-held view that 'an effective curriculum, appropriately differentiated to stimulate and engage the pupils, is a key factor in motivating children and maintaining an orderly learning environment' (DfE, 1994a: 13). Moreover, research into the views of pupils who misbehave is conclusive about their expectations of teachers (Wise, 2000). These pupils want a teacher who presents lesson content in ways that engage them, irrespective of their own preferred style of learning. They want their teacher to be interesting, well prepared and able to recognise that all pupils can contribute very effectively to their own learning.

A crucial element in this process involves a recognition that pupils who misbehave are frequently struggling because of specific learning difficulties. The *Code of Practice* (DfES, 2001b) is very explicit in stating that the first-line responsibility for addressing such difficulties is the class teacher. So it is very important that you move beyond the misbehaviour presented: as has been stated earlier, all behaviours are a means of communication. In many cases, the pupil is saying, 'I can't do this work,' and attempting to disguise this by 'displacement behaviour' – actions which are off-task and often disruptive to other learners.

As has also been mentioned, pupils are creatures of habit; they feel safe when a learning routine is established. But all teachers can expect a period of subtle 'negotiation' – this is the time, comprising the first few weeks of working with a group of pupils, during which pupils can be expected to test the boundaries that have been set out as a framework for their behaviour (Woods, 1990).

As I have indicated, there is now a huge literature of sound practical advice regarding the explicit routines (and their implicit meanings) of classroom management (for example, see Chaplain and Freeman, 1998). Figure 7.4, adapted from one set of guidances, provides a basic checklist. Whilst some of its recommendations may seem obvious, these common-sense approaches are sometimes overlooked as too basic to address complex interactions and behaviour. But it has to be emphasised that such guidance is the bedrock which both

Figure 7.4   Checklist for promoting learning behaviours

Classroom organisation	Classroom management	Rewards/punishment
All equipment accessible	Arrive on time	Relate to learning behaviour
Ambient temperature	Clear instructions	Fair and consistent
Lighting/ventilation	Acknowledge positive behaviour	Achievable and relevant
Materials labelled	Acknowledge achievement	Understood by all pupils
Facilitate easy movement	Act as role model	Understood by parents/ carers
Positive pupil grouping	Differentiated learning	Respond incrementally to pupil actions
Working environment purposeful, orderly, friendly, supportive	Varied pedagogy	
Work displayed	Use learning support (teaching assistants)	
Pupil involvement in class layout	Use peer support	
Routine for distribution of materials	Emphasise pupils' role	
	Set of rules/routines	
	Negotiated rules/routines	
	Displayed rules/routines	
	Reinforce rules/routines	

Source: QCAAW, 2000.

pre-empts many unwanted behaviours and insulates classrooms from the negative impact of pupil misbehaviour. Periodic reflection, therefore, on each of the issues highlighted in Figure 7.4 will pay significant dividends in helping to establish a learning classroom.

Establishing relationships

Further reference to existing research will confirm the long-standing belief in importance of the social role of the teacher (Polat and Farrell, 2002). Establishing – and maintaining – good relationships with all pupils is a vital insulating factor against problematic behaviours. In much the same way that adults draw inferences from the ways in which their friends or associates relate to them, so too do pupils in class. They formulate a profile of how their teacher communicates, and with whom, and they are quick to seize upon any inconsistencies and apparent favouritism.

One of the frequent protestations by such pupils is that a teacher is unfair and does not treat each pupil as an individual (Wise, 2000). There is also a lack of recognition that reward is a major motivational factor. Pupils who misbehave feel that they are unable to achieve in the terms recognised by the school: as sociologists would have it, they become 'status deprived'. This situation is fertile ground for pupils' seeking alternative means of recognition – by engaging in individual or group actions which disrupt the class.

You will need to continually review your social relationships with those pupils who are most at risk of misbehaviour. There is a tendency to view classroom relationships as fixed, but such a view fails to recognise that pupils arrive at a lesson bringing with them all manner of immediate experiences which might influence their behaviour. Nor should it fail to be acknowledged that the same would be true for teachers themselves. Understanding these systemic but changing linkages is a vital element of relationship building, and has been elegantly theorised by Bronfenbrenner (1979). It is a sad, but common, occurrence that the profile of a pupil who is inclined towards misbehaviour will usually highlight a background of domestic dysfunction, negative peer influences and the involvement of social service departments and/or the police. Securing a positive relationship against such an unpromising backcloth is obviously difficult, especially when the young person sees himself or herself as being incapable of doing so. But again, research evidence can assist us by showing that such pupils require:

- consistency in their relationships with adults;
- unconditional positive regard from their teacher;
- opportunities for pro-social relationship modelling (Sage, 2002).

Conclusion and dismissal

The conclusion of a lesson, ending with the dismissal of the class, is a potential trigger for problem behaviour. And yet it is frequently discounted in '… a sigh of relief that it is nearly over' (Gray and Richer, 1988). A pupil will experience as many as six or seven lesson endings during the course of a day in school. A noisy, unstructured or chaotic conclusion minimises any lasting effect of the learning that has taken place during the lesson. It also ensures that these pupils arrive at their next classroom in a frame of mind which is not geared towards effective learning.

Reflective task 7.5
Minimising unacceptable behaviours

Reflect on each of the four insulation phases described above. Construct a personal checklist of your actions which you believe

1   insulate against misbehaviour
2   might trigger unwanted pupil actions.

How might you be able to move checklist items from 2 to 1?

Once again, an ordered routine is paramount. Reviewing lesson content and pupil achievement as part of this process offers an opportunity to give positive feedback and recognition to pupils who otherwise might regard themselves as invisible. It also can be used to signal 'closure' to pupils; it is their 'signpost' to the next part of their day in school, and as such is an appropriate time for you to quietly reinforce, by instruction or praise, social behaviours that are acceptable.

MEETING THE CHALLENGE: RESPONSES TO INDIVIDUAL CASES

In spite of a proactive approach to classroom management it is sadly the case that a small percentage of pupils will misbehave. For some pupils this is an infrequent and uncharacteristic action; but some other pupils offer a greater challenge, such is the chronic nature of their misbehaviour. This section of the chapter examines possible responses in such cases. At the outset it is reassuring to return to the Elton Report's research on teacher opinion, which states that 'We find that most schools are on the whole well ordered' (DES, 1989: 11) and that serious incidents are rare. At the same time, the Report believes that '… even in well run schools minor disruption appears to be a problem'. So all teachers need to refine strategies for dealing with misbehaviour as soon as it occurs. What follows is a rehearsal of what will be familiar territory for some; but all teachers, whether newly qualified or experienced, are likely to benefit from continued reflection on these 'basics of behaviour'.

The ABC of behaviour is a good starting point. When confronted by a pupil who is misbehaving you need to address the (B)ehaviour in ways in which its (A)ntecedents are

Reflective task 7.6
Addressing unwanted behaviour

Write a short paragraph that describes one incident that you have recently had to deal with in your class. Then divide a sheet of paper into three equal parts – A, B and C – and place each of the key words or phrases you have used in your description into one, or more, of the categories, as described above. Is your description accurate enough to enable an intervention which is based upon 'evidence'?

recognised and its (C)onsequences are understood. Few teachers would argue that the unwanted action should be the focus of immediate attention. This is a 'public' performance, and all eyes in the classroom are on the teacher's response to this challenge. But it is the behaviour that is unwanted, not the pupil himself! All too frequently the two are merged in the mind of the teacher. If Rory's immature behaviour is publicly rebuked as 'Stop behaving like a five-year-old, Rory' it merely exacerbates the situation, as Rory needs to save face (and maintain his status with his peers) with a teacher-directed insult.

Avoidance of confrontation is essential, as a minor disagreement could escalate into a more serious form of disruption. But that is not to say that unwanted behaviour should be tolerated. Rather, it needs first to be neutralised so that effective learning can continue.

Typically such neutralisers involve use of a traffic light system, where a pupil is given feedback about his or her behaviour so that he or she can be involved directly in its own management. Where a pupil is working efficiently (green), communicate this with verbal approval, recognition that the pupil is retaining focus on the task set. Other rewards can follow continued positive behaviour. On noticing the first sign of non-compliance the traffic light shows amber, to alert the pupil to the fact that this inappropriate behaviour has been noticed. This can be reinforced by a verbal cue ('On-task, John … please') or a non-verbal signal. This should be followed by the use of choices: 'You can either do this work now, John, or you can complete it during break-time.' Further failure to comply means a red alert. Here is a pupil who may have learnt to off-task behaviour. The failure to comply needs to be *neutrally* acknowledged publicly as it happens (again, all the pupils need to know that you are in charge): 'John, I want to see you after this lesson to discuss your work.' This approach, which provides a structured approach in shared behaviour management, can be utilised in a range of cases where pupil misbehaviour is apparent. It should be the basis of a routine that all pupils come to regard as non-negotiable.

The class as a whole will be rating a teacher's performance in managing the classroom. The class, above all else, want its teacher to demonstrate confidence in managing any misbehaviour likely to be encountered in the classroom. The pupils do not want to be taught by a teacher who is easily rattled by the few pupils who appear unwilling to follow the rules of the classroom. In consequence you should always adopt a defensive and de-escalating approach in managing individual incidents by trying to offer the pupil at least one way out of a conflict situation. This is vital to the pupil, in that if a battle of wills between the two of you results in that pupil being 'shamed' in front of his peers, the relationship between you will be shattered, almost beyond the point of recovery.

The pupils also monitor your performance for any signs that you are becoming angry. Research by social psychologists indicates conclusively that human beings are much more influenced by non-verbal than by verbal communication (Argyle, 1983). It follows that, irrespective of the level of frustration felt on account of continued low-level disruption to a class; any tendency to interpret these actions as being directed at you personally must be avoided. If this is not done it greatly increases the stress and frustration felt by you, which in turn influences future teacher–pupil interactions. Concomitant to these feelings are visible signs of anxiety and anger. This has two equally negative effects: it reduces the capacity to think objectively in order to 'problem solve' the behaviour and it models unwanted behaviour for all the other pupils in the class. And of course, a teacher who is 'mad' is a gift horse to any pupil wishing to misbehave.

Much has been written of the need to identify sets of rewards and punishments (or sanctions). Whilst guidance on the nature and use of these are usually to be found in the staff handbook, it is worth noting a number of classroom principles. Firstly, that the most potent form of reward is verbal praise from the teacher (thereby indicating recognition of the pupil). Next, that rewards should be based on what has currency in the eyes of the pupils. Key rewards here, apart from verbal praise, are positive communication with the pupil's home, or to other teachers, display of pupils' work or recognition of progress or achievement during assembly or class discussion.

It is vital, in promoting a classroom ethos where learning can be accessed by all pupils, that a balance is struck between rewards and punishments. You should recognise that, in the pupils' mind, punishment is a legitimate response to wrongdoing. Equally, though, they are very aware that certain teachers make use of more punishment than rewards, and also that

Reflective task 7.7
Rewards and punishment

List the rewards and punishment that you make use of in your classroom. Does your list emphasise one or the other? How do you make sure that your preferred approaches in each case are effective?

these are often out of proportion to the wrongdoing. Punishment should be both directed towards an individual and explained in order that social learning might ensue from it. Punishing a large group of pupils, or even a whole class, is seldom productive and inevitably leads to pupil resentment. At all costs effective teachers avoid what some pupils refer to as revenge-punishment, which is destructive to both pupil and teacher.

In spite of these interventions some pupils are unable to follow the normal routines and rules of the classroom. Such pupils usually have associated emotional or learning difficulties and have been brought to the attention of the school's special needs co-ordinator (SENCO). In collaboration with the SENCO it is the job of the subject teacher to identify which behaviours are to be prioritised – usually in terms of their rate of occurrence, longevity, impact on the pupil's learning, impact on others and so on. The process usually involves an observation checklist, completed over several weeks. This then forms the basis of that pupil's individual education plan (IEP). A characteristic of the plan is its limited number of behaviour targets; care has to be taken to ensure that such targets are 'SMART' (Tod and Cornwall, 1998): those which are Specific, Measurable, Achievable, Realistic and Time related (can be reviewed and monitored in a sensible time span).

Finally, in those individual cases where pupils present the severest challenge, the role of the school as an active professional community comes into play. Colleagues on the staff will be very supportive – after all, there will be few experienced teachers who have not encountered at least one pupil whose behaviour was so extreme that they felt unable to cope. Experienced teachers in school can offer an opportunity for you to obtain non-judgemental feedback on the strategies they use in individual cases. And it is worth remembering that teachers learn as much from a failed strategy as from those that appear to work.

SUMMARY

Managing behaviour in schools is a topic which has been covered in hundreds of books, research papers and official documents. Much of what has been written has a basis in common sense. Rather than replicate the substance of that literature this chapter has sought to identify certain principles that help promote a learning classroom, in which pupils at risk of misbehaviour can thrive. What will be apparent is that much of this relates to your adopting a proactive approach to behaviour, in which conditions are established that minimise the likelihood of long-term problem behaviours arising by promoting effective engagement with learning. The existence of such conditions will also significantly insulate you and other pupils from widespread negative impact of misbehaviour. Placed in the context of both whole-school mechanisms for promoting good behaviour and of the clearly evidenced link between the curriculum and social learning, they offer opportunities for a more positive engagement with pupils who are inclined towards misbehaviour.

ACKNOWLEDGEMENTS

I acknowledge the support and helpful feedback from colleagues from the TTA Initial Teacher Training Professional Resource Network (Behaviour) in developing the focus of this chapter and in particular Dr Janet Tod from Canterbury Christ Church University College.

FURTHER READING

Hanko, G. (2003) 'Towards an inclusive school culture – but what happened to Elton's "affective curriculum"?' *British Journal of Special Education*, 30 (3), 125–31. This article emphasises the importance of establishing an appropriate set of conditions, or 'ethos', in your classroom in order to promote pupil learning. Hanko suggests that a deeper understanding of social and emotional factors will enable disaffected pupils to be more fully included within curricular and social processes, resulting in greater engagement in appropriate learning.

Visser, J., Cole, T. and Daniels, H. (2002) 'Inclusion for the difficult to include', *Support for Learning*, 17 (1), 23–6. This article reports on findings from a major study funded by government in England into what conditions need to be present in schools in order to meet the needs of children and young people who experience emotional and behavioural difficulties.

Part III

Consolidating Your Teaching Role

8 Assessment, Recording and Reporting

Alexis Taylor

Assessment has a two-fold purpose. It tells you (a) what individual (and groups of) pupils have learnt, but it also tells you about (b) yourself as a teacher. One way in which your newly qualified teacher (NQT) year is different from your initial teacher education (ITE) is that, as a full-time teacher, you know the pupils in the classes you teach better than you did during the short periods you were on school experience. This helps you to focus on the learning of individual pupils as well as on the teaching of whole classes. This change of focus presents you with some very important questions:

- How do you know when learning has taken place?
- How can you make sure you build on this learning?
- How can you let your pupils, and others, know about learning progress?
- Does learning automatically follow from teaching?

These essential, somewhat obvious, questions do not identify anything that you have not encountered in your teaching to date. Indeed, none of these areas is new. These questions lead you to focus your attention on the assessment, recording and reporting of pupil learning. Traditionally, teachers have always tried to find out whether pupils had learnt what was intended and have maintained records and written reports. However, the emphasis in the last decade or so on accountability in public services, especially education, has brought a renewed focus on assessment, reporting and recording. Parents, the general public and central government rely on the professional judgement of teachers about progression in pupils' learning, in addition to information provided by public assessment (e.g. Standard Assessment Tests [SATS] scores and General Certificate of Secondary Education [GCSE] results).

The purpose of this chapter is to explore issues inherent in the areas of assessment (both formative and summative), recording and reporting, to enhance your own thinking, and to build on your current understanding. Assessment, recording and reporting are professional issues, and this chapter aims to help you to set the issues in a wider sphere to help you move forward as a teacher who keeps learning at the heart of teaching.

OBJECTIVES

By the end of this chapter you should be able to:

- put into practice your developing knowledge and understanding of assessment, recording and reporting;
- become familiar and engage with some of the research undertaken in these areas;
- begin to develop your personal and professional thinking about these areas;
- be more confident of contributing to professional debate about these areas in a critical fashion;
- consider critically the inherent issues and conflicts about the nature and purpose of assessment, recording and reporting for pupil learning; and
- think about how you want to develop these areas as part of your own continuing professional development (CPD) as a teacher.

ASSESSING PUPIL LEARNING   NB

Assessment has featured prominently in change in education. Four periods of change were cited by Black (1998): the introduction of intelligence quotient (IQ) testing and use of standardised tests; national testing as part of the National Curriculum; the move to formative assessment; and the emphasis on assessment as transforming whole-school learning. Behind all these wider changes is how those 'receiving' assessment, i.e. the pupils, are affected.

When using assessment to inform pupil learning, i.e. to find out if pupils learnt what was intended, it is helpful if you understand pupils' experience of assessment. Consider your own experience of assessment as a pupil when you were at school. For example, did you always know what 6/10 (or 60 per cent or Grade B) meant? What did you do if you did not understand/agree with the teacher's assessment? Did you notice any differences in grading between subjects/between teachers? What assessment methods were used? How did you feel about being assessed? One teacher I knew often completed the homework and classwork tasks which he had given to his pupils. He argued that this practice gave him – the teacher – the opportunity to think about the experience of assessment by taking on the role of the learner who is assessed. You may find it helpful to try doing this (see also Reflective task 8.3).

That teachers use assessment to make a professional judgement about whether pupils have learnt what was intended appears to be a straightforward definition of assessment. However, this simplicity masks a range of complexities. For example, assessment can be:

- summative or formative
- written or oral
- formal or informal
- by individual or group
- norm referenced or criteria referenced

Reflective task 8.1
Reviewing your knowledge of assessment

This task is designed to help you work with increasing professional competence in assessment.

Re-visit some of the knowledge and information about assessment you have developed during your teaching experience to date and in texts you have used (e.g. Haydn, 2001). Make a list of those aspects you are confident about. Make a second list of those aspects you would like to enhance. For example, you may be fully confident in understanding the difference between formative and summative assessment, but you may wish to develop some further strategies for using formative assessment to enhance learning or may wish to work with a more experienced teacher on how to design and record summative assessments. You may wish to refer to http://www.tes.co.uk/online/assessit/. This is a website of the *Times Educational Supplement* which focuses on recent developments in assessments issues.

Look at your lists with your mentor and discuss ways in which you can gain experience and develop the areas identified.

- teacher led or pupil centred
- outcomes related or process related.

Your experience to date has enabled you to develop knowledge and understanding many of these aspects of assessment. If you need to refresh your memory refer to Haydn (2001). These aspects have been placed as alternatives in the list above. However, matters are not as easy as this, and such a straightforward way of looking at assessment may blur some of the contradictions and tensions inherent in assessment. Dilemmas come about for a number of reasons, including some which result when assessment is viewed only as an end product of teaching (assessment of learning) rather than part of the process of teaching (assessment for learning). For example, are end-of-year or key stage tests summative or are they (or should they be) formative within the five-year cycle of secondary schooling? It is important that you conceptualise issues like this concerning assessment as part of the process of your professional work. It is important to link thought and action, principle and practice, especially when you are following requirements that are sometimes beyond your control.

Reflective task 8.2
Conflicts in implementing assessment

Consider any conflicts you have encountered in having to implement assessments that have not been of your own making. Perhaps they have been connected to agreed departmental or school policy, or to national requirements related to the National Curriculum. Reflect on how you have resolved these conflicts and use this information to inform how you resolve conflicts in future.

When using assessments to find out what pupils have learnt, you need to look at what knowledge, understanding, skills and attitudes you plan for pupils to learn, i.e. your intended learning outcomes. On one level, these appear obvious. For example, the first of these – knowledge – may be interpreted as being about recalling factual information. The second – understanding – may be interpreted as the application of knowledge in terms of relationships, ideas, theories, connections. It may be easy to design an assessment that asks pupils to describe and explain. However, on another level, there are fundamental questions to be asked. Do pupils have to be able to recall something before they can understand it? In religious education, for example, a pupil may be able to understand why Muslims go on Hajj, but may not be able to recall the name of the city to which Muslims travel.

Assessing skills and attitudes may also create a dilemma. With regard to physical education, a pupil may be able to perform well in gymnastics, which can be assessed through demonstration, but how do you assess the extent to which the pupil has developed a health-related attitude to physical activity?

Assessment, especially formative assessment, may also show you that some pupils achieve learning outcomes which are different to those you had in mind. Perhaps you did not explain the activity adequately? Perhaps the activity was not suitable? Perhaps some pupils were ready to learn more than you intended? Can some pupils learn more working independently of you as a teacher? Is self-assessment by pupils something you would consider?

Assessment also tells you something about yourself as a teacher. If the pupils have not learnt what you intended, as a teacher do you:

- consider why not?
- adjust the learning context in some way?
- reconsider your teaching strategies?
- reconsider the content?
- reconsider individuals or groups of pupils within the whole class?
- redesign the assessment?
- think again about the marking/scoring of the assessment?

These questions show that assessment, whether formative or summative, links fundamentally with teaching and learning, and invites questions about your rationale for what and how you are teaching. For example, what is the purpose of what you have planned to teach? What are the pupils learning? Assessment then helps you to ask the questions: *how* and *why* does your teaching affect pupil learning?

Essentially, what you should have drawn from this section is that assessment is not a straightforward and mechanical procedure, but holds many questions and tensions that you need to think about. Thus, assessment should enhance pupil learning, but it also encourages you to question your professional values and actions and helps you to learn about yourself as a teacher.

RECORDING LEARNING

Recording learning appears straightforward (more so in summative assessment, which measures the end product of learning, i.e. attainment), but it also has its complexities. Much of your professional judgement about pupils is tacit. Recording things 'in your head' due to the 'busyness' of teaching is almost inevitable. However, it also carries with it difficulties, which make systematic recording a necessary obligation. Systematic recording:

- secures the evidence base on which you base your professional judgements;
- identifies areas of strength and development for individual pupils; and
- shows progression for individuals and groups.

Essentially, the way you record learning depends on the way you assess. Assessment using objective tests is fairly easy for you to administer. While it is easy to understand a recourse to this type of assessment which is not too burdensome for teachers, objective tests have some deficiencies with regard to pupil learning. For example, they are limited in the response that can be gathered and may focus on objective knowledge rather than conceptual understanding and application. They may also penalise pupils who want to do more than the test requires. Also, consider the pupil who may be able to explain what she/he understands but may not be able to write it as part of a formal test.

Learning is not static and is not always easily measurable and able to be recorded. As well as summative assessments, teachers collect information on pupil learning through a range of formative 'performance' assessments (Parkes, 2000): that is, where pupils are required to construct their own response to open-ended tasks, and where there is no one 'right' answer. Examples are discussion work, question and answer, investigations and compiling individual portfolios. Recording learning through using such formative assessment is not easy for a teacher. However, a study by Parkes (2000) investigated pupil learning outcomes using objective tests and performance assessments, and found that performance assessments captured more than objective tests, and that pupil learning was enhanced in performance assessments as pupils felt they had more control over them, rather than the objective tests which they perceived were 'done to them'.

Recording learning is not just a matter of collecting enormous amounts of data to put in a mark book or computer. You also have to make sense of pupil records so that you can monitor the progress of individual pupils against their own achievements and also against trends for groups within and between classes. Records also help you plan your teaching and pupils' learning: that is, assessment for learning.

REPORTING LEARNING

Besides your needing to make sense of assessment and assessment records, others need to make sense of it also. *Pupils* need to understand what you record about them (so that it can enhance their learning). One way to do this is to let pupils know how the information is used to help them to learn. You can do this by sharing with pupils:

- the intended learning outcomes of the lesson and the reasons for the activities in the lesson;
- the specific criteria by which the intended learning outcomes are assessed;
- what feedback is given; and
- how the learning is recorded.

Such activities give some degree of involvement to pupils for their own learning: this can influence their motivation and self-esteem, as well as build an atmosphere of trust and partnership in the classroom as you and your pupils work together to improve their learning as well as your own teaching. The LEARN Project (Bristol University, 2000) investigated the expectations of assessment requirements of over 200 pupils covering ages 3–13. The pupils found positive feedback and recording of achievement a crucial element in helping

Reflective task 8.3
Reflecting on recording
assessment

This set of tasks is designed to enable you to reflect on how you record pupil learning. Discuss these with your mentor, as appropriate, to enhance your teaching and learning.

2.1   Consider how you record your day-to-day assessment of pupils. One teacher tried a 'Day Book', making a few written notes each day on individual pupils who were thought to need focused attention. Would such a system work for you?

2.2   Consider the strengths of the departmental policy on recording. Do you think there are any improvements that the department may consider?

2.3   Consider the department's recording system from the pupil perspective. You may use grades or marks or comments or another system. Does the system make sense to pupils? How do you know this?

2.4   Have you considered using any of the following:
   • Marking codes – these might help you to record more information than you can using grades or percentages. For example, (+) might mean making progress following a discussion with the pupil.
   • Dialogue marking – making a comment into a question encourages pupils to read what you have said and respond in their book. This might also save you time, as it is quicker than having individual meetings. For example, 'Jean, you've managed to note all the main points here. What do you think of adding some more to the last section?'
   • Pupil marking – this could be done in pairs or groups, or by the individual who has completed the work.
   Would any of these work for you? What difficulties do you envisage with each of these strategies? If possible try to use some of them with a target class and then review the process.

2.5   Performance assessments should be designed to allow you as the teacher to assess whether learning has taken place, and for you to be able to record this learning in some way. Think how you record, for example, role-play, discussion work, answers to questions. Consider any difficulties you have encountered in recording learning in this way. How have you overcome these difficulties?

them improve their work. They also noted that constructive criticism was helpful as a way of improving present performance.

On the other hand, not all assessment records motivate pupils, and may even lower self-esteem. Consider how Jackie may feel when you review her half-termly progress recorded in Table 8.1. How would you give constructive and genuine feedback to Jackie about future progress in a way that is realistic but motivating? So, while you need to handle the data you record, you need to balance this by realising that this data links to individual pupils, who are dependent on you to handle such data carefully and sensitively.

It is necessary, and in England a requirement, to report results of pupil learning to parents/guardians at least once a year. Most parents and guardians want to know how their children

Reflective task 8.4
Handling record data

This task is designed to help you consider how you handle the data you record about pupils learning. Table 8.1 is an extract from a teacher's notebook. Read through Table 8.1 and make brief notes on what it tells you about the performance of each pupil, then answer the following questions. What does it tell you about:

- the assessment activities the teacher has used in the unit – how would you follow up on this?
- each individual pupil in relation to his or her own progress over six weeks?
- each individual in relation to the group?
- any identifiable trends you would focus your attention on?
- what the grades mean?
- what characterises progress?
- whether or not the extract provides you with more queries than answers about assessment of learning?

Table 8.1 Extract from an NQT's record book

Pupil	2/9/04 Home work (Q and A)	9/9/04 Work sheet	16/9/04 Group work	24/9/04 Survey	30/9/04 Role-play	7/10/04 Self-assessment of unit
Harshinder	A	A–	A	B	A	A
Jackie	E	E	D	E	C	B
Mandeep	C	C +	C–	E	C	B
Paulette	D	D +	D	E	C	C+
Rosemary	B	D	B	C	C	B

are progressing, and want to be informed by schools. Most schools go beyond this minimum statutory requirement. You probably have attended a 'parents' evening' following a formal report period, but in what other ways does your school report pupil progress to parents/guardians? For example, your school may operate a weekly diary system in which the pupils write down their homework, but which also acts as a channel of communication about progress. Your school may also invite parents/guardians to a meeting about individual pupils. Such meetings may report on progress but may also cover other pastoral aspects, such as behaviour and adjustment to school life.

Over the last decade central government in England has required that schools report to the *public* the results of formal examinations and nationally set key stage tests. A description of the data is published in the Package of Pupil Performance Indicators (known as the Autumn Package). This also contains the government's recommendations for the use of the data to support headteachers and governors with the process of target-setting and school improvement. It contains analysis of Key Stage 1, 2 and 3 assessments and GCSE/General National Vocational Qualification (GNVQ) exam results, including national summary results, information on value added between key stages and benchmark information. This enables schools to understand what progress they are making; compare the progress made by individual pupils with progress made by other pupils with similar prior attainment and compare their performance with similar schools. If you want to know more the website, http://www/dfes.gov.uk is useful for further information about the Autumn Package. It also provides recent information about government initiatives.

Reporting in ways such as the Autumn Package presents a number of tensions. One tension is that the information is published as performance indicators (referred to as 'league tables') which present results in comparison with national averages. Another tension is the use made of such data. Besides serving public accountability, the publication of such data is also used to make comparisons between schools. However, individual schools have different contexts in terms of:

- pupil/staff ratios
- resources
- intake
- subject organisation
- teaching methods
- prior levels of attainment at school entry.

This last factor has been found by some research studies (for example, Fitz-Gibbon, 1997) to be a major source of school differences as pupils enter secondary school with different levels of knowledge and information depending on their previous schooling during the primary stage. The extent to which secondary teachers accommodate pupils' prior levels of attainment and learning when they arrive and build on this learning or whether they repeat or leave gaps in the pupils' learning is important. Diagnostic assessment – that is, finding out the starting point of each pupil on entry to secondary school – is an essential part of the assessment process, therefore. Diagnostic assessment can be both a formative and summative assessment.

Because of these points some might contend that public reporting of results has moved away from being related to pedagogy and pupils into the realms of whole-school management. Blanchard (2003), for example, argues that there is '… a gap between the theory and practice regarding the relationship between whole-school targets and individual targets' (p. 257). Thus, some researchers have identified limitations to the comparison of raw results of the Autumn Package (see above) and have suggested that an approach based on value-added performance would be more acceptable. A value-added approach suggests that pupils' performance is measured against their own achievement as opposed to comparing this to others. If a pupil achieves 10 GCSEs at A★ after entering Year 7 with low SATs results, this may indicate something positive about the pupil, the department and the school, all of which may have contributed to improving learning. A comparison with national GCSE averages would not identify this. Such value-added assessment may indicate something about school effectiveness, and may be a way in which schools can be compared. Researchers (for example, Reeves et al., 2001) have also indicated that factors such as gender, English as an additional language (EAL) and ethnicity may be significant in determining pupil performance. For example, Tinklin (2003) investigated the 'gender gap' and attainment levels and found cultural factors were influential in creating differences. The implication of these findings is in their challenge to teachers to consider how low and under achievement is understood.

The type of school may also be influential. A recent research study using an analysis of national value-added datasets has provided some interesting data on the relationship between pupil performance and specialist school status (Schagen and Schagen, 2003). They found technology and language colleges performed slightly above the norm, while sports colleges were slightly above the norm at GCSE but not at Key Stage 3. Arts colleges were above the norm for English, but below the norm for mathematics and science. There was some evidence of a negative impact of the presence of specialist schools in a local education authority (LEA) for the value-added results of pupils in non-specialist schools at GCSE but not at Key Stage 3. The importance of these findings is what they imply for us as teachers about assessing pupils across schools and subject grouping.

However, the concept of value-added assessment also has difficulties. For example, is it possible to predict grades at GCSE or levels at key stages on the basis of previous performance at a key stage? How can a SATs result be compared to a GCSE result (see also Haydn, 2001)? Also, individual pupils perform differently because of a variety of factors, such as motivation, previous knowledge, personal strengths, and their needs as individual learners.

You will become increasingly aware that the use of data on pupil learning is reported beyond the school in which you work, and this may confront you with a number of related questions and issues. For example, do you think that the setting of attainment targets on a national and/or LEA basis and whole-school targets can sensibly produce targets for teachers? Do you think there are tensions between having national, LEA and whole-school attainment targets with the individual nature of learning? How, do you think, having to report attainment in relation to external targets influences the way you teach and relate to pupils in your class? Following a review using research evidence dating back to the 1980s, Goldstein (2001) identified some limitations in the usefulness of performance data for judging schools and teachers. For example, teaching may be increasingly determined by the need to show results that are externally measurable. Goldstein is useful reading for those starting out in teaching.

YOUR CONTINUING PROFESSIONAL DEVELOPMENT (CPD)

It is wider questions such as those mentioned above that you will address as your career progresses. During your induction period in England (TTA, 2003a; TTA, 2003b) you are consolidating your knowledge and understanding and need to reflect on how you can enhance your knowledge, understanding and practice in relation to assessment, recording and reporting. Such reflection will help you think deeper about pupil learning and of the impact of your teaching on pupil learning.

However, reflection is enhanced if you go beyond thinking about your own practice. Reflection is better informed by systematic investigation and data analysis and relating such findings to the literature. The website of the British Education Research Association (BERA) at http://www.bera.ac.uk provides a useful starting point to find out about recent research projects in assessment, recording and reporting pupil learning. For example, Torrance and Pryor (2001) carried out an action research project to develop formative assessment and you may find it helpful to read about this. Following their example, you may wish to establish your own action research project to problematise and study critically one of the aspects of assessment, recording or reporting you would like to enhance (possibly one identified in Reflective task 8.1). Approach the action research in the spirit of exploration and investigation as opposed to proving what you already think. Be ready to confront your own preconceptions. The results, in the form of an analytic framework, may inform not only your own teaching but also those of the department or school in which you work. You may find it helpful to work with another colleague and/or link with your local higher education institution to take this work forward.

SUMMARY

This chapter has considered some of the inherent tensions in the three related areas of assessing, recording and reporting pupil learning and shown that these are complex entities. You may not be able to 'solve' these tensions, but you can develop a principled framework in which to work. To achieve this you need to continue to ask yourself questions about pupil learning and your own teaching. You may also want to revisit some of your preconceptions, and to search for answers at a deeper level using action research as part of your CPD.

FURTHER READING

Black, P. (1998) *Testing: Friend or Foe? Theory and Practice of Assessment and Testing.* London: Falmer. This book uses international research literature to demonstrate issues connected with assessment and testing. Professor Black acted as Chair of the Task Group on Assessment and Testing (TGAT), which undertook initial work on the National Curriculum levels.

The website at http://www.qca.org.uk/ca/5-14/afl gives information about assessment for learning, and gives links to other websites concerning assessment issues.

The Assessment Reform Group has led the area of assessment in raising standards in schools. Their website at http://www.assessment-reform-group.org.uk/ gives information about the work of the group.

A useful journal is *Assessment in Education: Principles, Policy and Practice.* This provides evidence of research studies in the latest aspects of assessment from an international perspective.

9 Language in the Classroom and Curriculum

Tony Burgess

Language has been central to education since the ancient Greeks, but contemporary knowledge about the issues concerning schools is a great deal more uncertain than sometimes is supposed. Reasons are well set out by Colin Harrison in his review of recent research in literacy for the Key Stage 3 strategy team working in England: complexity of the issues, fragmentation of the field and the absence of a unitary theory. 'The problem in a complex domain,' he adds '… is that you cannot advance knowledge if you oversimplify … you need to pay the price of accepting that there may not be simple answers to complex questions' (Harrison, 2002: 7). So, while it is a start to recognise that language is important to many aspects of your teaching, you need to use your judgement in developing ways of working and treat cautiously the claims for certainty advanced for various methods.

Across the last few years, the focus in schools has been on literacy. Along with numeracy, and more recently behaviour, literacy is one strand in the government's Key Stage 3 strategy, with application not just to English but to all subjects that have a part to play in 'literacy across the curriculum' (Department for Education and Skills [DfES], 2001a, 2001b). The encouragement has been for teaching more explicitly to young people the elements and systems that are available to them, as users. So, work at word, sentence and text level, recognising language's different levels – from phoneme up to discourse – underpins the national framework for English and Department for Education and Skills (DfES) advice for work across the curriculum more widely. Engaging with these priorities is important, and you can gain from the strategies and detail in the materials provided as you proceed. The central work of classrooms, though, lies with the meanings that pupils make and with their use of language in their learning. Concentrating on these is your best starting point for the work that you are seeking to develop.

Two insights matter, here. Both come well attested, in studies of children's language development and in educational practice. First, language has a role in structuring and exploring learning; second, pupils come to grasp its powers through active use. It follows that your priorities should be for pupils' use of language and for supporting pupils' making meaning. It is the interest that you ignite – in the issues, problems and ideas within your teaching subject – which supplies the energy for use and hence the basis for development of language.

We propose below that you reflect on your own language autobiography, in order to review the range of understandings that are relevant to classrooms. In considering your story, it is helpful to begin your time line with your grandparents and your parents. This enables you to put yourself into a wider history and connects you to the diversity of the classrooms you will encounter. We should keep the word 'diaspora' for enforced migrations. But there are few of us who have not been part of some migration and who do not carry in our speech the memories of family lives in different times and different places. You could also try this exercise with pupils, to learn about them and to raise their interest in language.

It will become apparent from these reflections that, as a teacher, you need to find a balance between acknowledging how much children do for themselves in learning and not denying them instruction that can help. How best to keep this balance goes to the heart of much that is debated, at present. As children, or as parents, many of us will remember the actual moment of learning to read as a mystery. Most children who accomplish this transition from supported reader to reading do it for themselves. Their learning is not co-extensive with teaching. Yet teaching also mattered – the bedtime stories, the school reading book, the attention paid to print – the scaffolding, to use a word to which we will return. You will find this balance differently, in specific settings, with different pupils.

Your judgement in developing methods, priority for meaning, a reference point in autobiography and a balance between learning and instruction are then the points to carry forward. The chapter, which now follows, treads a path through various themes, pausing on some points where considerations about language weave into the fabric of the classroom, which should occupy you as teacher. In order to provide a context, some remarks about the history of interest in language in the classroom are included in the following section. After that, the chapter seeks to stand behind your shoulder, as you make your plans for classes that you are to teach.

OBJECTIVES

By the end of his chapter you should be:

- aware of priorities for language across the curriculum;
- in a position to organise your classroom so as to integrate aims for the language development of your pupils with those of curriculum learning;
- alerted to some strategies for encouraging pupils' use of language in the different modes – talking, listening, reading and writing.

Reflective task 9.1
Reflecting on your language
autobiography

Reflect on your own autobiography as a user of language.
 Consider the strands within the history of your language, how you learned to speak and read and write, the influences on your development.
 What impact did the language of school have on your own language, as you encountered different ways of speaking in the classroom and amongst your peers?
 Use the insights to construct biographies for your pupils.

THE AIM OF LANGUAGE ACROSS THE CURRICULUM

The Bullock Report (Department of Education and Science [DES], 1975) gave national currency to the idea of 'language across the curriculum'. One intention in the phrase was to place the more inclusive 'language' at the centre of teachers' attention rather than the specific, subject-centred 'English'. Bullock's general argument was for the role of language in learning. In the masterly phrasing of its central Chapter 4, the report held out a goal for all teachers: to exploit the role of language in learning in all its aspects as the surest means of helping children to achieve mastery of their mother tongue (DES, 1975).

Bullock's detailed recommendations were shaped by various research projects, which had preceded the report, funded by the new Schools Council. These projects, still influential today, included Wilkinson's (1971) work on oracy, Britton's work on writing (Britton *et al.*, 1975), Halliday on knowledge about language (see Pearce *et al.*, 1972) and Derrick and her SCOPE team on the teaching of English as a second language (see Levine *et al.*, 1972). The strengths of this original research background (and some of its omissions) have influenced the pattern of attention paid to language, subsequently.

Following the Bullock Report, many new initiatives emerged, considering the place of language in different curriculum subjects. There was work by different writers in science (Sutton, 1981; Carre, 1981), geography (Williams, 1981) and history (Levine, N., 1981). Other projects studied language across the curriculum as a whole (Marland, 1977; Torbe, 1980). A new emphasis on bilingual learners (see Levine, 1990) revised the teaching of English as a second language within this wider point of view. Work on reading showed that secondary teachers also needed to become involved in promoting students' literacy and not simply take for granted the development of reading and writing skills (see Lunzer and Gardner, 1979).

Other projects followed at the end of the 1980s and beginning of the 1990s. Of chief importance were the National Writing Project (1989/90) and the Oracy Project (Norman, 1992). This research breathed new confidence into teachers' uses of informal talk and work with writing. A third project, Language in the National Curriculum (Carter, 1990), introduced perspectives from contemporary linguistics, though it succumbed to government disfavour as the National Curriculum was introduced.

Thus, the notion that 'every teacher is a teacher of English', originally coined in the 1920s, has a long history. It is worth knowing something of how research and practices in classrooms have developed, since this provides a window on the different expectations that have existed at different times. The Key Stage 3 strategy is distinctive in seeking rapid system level change. It was felt that earlier initiatives, such as the development projects of the 1980s, left too much up to local development and often foundered on patchy take-up at school level. Detailed materials and training have been provided in order to implement all strands, including literacy, with the expectation that priorities for development be set, as part of whole-school planning. You should inform yourself of your school priorities for literacy in planning for your lessons. But you will also want to construct your own basis for thinking about the role of language generally, and the chapter seeks to address this, in the sections that now follow.

THINKING THROUGH YOUR PLANNING

One good point of entry is your schemes of work and lesson plans. You will have given much attention to planning, as a student teacher. It is not intended to repeat advice about this, here. However, as you review your plans for teaching it may be helpful to consider questions of language at the forefront.

One step is to think about the interest of your topic from a pupil's point of view. You want your pupils' active interest. You should think about the points where they will make connections. Identifying these will fine-tune your approach as you concentrate on how the pupils will take up the content you are offering and how you will assist them in making meanings from this.

A further line of questioning should turn round the linguistic means that you have chosen to explore this interest. You should aim to keep a balance here between talking, reading and writing. At the same time you may need to teach some of the language skills on which you intend to draw, for you can not presuppose them, and it is worth identifying these.

Working with your pupils' language, it is sometimes useful to expand frames of reference in ways that look beyond the classroom walls, for in this way you can enhance the quality of pupils' work and help to give it purpose. There may be room, in reading, for richer resourcing of your topics through texts that bring in materials from outside. In writing, pupils' texts can go beyond the usual exercise books and folders, central though these are, towards display or exhibition or production.

Such detailed thinking through of where the pupils' interests lie, and of the linguistic means you chose, helps consolidate your plans. Two further sets of questions should be added. You should use your early lessons to introduce procedures to support the use of language. It is open to you now to plan development of procedures for the conduct of your classroom, in a more systematic way than was available to you as a student teacher.

Finally, but fundamentally, you should think about your teaching from the point of using the different cultural vantages and expertise available within your classroom.

The following list should help you think through your planning from the point of view of language:

- What is the interest of the topic?
- What will be the pupils' take on it? What prior knowledge will they bring? What connections will they make with their experience?
- What will be the specific points of entry for their enquiry and for their classroom work?

- What will be the points of pupil expertise that you may use to take the topic forward?
- How culturally open is the topic – is there room for cross-cultural comparison or for contributions from different experiences?
- What linguistic means have you have chosen to develop and explore this interest? Will you need to teach these?
- How will you handle any text(s) you introduce?
- Is your lesson sufficiently and interestingly resourced? Is there room to supplement your principal text(s)?
- How will you orient the pupils towards their reading?
- Is there room for different or for critical readings of the material you introduce?
- How will you handle comprehension?
- How does pupils' writing figure?
- What will be the genre, or text type, for any extended writing?
- Will you need to teach this?
- What will be the audience?
- What is the interest of the task?
- Is there room for writing tasks to be expanded?
- Have you built into your planning a sense of the procedures that you are seeking to establish in your classroom work?
- Do you need to teach these?
- What will be the outcome for the work that is accomplished?

While concentrating on your planning, a number of more general issues have been raised about the sort of classroom you are seeking to construct. We have begun with interest, linguistic means, procedures and cultural openness. But accompanying these points are questions about the sort of climate and environment that can best support your pupils' use of language, and we now proceed to these.

DEVELOPING AN INTERACTIVE CLASSROOM

Your plans envisage opportunities for making meaning and for using language. It follows that you need to build an interactive classroom with a culture and a climate that supports your pupils' use of language and their learning.

We can think about this interaction as including several levels, such as pupils' interaction with the curriculum content you introduce; their interaction with each other (and with you); and the interaction of the tasks that they accomplish with longer-term aims and purposes. The point has been made earlier that you can build into your planning development of the procedures that you are seeking to establish. You will want to make explicit rules and procedures for getting down to work, movement, gaining attention, the conduct of relationships, homework and the management of class work. This setting up of rules and procedures will cover matters that you have thought about already but which can be profitably reviewed for their contribution to fostering interactive use of language.

Interaction does not simply happen, in classrooms. It is not already there, waiting to be managed. It has to be constructed. It can be relatively minimal, or maximised and given salience in the classroom you are seeking to develop. A main consideration is that the potential for interaction in the classes that you teach is something you develop over time. It is through experience of joint work, you and your pupils together, that procedures become settled ways of doing things and cease to be just plans made in your head. This is a memory to foster. As days and lessons turn into a class's history, present moments come to be informed by recollections, between you and your pupils, a source of learning that can be renewed and perhaps a source of pride.

Writing about 'what good differentiators do', the Education Department of the Scottish Office (1995) identified a list of ways towards promoting a positive classroom environment, which may usefully be considered, here. Good teachers:

- shared the management of learning with their pupils;
- promoted the belief that attainment could improve;
- used a wide range of sources of information;
- identified a range of needs;
- responded to these needs by agreeing targets and criteria for success, giving assistance with problems, boosting pupils' confidence;
- gave and received continuous feedback;
- used a range of sources of support.

If you think of maximising interaction as a goal, as an achievement to be deepened and developed, you will have a rationale with which to co-ordinate your planning and give direction to the ways of working that you seek to introduce.

YOUR LANGUAGE AS A TEACHER

We turn now to your language as a teacher. You need to maintain your own confidence and fluency in your new setting. As you know from practical teaching, your language as a teacher has to integrate attention to content with anticipating behaviour and indicating skills. Pre-thinking these different levels can be helpful. You could work on the following points outside the classroom:

- scripting longer inputs, such as your introduction to your topic, setting tasks or homework, feedback to the whole class on a piece of work, the plenary's review of key points in the lesson;
- pre-rehearsing questions;
- preparing ready answers to personal comments, intended to test you out or to destabilise you;
- preparing ready answers to predictable disruptions: lost pens, lost books, forgotten homework, calling out, complaints;
- having principled responses to more serious disruptions: arguments between pupils, individual misbehaviour, refusals to co-operate, where the goal may be to demonstrate your equity, to offer choices, and to distinguish between the person and the deed.

Alongside confidence and fluency, you also need to signal your enthusiasm, your equity and care for all pupils.

A good deal of attention was paid to teachers' handling of whole-class teaching in the early days of studying language in the classroom. Researchers drew attention to the conceptual level of language used by teachers in secondary classrooms and to the use of technical terms. They questioned the balance of closed and open questions. Students of classroom interaction pointed to the dominance of talk by teachers and to the guessing games that often featured, where pupils sought the answer that the teacher expected. There were useful criticisms in such studies, and you plainly want to work at getting your own language simple and effective, at concretising explanations and at diversifying ways of opening up discussion.

Yet, at the same time, closed questions can be a useful way of establishing security or of ensuring the involvement of everybody in the class. They can help to get discussion going, at a point where more demanding questions might be too challenging. Equally, the concepts of the subject may serve a necessary function and be a part of the excitement of the study. The point at issue here may be awareness of the need to teach the concepts of your subject and to engage the interest of pupils in this – to aim for the expansion of their vocabulary and their appreciation of the relevance of this.

Exploration of these and other points may be found in the publications of the National Oracy Project (Norman, 1992) which may be briefly mentioned here. One interesting argument is that of the psychologist, David Wood, who raises the issue of alternatives to teachers' questions, given the inhibitions which always exist from 'the strong asymmetry of power in interactions between teachers and children'. His argument is that 'pupils can be encouraged to take the initiative', but that this demands 'tipping the balance of control in the pupils' direction' (Wood, 1992: 207).

Wood points out that all questions constrain, to some degree, how pupils can reply. He invites consideration of alternative conversational moves such as a personal contribution by the teacher or just supportive, phatic response. (A 'phatic response' is one that encourages more talk, or seeks amplification, and is supportive of the speaker.) Wood adds:

> When a teacher tells a class something, makes a 'personal contribution', one might expect one of any number of things to happen. Pupils might simply acknowledge what has been said, offer a contribution of their own or discuss the teacher's contribution between themselves. They may even address a question to the teacher (a rare happening as we have seen). Similarly after an acknowledgement or 'phatic move' from the teacher pupils could offer an acknowledgement back, raise a new direction or topic of talk, contribute, question, or address each other. In many different classrooms, we have found that each of these eventualities occur. These 'low control' moves from the teacher engender the widest range, longest and most animated responses from pupils.
>
> (Wood, 1992: 207ff.)

Ways in which you can make such responses include:

- making a declarative (open-ended or provocative) statement which invites rejoinder or disagreement;
- inviting elaboration ('Could you say a bit more than that?');
- admitting perplexity when it occurs, whether about the topic itself or about a pupil's contribution to it;
- encouraging questions from pupils (rare in many classrooms);
- maintaining silence at strategic points (three to five seconds may be enough to draw in another pupil's contribution or encourage the previous speaker to elaborate on what was said.

(Edwards, 1992: 238)

There will remain times when you will find that traditional questions are advantageous, but there is considerable evidence from the project that moves of this kind, by you, can at times be generative of pupil questions and responses. Note also that these alternatives are possibilities for teacher–pupil interactions in small-group learning as well as in the whole-class setting.

Key issues for your language, then, will be protecting your own fluency and your capacity for ready answers in response, as well as giving thought to concepts, concreteness of explanation, questions and ways of generating discussion in the whole-class setting. We will return to other aspects of your teaching strategy, such as modelling and giving feedback, in considering pupils' language, in later sections.

YOUR PUPILS' LANGUAGE AND EXPERIENCE

Your pupils' making meaning should be the heartbeat of your classroom. It will follow that your principal concern is to work within the language that your pupils bring, exploiting their resources, in the exploration of the topics in your plans and schemes of work. You will best support development in using language with this as your priority. Equally, a picture of your pupils' needs as language users will be found through working with them, in contexts that encourage active use. Just as maximising interaction in your classroom is a goal for which you work, so quality in making meaning will need time to develop. As pupils gain in confidence, they come to know their skills more surely, in the tasks and contexts you provide. Shared management of learning with the pupils, agreed criteria for success, and all the countless ways in which you boost confidence and encourage, will be important here, as noted earlier.

Pupils also need your skill and your awareness in understanding their histories as language users and in identifying points for their development. They need your guidance here, as an aspect of your teaching, not just as part of an assessment regime intended for school target setting and evaluation, necessary though that also is. It follows then that you should get to know your class, through every means at your disposal, and aim to build on individual dialogues related to their needs.

Contemporary classrooms have many different language repertoires within them, many different language histories and many levels of ability, and experience, in literacy (including reading and writing but extending also to information technology and familiarity with different media). You should form a view of this diversity and develop strategies for working with the different needs of individual pupils. But you should work to keep alive your pupils' eye view of these concerns. Your pupils need your understanding of their challenges in comprehending text or in developing their writing, not just your diagnosis. Perhaps the central challenge you face is finding time and means to build the depth of dialogue with individuals that will support their learning.

It may help to set out for yourself some key points for your work, in short- and longer-term perspective, and balancing whole-class work with reflection on the needs of individuals. A start is offered in Reflective task 9.2 below. Initially you need to get your work in classrooms going and to establish ways of working for the class as a whole. You should also use this time to develop strategies for individual pupils as you consolidate your knowledge of them. The way you organise for differentiated work within specific lessons, or in sequences of work, should take into account these individual strategies.

Reflective task 9.2
Establishing priorities for
working with your pupils'
language

Review your own priorities in working with your pupils' language, making use of the suggestions below. Sequence these in chronological order, to help give a direction to your classroom work across a period of time.

Points to work at in your early planning:

- Gear lessons from the first to work with the resources that your pupils bring.
- Use your early lessons to form an initial picture of where the class's language needs will lie.
- Form relationships with individual pupils.
- Seek out pupils' expertise, and use it.
- Develop your own system for recording individual progress and achievements. For example, a day book for each class could be a method, or a column format for speaking, reading, writing, special points, behaviour, in your mark book.

Strategies for the whole class, over time:

- Balance whole-class objectives and individual targets in the classroom tasks you set.
- Use pupils' prior knowledge, and their own descriptions of this, as a way into material.
- Invite pupils to contribute to the resources of your lessons by bringing in material.
- Exploit the language resources of the class, where possible, for comparative insights into language, words and syntax and ways of speaking.

Preparing strategies for individual pupils:

- Construct a picture of individual language biographies, which registers their time in school, and work to put these in your head.
- Find out about your pupils' interests, and about their reading and their viewing.
- Find out about your pupils' patterns of achievement, as registered in tests and levels, and IEPs.
- Construct your own picture of your pupils' strengths and needs in language.
- Develop strategies for individual pupils, building on the dialogue with them that you have established.

In what follows, we take up in more detail working with bilingual pupils and concerns with literacy.

Working with bilingual pupils

Finding out about the languages of your pupils is necessary for an interactive classroom. This enables you to make provision for bilingual pupils and to develop strategies for their learning. They face a dual task: coming to terms with particular curriculum content and mastering English. By your knowing and acknowledging their wider resources in language, you will be better able to help them meet the challenges within your subject.

Reflective task 9.3
Finding out about the languages of your bilingual pupils

Your pupils have a lot of information about the languages they speak, which could be useful to you. Eliciting, in tactful ways, just some of their linguistic knowledge and expertise could also produce ideas for classroom activities.

Try to find out something about the following:

1   What other languages are spoken by pupils at home?
2   Find out who they speak their languages with, which language are they better at, when they would choose to speak English, say, rather than the other language.
3   Do they know stories or songs or poems in the other language?
4   Do they read in the other language? Do adults read to them in that language? Have they got books or magazines or videos in the other language?
5   Do they know where else in the world their other language is spoken?
6   In what ways do your pupils speak differently from members of their family or of their class?

Schools have used information like this in a number of ways. Consider whether any of those listed below might be appropriate for you:

1   They have invited parents to make books for their pupils in the home language, and some of these have been published for classroom use and translated into English.
2   Adults from particular communities have been invited into class.
3   Pupils have made charts from their research into the languages spoken by the class.
4   Pupils can be asked to teach the class or group in their other language, to say something in a new language.
5   Pupils have used their skills in writing another language to show other pupils.
6   Pupils' knowledge about being bilingual, about having difficulties understanding or expressing oneself and about cultural differences has been used effectively in the classroom.

Bilingual learners may require that tasks be modified at times and be differentiated for them. But it is also vital that they keep in touch with the central meanings in the classroom. Much can be achieved by thinking through the main tasks of the classroom with their needs in mind and by seeking to explain these, in explicit and focused ways. Some ways of doing this are indicated below:

- Anticipate what demands are made by curriculum tasks – for narrating, talking about experience, reasoning, arguing, speculating.
- Suggest particular roles for pupils, which will help them to make their way in group work or discussion settings.
- Offer concrete formats for your pupils to work on collaboratively: e.g. charts, diagrams, contrasting statements, matrices.
- Anticipate difficulties and demands in the reading material provided, and be clear about the kinds of written language your pupils require.
- Unpack longer tasks (curriculum units, or reading and writing tasks) into steps and stages, where this is helpful to your pupils in reducing uncertainty or complexity.

The recommendations here for working with bilingual learners are for finding about the languages of your pupils, anticipating language needs in preparing lessons and materials, and developing individual strategies. There is much that could be added, which you can follow up in further reading. A useful schedule of language-linked strategies, for working with bilingual learners, is given by Josie Levine (1990), in her book on *Bilingual Learners and the Mainstream Curriculum*. Another excellent source is Deryn Hall's (1995/2002) *Assessing the Needs of Bilingual Pupils*.

WORKING WITH YOUR PUPILS' LITERACY

Your pupils' literacy needs will be of different kinds. Within the classes you are teaching, all pupils will need help in mastering conventions in the discourse of the subject you are teaching, especially in written language. Some pupils will have greater difficulties with their reading and their writing than others. In your planning, then, you need to think about what opportunities for reading and writing will be on offer and how you will develop tasks and procedures that support your pupils in mastering these literacy skills.

We consider in this section some general ways for encouraging reading and writing and come to more specific procedures for handling texts in the section that follows.

Your procedures for handling class work, and for homework, will form one strand in your approach to literacy; and as was mentioned earlier it will help to build your expectations about this into your lessons early on. In your school, it is probable that there will be some well-established routines about use of exercise books and rough books or paper, and you should follow these. But it is also worth reflecting on points that you might want to introduce. Many schools, for example, paste instructions about completing class work or marking policy into the front of pupils' exercise books, and you may want to think about such practical ways of signalling your routines.

The key point is to establish expectations about how class work will be conducted. It is likely that your work in all classes will move between spoken and written language, board work and discussion and writing. Your pupils' exercise books become their written records and their instruments for learning, and the values and procedures that surround them need identifying and asserting, and, at times, protecting.

To encourage reading generally, you need to know your pupils' current reading and viewing interests. It is helpful to devote some classroom time across the year to promoting and discussing these interests. You should set your own concerns with reading in your subject within a sense of pupils' reading for wider purposes. Some ways that you might consider are given in Reflective task 9.4.

Reflective task 9.4
Organising literacy in your classroom

Using the suggestions listed below, consider ways in which you might promote the literacy of your subject, as well as encourage reading and selective viewing more generally:

- compiling a reading and a viewing survey conducted as part of classroom work;
- developing a classroom library related to your subject, combining books and other materials, being open to contributions and suggestions from your pupils;
- devoting classroom time to discussing reading and the 'literacy' of your subject, and making time available in class which is specifically for pupils' reading;
- devising a system for promoting, monitoring and sharing reading through the year, such as book reviews, a notice board, reports offered to the class by pupils on interests that they are developing;
- developing different ways of using the school library for reading in your subject and for research;
- mounting displays and exhibitions in the classroom, combining pupil work and other related material.

Your pupils need to see how writing and public enquiry is conducted in your curriculum area, in ways that go beyond just text books and work sheets. Equally, your pupils' own work can become a part of the literacy environment that you are seeking to establish.

It follows also that you need to make clear your concern for writing in your subject, as an essential part of its communicative resources. Your interest will need to go beyond just using writing for testing purposes, or for recording, or answering questions in the context of your class work. Perhaps a reasonable aim is that in every unit of your work, there should be at least one piece of writing that offers wider opportunities for your pupils.

We consider later some options in the different genres of writing that might find a place in writing within your classroom over time. The point to make at this stage is that pupils will need your guidance in the written work to be attempted and procedures established in the classroom governing how writing is accomplished.

One recognised approach at your disposal is to build attention to the writing process into your ways of working, through establishing your classroom as a writing workshop, at the point where pupils work on longer writing tasks. The emphasis here is to encourage pupils' recognition that written texts take time, and may go through different drafts on the way to their completion. In such a way of working, as developed in America by writing teachers such as Donald Graves (1983) or Nancie Atwell (1984), you intervene within the preparation of writing drafts principally as consultant. You give classroom time to pupil editing of colleagues' drafts and seek to train your pupils as good editors and readers as part of their development as writers. The goal here is substantial outcomes in writing, accomplished across a period, and it follows that incentives are needed in order to maintain the energy of the process.

Accompanying this approach there is an emphasis within the literacy strategy in England on modelling writing in different genres and on 'shared writing'. Such modelling needs to start with a clear focus on the type of writing pupils are working on and then take pupils through the kinds of choices to be made in constructing such a text, working in small units. There is clearly value in such focused work, and you may want to look at how such concentrations on the writing process and on shared writing can usefully be brought together.

In this section about the language and experience of your pupils we have focused on some key components of your work. Key points have been to focus on making meaning within the language that the pupils bring and to use your early lessons to form a view of language needs and of strategies for individual pupils. We have also considered some key moves to make in working with your pupils' literacy. We have emphasised the need for working over time. Against this background, we can look in greater detail at the handling of spoken and written texts. We turn to this within the sections that now follow.

TALK AND COLLABORATIVE WAYS OF WORKING

Working on your own language as a teacher, reviewing explanations and questions, and experimenting with low control moves, were points considered earlier in relation to whole-class ways of talking and discussion. Your emphasis in pupil/pupil talk should be mainly on the provision of worthwhile activities and on developing the expectation that pupils help each other. When classrooms are organised round collaborative ways of working, talk will occur most often between pupils within joint undertakings.

The spectrum of pupil/pupil talk can extend from pair work to more formally organised groupings. Your sense of what is manageable is important, while looking to offer opportunities for talk of different kinds. Reflecting on the work of the Wiltshire Oracy project, Howe (1992: 30 ff) emphasises the importance of designing settings for talk, so that the pupils' sense of purpose can positively affect the quality of talking and thinking.

There should be:

- the right amount of choices within a task – an overall direction but opportunity for negotiation and room for interpretation;
- time to think and get to grips with a task but also on occasion a degree of 'pressure', in order to help focus the work;
- a purposeful job to do;
- audiences and purposeful outcomes – talk contributing to ongoing work rather than occurring in a vacuum.

Jobs that talk can do

The kinds of job that you want pupils to do in talk will vary, and different starting points will draw on different skills. It is worth considering then the kinds of talk that matter most within the teaching of your subject and looking to develop these, in planning for your class's work across a period of time. Again, the Wiltshire work is useful, in setting out a range of possibilities, and the list that follows has been adapted from Howe (1992: 31–2).

To encourage speculating and hypothesising

Pupils might:

- solve a problem;
- make a list of possible reasons for …;
- come up with a group theory;
- choose a section that they find interesting/difficult, and devise some questions for another group on it;
- make some predictions about what is likely to happen next;
- build in a planning stage for an activity before they are allowed to get their hands on any equipment or materials.

To help pupils make connections with their own experience

Pupils might:

- bring a personal object to school that has particular meaning for them, and then talk in a group with others about the object;
- choose a section that reminds them of a time when they …;
- take it in turns to tell others about …

To help pupils develop arguments and explore reasons

Pupils might:

- in pairs, take one side of a topic or argument and build up a case. Then join up with another pair who have taken the other side and talk it out;
- select a number of items, or ideas from a longer list;
- put a list of items into order of priority;
- organise a number of statements into three piles: 'Agree', Disagree', 'Can't agree'.

To develop skills in explaining and describing

Pupils might:

- compare and contrast two different things: two maps of the same area, two accounts of the same event, or concept, or design;
- devise and swap questions with other groups;
- talk something through (as above) and then regroup.

The list above draws on a number of different ways of working developed in recent years. Much useful talk can take place in interpreting a text, in 'reading groups' formed for that purpose, or in the joint construction of a piece of writing. By building talk tasks into reading and writing, talk can also contribute to your pupils' literacy. It should be made explicit too that pupil/pupil collaboration in such tasks provides a base for work with bilingual pupils in your class, or those with reading difficulties, though how you handle this will vary.

READING IN CURRICULUM LEARNING

Your work in building general awareness of literacy in your subject, suggested earlier, should form the background for your handling of specific texts within your schemes of work. For pupils to be aware of your concern for reading, as central to communication in the subject you are teaching, will aid transition to the texts that you are putting before them. Your central tasks are then to encourage the active making of meaning in the reading that your pupils undertake and to develop critical reflection on the material that they are meeting.

In a recent study of reading in a range of secondary classrooms, a group of Bristol researchers (Webster *et al.*, 1996: 123) make a key point about reading, while identifying recurrent shapes in lessons:

> A highly characteristic format, occurring in almost all of the lesson scripts (in secondary classrooms), was for two or three teacher-controlled tasks to be introduced with supporting information in a text-book, blackboard notes, handout or worksheet.

As they comment further:

> In the lessons we observed, reading and writing were most likely to be used for following or responding to teachers' instructions. Occasionally, pupils read as they followed the teacher's exposition, listening to new ideas in science, mathematics or humanities, whilst looking over a text ... There were very few opportunities to pre-read texts, to read continuously or to interrogate textual evidence. Very rarely were pupils able to read critically, analysing and evaluating their reading sources.
>
> (Webster *et al.*, 1996: 132)

The findings of this study point towards the need for more developed treatment of the ways of studying texts in classrooms. Teachers in the sample would quite often base their lessons round diverse stimuli – newspaper extracts, poetry, letters, video and TV recordings. However, the characteristic patterns of managing reading were relatively unconsidered. They tended to confine literacy-related tasks to extracting information, rather than encouraging active interrogation of the material, and limited opportunities for critical examination and reflection.

To assist the ways in which you handle texts in classrooms in your regular teaching, a body of work now exists devoted to promoting reading which is active and critical. These activities can be useful, and can offer ways of bringing pupils' resources in spoken language into development of meaning in their reading. It is important that the point of such activities is understood and that they are linked to larger purposes for pupils and to opportunities for feedback and consolidating understanding. Otherwise, the doing can take over, with loss of the connections and wider understandings that formed the original intention.

**Reflective task 9.5
Working with texts in
curriculum learning**

After looking at the suggestions given in the two lists below for methods of active comprehension and encouraging a critical examination of texts – 'Ways of encouraging active interrogation of texts' and 'A framework for looking at texts' – identify points in your schemes of work where these might be appropriately introduced.

Ways of encouraging active interrogation of texts

- *Sequencing*: Cut the text into parts a few sentences long and shuffle them. In groups of two or three, your pupils try to work out the most coherent sequence.
- *Prediction*: Pause in reading through a text and ask your pupils what comes next in the argument or story; or stagger the text, in a photocopied version, and ask for predictions at the end of reading each part.
- *Group close*: Prepare a passage with words deleted. Your pupils are required to think of words that would restore the sense of the original, not necessarily the exact word.
- *Devising questions*: When they have read a passage, each group of pupils devises two questions which, if given to someone else, would prepare them to think about the topic, or each group devises two questions which could be asked to test if another reader has understood the passage.
- *Underlining and theme finding*: Your pupils underline the two, three or four most important sentences, and/or devise a heading for each paragraph.
- *Labelling parts of the text*: You provide labels such as 'statement of fact', 'statement of opinion' or 'applications of the idea'. Your pupils examine the structure of what they are reading and find where these labels could be appropriately attached.
- *Diagramming*: Your pupils' task is to represent the text by some form of diagram.
- *Constructing tables or charts from information in the book*: You provide an outline, for example headings under which to compare say canals with railways, or Tudor life with that in the present day. These outlines will require not only close reading of the text by your pupils, but also analysis.

(Adapted from O. Watkins in Sutton, 1981: 71–3)

Pupils' critical reflection on their reading will arise more readily in a classroom where reading has already come to occupy a prominent place, with an expectation that texts of different kinds are likely to be encountered. It is important that your pupils come to recognise that texts have histories of making that exist in the public world, and are not just transparent vehicles of information. They need to know that texts can be examined for meanings that are excluded as well as for the ones that are selected. Increasing sophistication about sources of evidence and the forms of writing in subject areas are important aspects of young people's development as readers.

A framework for looking at texts

You may find helpful, in developing your pupils' reflections, the framework that was prepared in the course of the Language in the National Curriculum Project (Carter, 1990), an adapted version of which is set out below. These points for analysis were originally designed for teachers among a number of initiatives intended to promote knowledge about language. However, the moves proposed could also form a basis for useful work in your classroom designed to foster a critical literacy in your subject area.

- *Who speaks this text?* Is there an 'I' or a 'we' in the text? What kind of voice if this? Does the writer address me directly or through an adopted 'persona'?
- *Who is being spoken to?* Is there a 'you' in the text? What kind of audience is being addressed, and how can we tell? Am I prepared to include myself in this audience?
- *Where does the text come from?* What do we know about when, why and how it was produced? Does the text itself disclose these things? What status does it have? What values does the text assume?
- *What kind of text is this?* What other texts does it remind me of? What form does it take? What recognisable conventions has the writer adopted?
- *What does the text want?* What do I deduce about the writer's intentions? Are these intentions openly stated? What kind of reading does this text invite?
- *What does this text mean to me?* What are my motives as a reader of this text? How have I chosen to interpret it? Do I share its values? What thoughts has it prompted?

You might like to ask all these questions of the page you are now reading.

In discussing these questions with colleagues, it might be helpful for your lesson planning to consider some of the detailed rhetorical choices which writers make:

- *Presentational*: e.g. choices of layout, typeface, illustration;
- *Organisational*: e.g. choices of narrative, logical, metrical or figurative pattern;
- *Grammatical*: e.g. choices of tense, mode, person, syntax, punctuation;
- *Lexical*: e.g. choices of vocabulary, idiom, metaphor.

WRITING IN CURRICULUM LEARNING

Writing in curriculum learning gains from being seen in the context of literacy more generally. Where attention is paid to developing pupils' reading strategies, and to their critical examination of texts, there is a basis for developing equivalent concerns for choice and processes in composing writing.

Despite the ambitious aims for writing that many teachers have, the evidence is that kinds of writing in classrooms are often fairly limited in scope – answers to questions, notes, copying from the board, tests of different kinds. A main task for you, as a teacher, is to find a way of reconciling the need for these relatively bread-and-butter kinds of writing with writing of more ambitious scope, as was noted earlier in the remarks on working with your pupils' literacy.

What can often limit writing in school is the pupils' sense that only one text type or genre is suited for a particular purpose, coupled with an overdependence on writing for the teacher as audience and sole reader. In the course of school learning, the purposes of writing

Figure 9.1 Thinking about writing

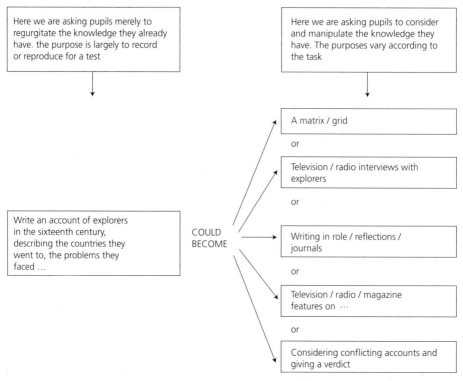

Source: Adapted from Radcliffe (1989/90).

are often to engage with new information, to develop interpretations, to construct arguments – to inform, to argue, to explain. Too often, given these purposes, the essay written for the teacher can become the 'default genre' (as it has been called) of school writing, where choosing among different text types, and considering other possible audiences, might better serve the writer's purpose.

It is helpful then to think about the wider possibilities for writing by pupils, which could arise from the topics you are teaching. Some choices are set out diagrammatically in Figure 9.1. The structure suggests a way of thinking about learning activities for your curriculum area, and helps envisage different ways in which they might be deepened by writing. For your pupils, deciding how to communicate and to whom – considering the demands of different genres and different contexts – are matters in their development as writers. So, building in some element of selection over writing tasks is worth considering. For you, being specific about purposes, and differentiating between these purposes and the types of text to be produced, will allow you to discuss with pupils the demands of particular tasks and engage with their development as writers.

Accuracy and precision in using written language, control of sentence structure, punctuation, spelling and presentation are all best handled by your pupils in the context of drafting actual pieces of work. But this does not mean that clarity about requirements and mini-lessons on selected points concerning good writing are not important. The techniques of modelling in the national literacy strategy make a contribution here.

Table 9.1   Literary genres across the curriculum

Types of genre	Characteristics	Curriculum area
Personal account	First person account of direct experience. Writer organises material by time to tell about events, e.g. account of a family holiday.	All subjects particularly English, PSE, CDT
Report	Objective account of an incident or activity. Third person account of what took place, specifying actions or information in a time sequence, e.g. experiment to find the boiling point of different liquids.	All subjects particularly science or geography
Imaginative	First person account of an imagined experience involving writer in role of another. Creation of a context, characters and time sequence, e.g. letter from the trenches during World War I .	English, history, PSE
Instruction	Instructions which direct reader to a goal. Specification of steps and ordering of information in a chronological sequence, e.g. operating procedure for a video recorder.	Science, CDT, home economics mathematics
Explanation	Objective interpretation of events or mechanisms. Causal relationships and technical vocabulary in a sequential chain of events, e.g. effect of crop failure in Brazil on High Street coffee prices in the UK.	Geography, science, CDT
Description	Selection of information which describes appearance or properties of an object or phenomenon. Third person factual, objective style, e.g. description of an Iron Age hill fort.	Science, history, geography, CDT, home economics, modern languages
Opinion	Presenting a personal viewpoint supported by arguments or examples. Selection and organisation of subjective information around a theme, e.g. article on the effect of violent videos on young people.	All subjects

continued ...

Table 9.1 continued

Types of genre	Characteristics	Curriculum area
Narrative	Relating a story with plot, characters and sequence of events to entertain an audience, e.g. science fiction story.	English
Information	Formal objective writing emphasising factual information. Attempts to classify, using technical vocabulary or graphic devices, e.g. information on pollution of British beaches.	All subjects
Persusasion	Attempt to influence reader to a particular course of action or belief, e.g. advertising leaflet.	English, history, PSE, religious education
Compare and contrast	Balanced and objective treatment setting out similarities and differences between two or more topics, e.g. properties of metals/non-metals.	All subjects
Reflection	Personal response to experience, organised thematically, e.g. views on living through a bereavement.	English, PSE religious education
Argument	Development of a logical argument supported by evidence, e.g. case for legalising euthanasia.	All subjects
Analysis	Impartial and systematic exploration of a problem, evaluating conflicting evidence to draw objective conclusions, e.g. patterns of poverty and health in different social groups.	All subjects

Source: Adapted from Webster, Beveridge and Reed (1996, pp. 154–5)

Note

PSE: personal and social education; CDT: craft, design and technology

Your pupils may gain confidence from collaborative drafting at times, and such collaboration can take place at different stages in the emergence of a piece of writing. An extended piece of writing may need to pass through a number of drafts, with different opportunities for editing and rewriting sections in its progress, in discussion with peers or with you. There can be first-stage audiences as well as final ones and peer work does not have to be an all-or-nothing option. Different permutations of editing and joint work are possible, and can be planned ahead, as stages in the process.

Schools and subject departments vary in their policies and procedures for writing in how these are worked through in curriculum planning and schemes of work. The advice here draws on research in composing (Graves, 1982) and on the work that you can find developed in the National Writing Project (1989/90) and in the national literacy strategy (DfES Standards and Effectiveness Unit, 2001b). It assumes that work with writing will arise in an overall climate where collaboration and discussion are expected and where your pupils are perceived as learners in their use of language as well as in curriculum content.

In their investigation quoted earlier, Webster *et al.*, (1996) identified a list of the writing genres that they found were actually employed in secondary classrooms, which is given in Table 9.1. In their list, 'type of writing' is rather closer to what has been called 'purpose' here, and their notes on 'characteristics' might be developed to include further examples of texts of different types and more consideration of different audiences. It is an interesting snapshot, though, of writing in different curriculum subjects at the present time. You might reflect on these examples as you clarify your own priorities for your pupils' writing and plan the tasks that you will introduce.

Reflective task 9.6
Planning your pupils' writing

Consider the list of literacy genres across the curriculum given in Table 9.1. Use it to identify:

- which you presently use, and why;
- which others might be suited to your curriculum area;
- which would not be suited to your work;
- where you might further specify the characteristics of particular genres, by adding alternative types of text and different audiences.

SUMMARY

Two priorities were identified to guide your work with language: to exploit language's role in learning and to promote active use. Following from these priorities, we suggested you review the place of language in your schemes of work and set goals for an interactive classroom where language use can flourish. Other advice included preparing your own use of language, as a teacher, finding out about the diverse language repertoires of your pupils and developing individual strategies based on your assessment of their needs. Under the pressure of curriculum content, abilities in reading can sometimes come to be assumed by teachers, without sufficient attention being paid to developing a climate in which books and other writings in the subject are regularly handled by pupils, talked about, interrogated and shared. Methods were considered for developing a literacy environment and for encouraging active and critical approaches to reading. In their writing, too, pupils need procedures that encourage them to see themselves as writers, with choices to make about the way they write and how their texts are prepared. It was suggested you review your use of different writing genres within your subject. You need to find out literacy priorities determined in your school. The focus here has been a framework of considerations about talking, reading and writing, which you can develop further.

FURTHER READING

Harrison, C. (2002) *Key Stage 3 English. Roots and Research,* date of issue 06/02, Ref. 0353/ 2002. London: DfES. Colin Harrison's review of the research underpinning the Key Stage 3 strategy for literacy is balanced and authoritative.

Levine, J. (ed.) (1990) *Bilingual Learners and the Mainstream Curriculum.* London: Falmer. This book contains an essential account of partnership teaching, much good advice and examples of appropriate work.

Norman, K. (ed.) (1992) *Thinking Voices. The Work of the National Oracy Project.* London: Hodder & Stoughton. This project provides suggestions for 'working with talk' in classrooms and includes many thought-provoking transcripts.

10 Towards a Better Understanding of the Needs of Pupils who have Difficulties in Accessing Learning

Richard Rose

I think differences make the world go round, kids need to know that. They need to learn that more than 'the rotation of the earth' in science! I think schools must teach differences and celebrate them. At the moment schools do the opposite, trying to make everybody normal.

Kate (a secondary pupil from London) in Burke and Grosvenor (2003)

All teachers are invariably confronted in their classes by pupils who display a wide range of needs and abilities. As a teacher you are responsible for ensuring that you provide each pupil with an opportunity to learn and, where possible, to maximise their potential. Whilst this maxim would find the support of most teachers, there are few who would pretend that this ideal is easily achieved, and the majority would suggest that there are many pupils who require approaches and teaching strategies which extend the repertoire of even the most experienced.

As a teacher, you can learn to deploy teaching approaches which enables all pupils to gain greater access to learning. However, as the quotation from a secondary school pupil at the beginning of this chapter demonstrates, the perception that not all teachers are able to empathise with those who find learning to be a struggle is not uncommon in our schools. Many teachers have dedicated large parts of their lives to developing innovative approaches that enable pupils from marginalised groups, or those with special educational needs, to become more effective learners. This has resulted in considerable progress towards a better understanding of how all pupils may be enabled to access the curriculum and learning. However, even these committed teachers admit to not always succeeding in their efforts to reach all learners. Such committed teachers also ensure that they have a good understanding of those cultural and social influences which may influence expectations in relation to pupils from specific groups. For example, the government intention to increase access to higher education requires that young people and their families from communities where there has been no previous expectation of progress to education. beyond the age of 16 receive support in understanding the opportunities available to them. Underperformance of pupils from some ethnic and socio-economic groups has been a major obstacle in enabling all pupils to reach their potential. As a teacher confronted by a diversity of needs, attitudes and abilities, you will often be frustrated by a seeming inability to enable every pupil to make the progress which you believe they should. It is almost certainly the most conscientious teachers who find themselves worrying about the progress of pupils who, as result of, for example, learning difficulties, language or cultural problems or issues associated with mental health, seem to find learning particularly burdensome. Whilst you should not be surprised when you discover pupils who challenge your established teaching strategies, you should be prepared to adjust your methods in an attempt to gauge how you may more effectively engage with all the pupils in your class.

This chapter provides some guidance related to good practice in addressing the needs of all learners, with an emphasis upon promoting positive attitudes towards learning, and working collaboratively to address the needs of individuals within whole-class situations.

OBJECTIVES

By the end of this chapter you should have some idea of:

- ways in which you can plan to ensure that the individual needs of pupils are addressed in your lessons;
- where you can expect to find support for pupils who have difficulties in accessing learning;
- how to make effective use of that support.

FACTORS THAT MAY IMPEDE LEARNING

As a teacher you must be aware of the many dangers associated with stereotyping which may exacerbate difficulties in accessing learning. Self-fulfilling prophecies have played a significant part in inhibiting learning in some pupils as a result of teachers having low expectations with regards to their potential. Cooper (1993) has demonstrated the ways in which a particular identity or label attached to a pupil can contribute significantly to the preconceptions and assumptions held by teachers. Pupils who arrive in school with a label which describes them as having a learning difficulty, or behaviour problem, or as a gypsy traveller or refugee are often subjected to a series of expectations which differ considerably from those attached to their peers. Writers from minority communities, including those with disabilities (Rieser, 1992) or from marginalised racial groups (Gurnah, 1989), have described their experiences of education as at times impeding rather than promoting opportunities for learning. Teachers' attitudes and expectations make a significant contribution to the progress made by all young people. Where expectations are low this can result in underachievement, negative attitudes to learning and disaffection. Kerry Noble, a disabled writer and consultant, describes her personal experience of schooling in the following terms:

> When teachers set me a piece of work I began to realise that certain teachers would praise my work regardless of the amount of effort I had made or the quality of the work produced. As a consequence of this I became lazy and did not make as much effort as I should. I suspect that if I had been able-bodied they would have had a different attitude.
>
> (Noble, 2003: 60)

Teachers can impact positively upon the learning of all of their pupils but can only do so when the first important step of establishing a relationship based upon trust and appreciation has been achieved.

Inevitably some of the pupils in your class will experience factors which impede learning. Many of those described as having special educational needs or for whom English is an additional language require that you take specific measures in order to assist them in becoming effective learners. There is a temptation for a teacher to dwell upon those factors which may impede learning rather than look for the preferred learning style and strengths of the pupil and to adjust teaching accordingly. The match between teaching and learning styles is probably the most significant factor in determining whether a pupil will succeed as a learner and is therefore one to which you need to devote considerable time. Some pupils require additional materials which recognise their strength as visual learners, whilst others prefer increased opportunities to engage in discussion through group activity. Learning styles are closely related to confidence: the pupil who has difficulties with reading may well be able to demonstrate their competence verbally whilst feeling inadequate if given large amounts of written text. As a teacher you need to be aware of the intended learning outcomes and provide opportunities for pupils to demonstrate their ability rather than their limitations, which may result from limited teaching approaches. Multi-sensory approaches to teaching which recognise that different pupils exhibit different strengths in respect of visual or auditory learning often prove most successful. As a teacher you should examine how you can present your reading materials and develop concepts through a range of channels.

Research conducted by Florian and Rouse (2001) identified a number of teaching strategies which had proved successful in enabling pupils with special educational needs to be successfully included in secondary classrooms. These included the promotion of co-operative learning between pupils of all abilities, peer-mediated instruction, the careful management of learning support and well-differentiated planning and delivery of lessons. These are all described as positive actions which may enable pupils with special educational needs to learn but which at the same time bring benefits of participation to all pupils in a class. Robertson (2000, 2001) has identified similar strategies as being critical when addressing the needs of pupils who enter school with limited English language ability. She suggests that teachers need to concentrate more time upon those learning outcomes which, whilst not being measurable, may have a significant impact upon pupil participation. In particular, enhancing self-esteem by identifying the means of communication and learning approaches with which pupils feel most comfortable is likely to reap many rewards. Self-esteem is not promoted in classrooms where pupils feel excluded from their peers or from the lesson content and an emphasis upon strategies to promote their inclusion must therefore be a prime consideration in your classroom.

If attitudes and difficulties in identifying learning styles can prove to be impediments to learning, there are at least some steps which you can take to overcome these. Some steps are discussed later in this chapter, but one which merits mention from the outset, because of its potential impact upon the teacher–pupil relationship, is that of pupil participation. In determining how best to plan and differentiate for learning, teachers are well advised to listen to the pupils for whom they are planning. Pupil participation in setting their own learning targets and identifying their preferred approaches to working can have a significant impact upon learning (Rose, 1999; Fletcher, 2001). Involving pupils in decision making not only provides you with useful insights into their perceptions of their own learning needs, but also enhances your relationship with the pupil and fosters the respect of the individual pupil.

Reflective task 10.1
Using pupil perceptions to support planning and teaching

Identify a pupil in a class that you teach who has difficulties with learning. This may be as a result of a special educational need or a difficulty with English, or possibly for reasons which are not easily determined. Through discussion with this pupil, identify those aspects of school that he/she enjoys or finds less enjoyable and try to find out the reasons behind these attitudes. See what the pupil can tell you about his or her preferred learning style and what teachers do that either encourage or inhibit learning.

Having gained this information, consider your own teaching approaches and how these might impact upon this pupil's abilities to access learning.

SEEKING AND USING SUPPORT IN THE MANAGEMENT OF LEARNING

When starting out on a teaching career or joining a new school it is possible to feel quite isolated and to be unsure of how to address the specific needs of individual pupils who challenge your teaching approaches. Most schools contain a mixture of well-established and less-experienced teachers and whilst you may feel overwhelmed by having so much to learn, you should normally be able to find someone who is prepared to give you the benefit of their experience and to offer advice. It is, of course, important to identify the roles and responsibilities of specific colleagues within the school, but also to become familiar with the procedures required to access and make effective use of these colleagues.

With regards to pupils with special educational needs, the special educational needs co-ordinator (SENCO) is an obvious first port of call. All schools are required to have a SENCO and in most secondary schools he or she manages a small team of support staff. The school is likely to have set procedures for seeking the support of the SENCO and it is important that you familiarise yourself with these as soon as possible. It is likely that when you take over a class the SENCO will provide you with information related to any pupils with special educational needs with whom you are likely to come in to contact. You should familiarise yourself with the needs of these individual pupils through an examination of their individual education plans (IEPs) and through discussion with the SENCO and other staff who know them well. An examination of pupil's work often provides a useful starting point with indicators of how other teachers have adapted or differentiated work to meet their needs. This rule should also be applied to other pupils who have difficulties with accessing learning because of, for example, difficulties with spoken English. Pupils with special educational needs are, in England, managed under the arrangements of the Special Educational Needs Code of Practice (2001) with which you need to be familiar. It is also important that you are well prepared before seeking the advice of the SENCO, who is likely to be a hard-pressed colleague whose time is at a premium. In order to make effective use of the SENCO, before approaching him or her about an individual pupil prepare a list of specific questions. It helps to be able to provide exemplars if you are seeking help with regard to specific behaviours in situations. You will also find the SENCO to be more responsive when you can demonstrate your own thinking about a problem and describe any tactics which you have used in an attempt to solve problems. Be aware that the SENCO may well have limited knowledge of a pupil and that you may see this pupil far more often than the SENCO.

Pupils who have difficulties accessing learning often receive some support from one or more teaching assistants (TA) (note: the term 'teaching assistant' has largely subsumed the earlier descriptor of learning support assistant [LSA] which was in common use until recently). The ways in which these colleagues are managed varies from school to school. Often they are attached to a department or faculty, but in some instances they are attached to a specific pupil. It is the responsibility of the teacher to manage TAs and to organise work for pupils. Often the TA who has worked for some time with an individual has knowledge of and information about a pupil which is critical to your ability to be able to plan effectively to meet individual needs. At first it may appear anomalous that you are the teacher but appear dependent upon the TA in order to be able to address the needs of a pupil with special educational needs or other difficulties. It is important to regard all TAs as critical professional colleagues and to develop a team-work approach to working with them. By involving them in planning, discussing assessment and ensuring that their experience and opinions are valued, you not only develop a positive relationship with a colleague who can play a vital role in supporting your lessons, but also are ensuring the most effective support for pupils.

The management of TAs to provide the most effective support is never easy. Research suggests that in too many instances the use of classroom support can create dependency where it is inappropriately managed. Tennant (2001) observed the use of learning support which was seen by some pupils to inhibit rather than promote learning. In the findings of his research he describes examples of approaches to learning support which, whilst being well intentioned and organised, denied pupils access to appropriate learning. He cites, as an example, a pupil with 'less than perfect English' who was being provided with one-to-one support which isolated him from access to his fluent language-using peers. He suggests that contact with these peers would have been beneficial both socially and in terms of providing language role models. Thomas, Walker and Webb (1998) have identified the effective use of learning support as an essential feature of inclusive classrooms. However, they identified three major obstacles to the efficient management of TAs, these being:

- Class teachers make invalid assumptions about the preference of the LSA to work solely with the 'designated individual'.
- They may assume academic expertise held by the LSA which the latter does not in fact possess (particularly in the secondary school).

- The LSA may, because the classroom teacher is 'in charge', be inhibited from making suggestions about appropriate ways of working.

(Thomas *et al.*, 1998: 29)

Each of these factors seriously impact upon the ability of the pupil to become an independent learner. As Thomas and his colleagues emphasise, this difficulty can only be overcome through a clear commitment to involve the TA in discussion about what is to be taught and how. It is necessary to provide a clear definition of tasks, but also to ensure that the pupil has access not only to the TA but also to you as the class teacher.

Reflective task 10.2
Developing rules for effective in-class support

Meet with a TA with whom you regularly work. Identify a pupil who receives support from this colleague during your lessons. Allow the TA time to describe how they perceive their role in relation to supporting this pupil. Encourage them to talk about the learning strengths and weaknesses of the pupil and consider how these match up to your own perceptions. With the TA, draw up a plan for effective support of the named pupil under the following headings:

1   the needs of the pupil;
2   when support is required;
3   the role of the teacher;
4   the role of the TA;
5   what the pupil sees their need for support to be;
6   how will we know that the support provided has been effective?

Return to this sheet after a period of teaching and see if it needs to be reviewed.

In addition to support from a TA, some of your pupils may receive input from outside agencies. These might for example, include social workers, therapists or a teacher from a local education authority multi-cultural service. Lacey (2001, 2003) has identified potential tensions which can occur in these circumstances. Whilst each professional involved has the interests of a pupil in mind, it is likely that they see the needs of this individual from the perspective of their own disciplinary background. It is essential that pupils receive support through well co-ordinated multi-disciplinary teams based on effective channels of communication and a clear definition of the roles to be played by individual professionals. You will increase the potential for effective team work if you follow a set of procedures which not only benefits the pupil concerned, but also protects your own ability to work in a professional manner. When dealing with colleagues from other agencies maintain a written record of what has been agreed and who will take actions. Share this record with someone in a management position within the school: in the case of a pupil with special educational needs this is likely to be the SENCO, in other cases it may be a deputy head teacher or head of faculty with pastoral responsibility. Ensure that all issues of confidentiality are maintained. Keep a record of the actions which you take in order to support any agreement made between agencies. Where unsure about what to do, or if decisions made are unlikely to be manageable, seek advice.

Working with other agencies is never easy and should not be undertaken by you as a teacher in isolation. Whenever you are unsure of how to proceed you should seek the advice of a colleague who is in a position to make decisions.

TEACHING TO ENHANCE THE LEARNING OF ALL PUPILS

Amongst the many challenges which face teachers in their everyday practice, that of addressing individual needs in whole-class situations is one of the most challenging. Corbett (2001) conducted research examining successful teaching approaches that enabled pupils of diverse ability and need to be included in mainstream classrooms. Her work, and that of Lewis and Norwich (2000), recognised that there may be a range of pedagogic approaches which enable teachers in mainstream classrooms to meet effectively the needs of all pupils. They suggest that this begins with recognition of individual needs, which they term 'unique differences', which may require more intense or explicit teaching in order to be adequately addressed.

The identification of individual learning needs must mean more than simply knowing what a pupil can or cannot do. This is, of course, important, but often the assessment of pupil abilities fails to provide teachers with adequate information related to how deficits in learning may be addressed. As a teacher you are likely to have greater success with pupils who have difficulties in accessing learning if you adopt a more holistic approach to determining learning needs. When planning to address the needs of an individual pupil you should consider:

- the current performance, abilities and deficits of the pupil in relation to your subject and current teaching objectives;
- the pupil's preferred learning style and opportunities to address this in your planned lesson;
- the principles by which any learning support will be used;
- your criteria for a successful learning outcome for the individual in relation to your subject for a period of teaching;
- the ways in which the organisation of the learning environment may promote effective learning.

Each of these factors is likely to impact upon your ability to successfully address individual needs within whole-class teaching situations.

When considering the current performance of individual pupils it is essential that you attempt to focus upon the positives and emphasise what pupils can do. Most pupils when discussing their own learning needs and abilities will tell you about their difficulties and what they find difficult. Motivation and confidence are essential features of becoming an effective learner and is best achieved if you can demonstrate to pupils some of their successes in the classroom. In so doing you need to be aware of the peer pressures which pupils often experience and ensure that the ways in which you provide support or discuss learning needs enhance rather than inhibit learning. It may help to celebrate the successes of a pupil in front of the class, but if these successes are related to work which is of an easier level than that undertaken by the pupil's peers it may be better celebrated quietly and with the pupil alone.

Talking to pupils in advance of a course of lessons, explaining what your expectations are and helping the pupil to identify where they may have difficulties, can reap many rewards.

Such a discussion should also enable you to assist the pupil in setting appropriate targets related to your expectations for their individual learning outcomes. Consider the experiences of Kerry Noble quoted earlier in this chapter (p. 141). Had teachers spent more time discussing their expectations and entering into negotiation about required outcomes with her, they would have commanded greater respect and provided motivation for learning. Pupils must know that it is acceptable for them to be working at a level which is different from that expected of others in the class, but they must also be aware of your demands and feel that they are challenged by your expectations.

TAs and the pupils themselves will provide you with many insights into how they learn. All learners have preferred methods of learning and these may well vary according to situation, lesson content or confidence in the subject. Pupils are often able to describe how they like to have work presented which may assist you in differentiating your lessons. They will also provide valuable insights into who they work well with, when they feel they need support and the kind of resources which may make life easier for them. Differentiation must be perceived as being more than simply providing a pupil with a different worksheet or materials. Lewis (1992) has identified 11 types of differentiation which she believes should form part of every teacher's armoury, these being:

- *Differentiation of content*: e.g. pupils in a group all work towards a single aim, such as reading a novel, but use several different versions of the novel, including simplified texts.
- *Differentiation of interest*: e.g. all pupils are producing graphs, but their graphs represent different data according to personal interest.
- *Differentiation of pace*: all pupils work at the same task, or with the same materials, but the teacher has different expectations of the time required for completion.
- *Differentiation of access*: materials or methods of working are different for individual pupils, e.g. whilst one pupil writes with a pencil another uses a computer and another produces pictorial work.
- *Differentiation of outcome*: e.g. one pupil writes a story, another draws a picture to tell the story and another records the story on audio tape.
- *Differentiation of curricular sequence*: pupils enter the curriculum at different points or take part in the curriculum in a different order from that of their peers.
- *Differentiation of teacher time*: the teacher gives more time to some pupils during specific tasks in order to ensure access.
- *Differentiation of teaching style*: e.g. some pupils may require individual instruction whilst others can work in small groups or pairs.
- *Differentiation of structure*: some pupils work on a step-by-step (task analysed curriculum) whilst others work on 'chunks'.
- *Differentiation of level*: all pupils work through a similar sequence, in maths for example, but at a variety of levels.
- *Differentiation of grouping*: the teacher groups particular pupils together for specific activities. Pupils act as supporters, or work with peers with whom they are comfortable or confident.

By having an awareness of these forms of differentiation you gain confidence in knowing which is appropriate at a particular time and for an individual pupil. There will be many times when pupils benefit from your use of several forms of differentiation. For example, you may well combine differentiation of grouping with that of interest and outcome in order to ensure that a pupil can engage with the lesson content. O'Brien and Guiney (2001) have demonstrated that effective differentiation is not simply about singling out a learner with difficulties, but being aware that a differentiated approach to teaching enables all pupils in a class to access learning at a level that is appropriate to their individual needs. It is rare to have the kind of homogeneous group where all pupils learn at the same pace, in the same way and from the same teaching approach. The teacher who has developed a thoughtful approach to differentiation can enable all pupils within a class to feel comfortable with learning. Increasingly, schools are able to provide teachers with data which can be used to gain insights into the learning journey of individual pupils throughout their schooling.

Careful differentiation also enables you to identify intended learning outcomes for individual pupils and to ensure that they are familiar with these. Such information is vital in enabling you to structure your lessons in a way that ensures that pupils are challenged without feeling excluded from the contents. Howley and Kime (2003) have presented case studies which illustrate how two pupils of considerably differing needs were enabled to be included in mainstream classrooms through careful structuring and differentiation. One of these pupils, a boy with dyslexia and behaviour difficulties, benefited from a rearrangement of the classroom environment and the provision of individualised pictorial and written instructions which enabled him to be perpetually reminded of the teacher's expectations. The second pupil, a girl with autistic spectrum disorders, required the use of a personalised timetable which indicated what would be expected of her at various times during the day and within lessons. Both of these pupils were described as providing particular challenges to their teachers but were able to be successfully managed within classes by having personalised adaptations made which assisted them with feeling comfortable about learning.

Reflective task 10.3
Planning for individual needs

After a lesson discuss with a pupil who has difficulties accessing learning those aspects of the lesson which they found easy or hard. Re-plan the lesson with the pupil and identify how you might have adjusted your practice to make learning more effective for this individual.

Consider how any modifications which you might make could benefit other pupils in the class.

SUMMARY

All teachers find having pupils who have difficulties with learning challenging. This applies to experienced teachers as well as those who are starting out in the profession. The effective management of such pupils is dependent upon careful planning, well co-ordinated team work with colleagues both in schools and from other agencies, and a commitment to being flexible with regard to teaching style. Effective planning and teaching for pupils who have difficulties with learning, possibly because of a special educational need or limited under-standing of English, is likely to benefit all pupils in a class. A commitment to an inquiry-based approach to teaching (see Chapter 16), where you are continually asking critical questions about the impact of your own practice, is likely to enable you to gain a greater understanding of what works for a wider range of pupils.

FURTHER READING

Hall, D., Griffiths, D., Haslam, L. and Wilkin, Y. (2001) *Assessing the Needs of Bilingual Pupils*, 2nd edition. London: David Fulton. This book considers the strategies which teachers may adopt in order to support pupils for whom English may be an additional or new language. It provides practical help through exemplar lesson plans and advice on resources.

Jones, C. and Rutter, J. (1998) *Refugee Education: Mapping the Field*. Stoke-on-Trent: Trentham Books. This text provides insights into the challenges faced by refugees when entering the UK education system. It offers sound advice on the ways in which teachers can make life easier for pupils from refugee families.

O'Brien, T. and Guiney, D. (2001) *Differentiation in Teaching and Learning*. London: Continuum. This text not only discusses a wide range of approaches to differentiation, which enables pupils to be well included in learning, but also outlines the principles upon which effective planning should be founded.

Tilstone, C. and Rose, R. (2003) *Strategies to Promote Inclusive Practice*. London: Routledge Falmer. This book examines a range of situations where teachers find it challenging to include pupils in learning. Chapters provide case studies and advice on a wide range of issues including managing learning support, working with other agencies and planning for individual needs.

11 Key Skills

Developing Transferable Skills Across the Curriculum

Julia Lawrence

Education has for many years been seen as an opportunity to provide individuals with the skills necessary to become effective members of the workforce. Such beliefs reflected the industrial development of British society, with the introduction of apprenticeships and vocational courses (Kelly, 2001). Over recent years there has been an increased emphasis on the development of those key skills felt to be most appropriate within the workforce, resulting in their integration into the educational programmes currently in existence, such that nationally recognised qualifications are now awarded for them. This chapter aims to provide you with an overview of the key skills currently identified within education. Whilst most examples are provided using the English National Curriculum, it is anticipated that teachers from other countries will be able to apply the practical examples within their own education curriculum. Consideration will also be given to the development of other related skills through the chapter.

The chapter begins with an overview of the need for key skills, with the identification of what are currently seen as key skills in England. This discussion is expanded, with practical examples given as to ways in which they can be taught in different curricular subjects. The tasks included in the chapter are designed to give you opportunities to reflect on your current approaches to the teaching of key skills, and offer opportunities for you to make modifications to your teaching. Case studies are also provided which demonstrate activities that can be undertaken and provide the opportunity to use a range of key skills.

OBJECTIVES

By the end of this chapter you should be able to:

- identify key skills appropriate for inclusion in the curriculum you teach;
- provide opportunities for these key skills to be developed in your curriculum subject area, through the use of a variety of teaching strategies;
- reflect on the implementation of these strategies within your teaching.

KEY SKILLS IN EDUCATION

Whilst not a new phenomenon, the integration of key skills in education signals a focus on vocational qualifications in England. Importance is now given to the promotion of such skills within all curriculum subjects. The development of key skills is integrated into many university courses. Thus the introduction of these skills at an early age provides the basic building blocks for continued learning.

It can be argued (Farmer, 1999) that most curriculum subjects can be used to enhance the development of key skills, and that they should become embedded in the curriculum. The development of key skills is evident in educational programmes around the world. Table 11.1 shows the key skills identified within the Australian, Canadian and English school curriculum.

As can been seen in Table 11.1, six key skills have been identified in the English National Curriculum, these being communication, application of number, information technology,

Table 11.1 Key skills identified in Australia, Canada and England

Australia	Canada	England
Language and communication	Communication	Communication
Mathematics	Numeracy	Application of number
Scientific and technological understanding	Technological literacy	Information technology
Personal and interpersonal characteristics	Personal and social values and skills	Working with others
Cultural understanding	Independent learning	Improving own learning and performance
Problem solving	Critical and creative thinking	Problem solving

Source: Adapted from the International Review of Curriculum and Assessment Frameworks Internet Archive, available online at http://www.inca.org.uk.

Table 11.2   Key skills in the English National Curriculum and their application

Key skills	Application
Communication	Speaking, listening, reading and writing
Application of number	Mental calculation, data processing, application to everyday situations
Information technology	Use of information sources
Working with others	Small groups and whole classes, social skills, understanding
Improving own learning and performance	Critical reflection and ways of improving
Problem solving	Planning, testing, modifying and reviewing

Source: Adapted from DfEE, 1999: 22–3.

working with others, improving own learning and problem solving. It is important to understand what is included within these key skills (see Table 11.2).

Why key skills are included in the curriculum and what are they?

According to Moran (1999), 'The list of key skills meets the concerns of those including, but not only, industry and commerce who want to see evidence of achievement in skill areas that correlate with being effective workers and citizens' (p.13). Thus the inclusion of key skills within education can be seen as a response to the need for the production of an effective workforce as identified by Kelly (2001) who defines the key skills in England as 'generic, transferable skills that people can learn and develop in a wide variety of situations, whether in education or in the workplace ... Individuals need them in order to be effective, flexible, adaptable and mobile within the labour market' (Kelly, 2001: 21). It is important to acknowledge that these key skills do not necessarily reflect all skills required to prepare individuals for work, and in fact later in this chapter consideration will be given to the development of other skills that are not currently acknowledged in the context of the key skills.

Although the development of key skills reflect a means to an end whereby the end product is an effective worker, they highlight the need within education to promote transferable knowledge and skills across curriculum subjects, as pupils are given the opportunity to utilise the skills they develop in a wide range of situations. Consequently the teaching of key skills needs to be adopted as a whole-school approach, although it must be acknowledged that some curriculum areas are potentially better suited for the promotion of some skills, for example working with others in physical education through team activities, or the use of communication through English. The adoption of a whole-school approach should allow for the facilitation rather than restriction of skill development. Thus, in order to enhance pupil opportunities, teachers need to adopt a horizontal (cross-curricular) rather than a vertical (within-subject) approach to their promotion.

INTEGRATING KEY SKILLS INTO THE CURRICULUM

Table 11.3, taken from Department for Education and Skills (DfES) Standards Site (http://www.standards.dfes.gov.uk), provides an overview of how the six identified key skills can be integrated into curriculum subjects. Whilst not specific to all skills, the table allows us to identify tasks that are generic across subject areas, for example the use of oral work to promote communication and the use of group work to develop the ability to work with others. Other skills may appear more daunting, in particular the need to improve learning. You should give consideration to the development of these skills over time, in order that pupils have opportunities to reinforce their knowledge, skills and understanding evident within curriculum subjects. It is also important that your teaching of key skills demonstrates continuity and progression, so that pupils can recognise their relevance within the wider education context. The next section of the chapter provides more detailed explanations of how you can introduce activities to promote the development of key skills.

Communication

As Table 11.3 identified, the key skill of communication refers to the development of an individual's ability to speak, listen, read and write. The examples provided within the table demonstrate opportunities across curriculum areas for the promotion of such skills. Parallels can be drawn between the development and promotion of these skills and the basic literacy strategies implemented within the current education curriculum in England. In respect of the English National Curriculum there is a requirement by teachers to provide opportunities within lessons to further develop pupils' skills in reading, writing, speaking and listening. The increased emphasis on the teaching of these skills, in particular within primary schools, has meant that teachers in secondary schools need to ensure continuity in the successes achieved. Consideration therefore needs to given to this when planning lessons integrating the development of communication skills.

Application of number

To develop the application of number you should be looking to build upon the basic numeracy skills pupils are taught within your curriculum area. As with the key skill of communication, it is possible to suggest that some subjects are better suited than others for the promotion of these skills. For example, if we were to develop such ideas further when teaching design technology, we could identify the need to use measurements when weighing contents or building structures. Perhaps it is more difficult to look at ways to apply such skills to modern foreign languages, although suggested activities may include the playing of number games, or the application of number in respect of foreign currency. However, as you are developing these skills for later life, it is a requirement that opportunities to apply them are built into activities across the curriculum, as exemplified in Table 11.3.

Table 11.3 Key Skills and opportunities to apply them across the curriculum

	Communication	Application of number	Information technology	Working with others	Improving own learning and performance	Problem solving
Design and technology	Oral work Reading to extract information Written reports Display work	Use of calculations Communicating data and concepts Production of scale drawings	Interpreting, exploring and analysing information Developing and displaying data using computers	Sharing ideas Group work	Keeping a log of work Adapting work methods to changing situations Reorganising work loads	Researching Formulating and testing ideas Suggesting approaches
Geography	Oral work Reading to extract information Presentation of work	Use of calculations Presentation of results	Interpreting, exploring and analysing information Developing and displaying data using computers	Sharing ideas Group work	Plan–do–review cycle Identification of what needs to be done Reviewing and improving	Researching Formulating and testing ideas Suggesting approaches
History	Extended writing Presentations	Interpretation of data Use of timelines	Use of databases Presentations	Sharing ideas Group work	Reviewing work completed	Planning and carrying out investigations
ICT	Use of emails Reading	Use of numerical data		Group work	Reviewing/ modifying and evaluation	Researching Formulating and testing ideas Suggesting approaches
Modern foreign languages	Listening, observing, speaking Discussion Reading	Number games Foreign currencies	Research using internet Presentations	Group work	Target setting Organisation of work	Applying and adapting knowledge

continued ...

Table 11.3 continued

	Communication	Application of number	Information technology	Working with others	Improving own learning and performance	Problem solving
Music	Presentation of music Use of materials to suit intended purpose		Research Presentations Composition	Different roles Group work	Time management Organisation of work	Composition
Physical education	Plan and work together within games situations Emotions and feeling through dance and gymnastics activities	Use of bearing and grid references Collection of data during athletics activities	Use of data collected Use of related resources	Group work	Use of evaluation and improving	Applying and adapting knowledge
Religious education	Discussions Presentation of information		Research Presentations	Group work Sharing ideas	Planning to do review cycle Identification of what needs to be done Reviewing and improving	Applying and adapting knowledge
Science	Discussions Presentation of information Reading	Use of calculations Presentation of results	Research using internet Presentations	Group work Sharing ideas	Planning to do review cycle Identification of what needs to be done Reviewing and improving	Researching Formulating and testing ideas Suggesting approaches

Source: Adapted from the DfES Standards Site at http://www.standards.dfes.gov.uk/schemes2.

Reflective task 11.1
Working with the school's
literacy and numeracy policy

This task relates to the key skills of communication and application of number:

1   Think about the skills of communication and application of number.
2   Read through the literacy and numeracy policies produced within your school.
3   Use the policies to identify opportunities within your teaching to develop the activities associated with refining these two key skills.

Information technology

Pupils now have an increasingly wide range of opportunities and resources at their disposal to develop their information technology (IT) skills in school. Consideration needs to be given to constructive ways in which pupils can use these resources across curriculum subjects to develop this skill. The main ways in which IT is commonly applied is the collection of information – usually through use of the internet – the handling of the data collected and the subsequent presentation of data, using word processing. As teachers you should be critical of the applications you offer and look to develop pupils' ability to access a wide range of media opportunities. Advances in technology now allow for the videoing of performance, for example in physical education, or the use of computer-assisted programmes in design technology. The use of IT can also provide pupils with an additional method of presenting findings, for example in producing a video diary (see Chapter 13).

Working with others

Out of school and in the workplace pupils are expected to work with a range of other people. The development of this skill within the classroom setting can take a number of forms. Whilst the most common practice is pair or group work, opportunities may also arise whereby pupils can collaborate with other pupils, either between classes or between schools. A number of schools provide opportunities for older students to act as mentors to younger pupils, whilst others may provide opportunities for secondary school pupils to visit and assist within the primary school setting. Further opportunities may be provided through work experience. Consideration must also be given to the differing roles that exist within society, which you should reflect in your planning. A further way in which pupils can work together is through observation and evaluation, and is reflected in the next identified key skill.

Improving learning and performance

To improve their learning pupils need to have knowledge about what they are to learn, thus providing a framework from which they can evaluate success. Table 11.4 provides a training

Table 11.4   Practical examples of promoting learning within the curriculum

Key characteristic for assessment of learning	Examples of teaching strategies in lesson	Impact on learning
Sharing learning objectives with pupils	Teacher: Explains objective; Provides sheet with learning objectives for pupils to refer to; Questions pupils to check understanding; Ensures teaching assistant is clear about objectives.	Pupils: Gain clear understanding of what they are to learn.
Helping pupils to know and recognise the standards they are aiming for	Teacher: Explains success criteria; Models success by providing examples of previous work; Ensures teaching assistant is clear about standards being aimed for; Teases out, through whole-class discussion, what is good about work presented.	Pupils: Gain a clear understanding of the standards they are aiming for; Recognise features of good work.
Involving pupils in peer and self-assessment	Teacher: Provides sheet with success criteria for pupils to refer to; Ensures teaching assistant is clear about success criteria; Helps pupils interpret learning outcomes in the context of their own piece of work; Provides opportunities for discussion so that pupils can comment on and improve their work; Provides time for pupils to reflect on what they've learned.	Pupils: Assess progress they have made; Identify how they can improve their work; Act as critical friends.
Providing feedback which leads to pupils recognising their next steps and how to take them	Teacher: Questions pupils in groups about their work; Provides oral feedback; Builds on responses to help them take the next steps in learning; Works in partnership with teaching assistant; In whole-class discussion, uses examples of work to highlight how different aspects of compositions can be improved.	Pupils: See more clearly what they need to do next; Are able to discuss next steps with each other; In whole-class discussion, learn from each other.
Promoting confidence that every pupil can improve	Teacher: Provides positive and constructive feedback; Matches learning objectives to needs by pitching them at a level which challenges individuals; Celebrates success and sets appropriate targets; Works in partnership with teaching assistant.	Pupils: Remain engaged and on task; Gain satisfaction regarding their own progress; Have a sense that they can continue to improve.
Involving both teacher and pupils in reviewing and reflecting on assessment information	Teacher: Maintains continuous dialogue about progress being made; Frequently reminds pupils of learning objectives and success criteria; Works in partnership with teaching assistant; Balances teacher assessment with self- and peer assessments; Makes effective use of plenary for reflection – for example, 'no hands up' questioning and paired discussion.	Pupils: Reflect on learning; Focus on learning objectives and success criteria; Measure own progress and that of their peers; Take responsibility for their learning; Perform to a high standard and make good progress.

Source: DfES, 2002c: 36–7.

sheet from the English Key Stage 3 strategy. Whilst this chapter does not permit us to expand on this strategy, one of its aims is to improve the quality of teaching and learning in schools, and it focuses on allowing pupils opportunities to reflect on their learning.

The key characteristics identified in this training sheet provide guidance on how pupils can be encouraged in this reflection on their learning. As teachers, we are aware of the need to provide pupils with the objectives of the lesson, thereby giving them an indication of what they will experience during the lesson or scheme of work. We are perhaps less likely to provide examples of what we are expecting work to look like. In practical subjects, for example physical education, design technology and art, this may be overcome through the use of demonstrations, whilst in English, history and geography the use of model answers can be developed, so that pupils can see what they are aiming for. Opportunities should also be given to pupils to reflect on what they have learnt.

In order to engage in this reflection, pupils may require opportunities to further develop their thinking skills. DfEE (1999) acknowledge that such skills complement the key skills already identified, which are also embedded within the National Curriculum. Table 11.5 provides a description of these thinking skills.

Table 11.5 Thinking skills embedded in the National Curriculum in England

Information-processing skills	These enable pupils to locate and collect relevant information, to sort, classify, sequence, compare and contrast, and to analyse part/whole relationships.
Reasoning skills	These enable pupils to give reasons for opinions and actions, to draw inferences and make deductions, to use precise language to explain what they think, and to make judgements and decisions informed by reasons or evidence.
Enquiry skills	These enable pupils to ask relevant questions, to pose and define problems, to plan what to do and how to research, to predict outcomes and anticipate consequences, and to test conclusions and improve ideas.
Creative thinking skills	These enable pupils to generate and extend ideas, to suggest hypotheses, to apply imagination, and to look for alternative innovative outcomes.
Evaluation skills	These enable pupils to evaluate information, to judge the value of what they read, hear and do, to develop criteria for judging the value of their own and others' work or ideas, and to have confidence in their judgements.

Source: DfEE, 1999: 23–4.

Table 11.6 provides suggestions of ways in which thinking skills can be taught within curriculum subjects. Thinking skills require pupils to question themselves and thus enhance their own learning. They also facilitate pupils' development in respect of their ability to solve problems.

Problem solving

Problem-solving skills require individuals to question decisions in order to solve a given problem or situation. Consequently such skills will build upon those developed through

Table 11.6 Thinking skills and their application across curriculum subjects

Subject	Information processing skills	Reasoning skills	Enquiry skills	Creative thinking	Evaluation
Design technology	Use ICT to collect information.	Encourage the making of deductions; Use evidence to support reasoning.	Predict what they think will happen; Pose questions.	Apply imagination.	Create criteria to evaluate performance; Develop confidence in judgements.
Geography	Use ICT to collect information.	Develop ability to give reasons for ideas.	Predict what they think will happen; Pose questions.	Give opportunities to develop hypothesis; Use imagination	Create criteria to evaluate performance; Develop confidence in judgements.
History	Use ICT to locate and use information.	Develop opportunities for discussion to make deductions.	Predict what they think will happen; Pose questions.	Give opportunities to develop hypothesis; Use imagination.	Create criteria to evaluate performance; Develop confidence in judgements.
Physical education	Use ICT to locate and use information.	Provide opportunities to observe and comment on tactics used within games situations.	Predict what they think will happen; Pose questions.	Use imagination in the composition of dance and gymnastics.	Create criteria to evaluate performance; Develop confidence in judgements.

Source: Adapted from the DfES Standards Site at http://www.standards.dfes.gov.uk/schemes2.

**Reflective task 11.2
Developing thinking skills in
curriculum subjects**

1   Access the the DfES Standards Site at
    http://www.standards.dfes.gov.uk/schemes2.
2   Use the website identified above to access your specialist subject.
3   Within that subject compare how you currently teach the key skills
    in your lessons, with examples provided.
4   Reflect upon your current practice and make modifications to your
    subsequent planning.

improving their own learning and performance by reflecting on action through a learning cycle. (See Chapter 1, Figure 1.1 and also p.246 of *Learning to Teach in the Secondary School*, 3rd edition, in which the topic is discussed.) However, you may need to develop pupils' questioning skills further. Perhaps the most established method of teaching questioning is through the use of Bloom's taxonomy of questioning. Developed primarily as a tool to classify educational objectives, the taxonomy encourages the development of individuals' cognitive domain, and subsequently their intellectual skills, through the use of questions. Six levels of questioning are identified: knowledge (describe, identify, who, when, where), comprehension (translate, predict, give reasons, or say why), application (demonstrate how, solve, try it in a new context), analysis (explain, infer, analyse), synthesis (design, create, compose), evaluation (assess, compare/contrast, judge). Further information regarding types of questions that can be used can be found in Bloom (1956).

CASE STUDIES

Case study 1: Developing ability to work with others and improve own learning in physical education

Pupils are introduced to a skill through the use of a practical demonstration and verbal explanation by the teacher. Following this demonstration, pupils practice the skill with a partner. In order to enhance learning, a visual aid is provided which shows each phase of the skill being learnt with key learning points for each phase. As one of the pair perform the skill, their partner observes their performance and provides feedback based on the aid they have been given. The performer takes on board this information and is given the opportunity to perform the skill again to see if any improvement can be made. The teacher interacts with the observer to aid him or her in giving feedback to the performer.

The type of learning identified in case study 1 is referred to as reciprocal teaching by Mosston and Ashworth (1994) as one example in their spectrum of teaching.

Case study 2: The use of the key skills in science

With a partner, pupils have conducted an experiment looking at the height of pupils within their class. They used the data they collected to produce a graph to represent the different heights and then calculate the average height of the class.

A framework is provided by the teacher to show how the written experiment should be set out, with pointers as to what should be included under each section. These reflect the mark scheme for the piece of work. On completion of the task, pupils are asked to give their piece of work a grade based upon the mark scheme provided.

Adaptations to this may be that the pupils present their work using computers, or the pupils are given a title and have to devise their own experiment, thereby developing their problem-solving skills.

SUMMARY

The teaching of key skills across the curriculum is an important element of current educational practice. As teachers, it is important that we strive to incorporate them into our planning in order that pupils develop the skills deemed necessary to become effective members of the workforce. Whilst the chapter starts with the identification of six key skills, it is perhaps more realistic to acknowledge that such skills require the enhancement of other skills specific to that focus, for example in the form of thinking and questioning skills.

The chapter aimed to provide an overview of those key skills which have currently been identified and emphasised within educational programmes, including the school curriculum, and to provide practical examples of how these skills could be taught across curriculum subjects. Some techniques and strategies to promote the development of key skills have been outlined. Opportunities have also been given to reflect on individual practice to enable you to build in opportunities to promote pupils' development of the key skills which have been discussed.

FURTHER READING

International Review of Curriculum and Assessment Frameworks Archive (INCA) website at http://www.inca.org.uk. Developed by the Qualifications and Curriculum Authority in conjunction with the National Foundation for Educational Research, the website provides information regarding the curriculum taught in 18 countries. As well as providing comparable information, the website provides links to resources in specific countries.

DfES Standards Site at http://www.standards.dfes.gov.uk/schemes2. Provides detailed examples of how key skills and thinking skills can be integrated into curriculum planning. Resources are downloadable and the site includes access links with other curriculum areas.

Qualifications and Curriculum Authority website at www.qca.org.uk/nq/ks. Provides examples of key skill tests.

12 Values and Citizenship Education

Graham Haydon and Jeremy Hayward

This chapter will give you an overview of the areas of values and citizenship education that are frequently linked in debates on educational policy and the curriculum. The exact term 'values education' is one that you may or may not have encountered in your study and teaching so far. In most countries it is not a term used to denote a distinct part of the curriculum; in Britain, for instance, there are probably no teachers actually employed to teach 'values education' under that name, although there are teachers employed to teach, or to co-ordinate, areas of the curriculum which certainly involve values, including religious education, personal social and health education (PSHE) (which has been discussed in Chapter 4) and citizenship education.

At the same time, it is likely that you have encountered the idea that teachers should be teaching values. Many parents, politicians and teachers express the view that schools should be teaching (or 'transmitting' or 'inculcating' or helping to develop) values. The discussion on values education poses key questions on the teachers' role. Because values underpin the whole curriculum these are questions with which teachers, parents, heads, advisors, policy makers and everyone involved in education is concerned.

This discussion then forms the setting for that on citizenship education, which follows in the second part of the chapter. You may be required to teach some aspect of citizenship education in your school or it may form part of other work you do, in teaching your specialist subject or as a form tutor. The chapter goes over the background to citizenship education (or civics) and the example of the English citizenship curriculum is used as a case study to examine some of the main choices and challenges surrounding the subject. The context for the discussion lies in the enormous changes which societies have undergone everywhere over the past two decades. An increase in social, political and economic migration within and across boundaries has led to increasingly diverse societies, and corporate and economic globalisation has seen the nature of work and the patterns of life change throughout the world. Ideologies have withered and died and countries have fragmented under regionalisation and been united under transnational umbrellas. Key concepts caught up in these changes include those of *citizenship* and *citizenship education* and in these areas important questions have been raised that remain largely unanswered, e.g. what is meant by citizenship in increasingly pluralistic societies? How should a citizen react to opposing forces of devolution and globalisation? How will the forces of devolution and globalisation impact on the way we view ourselves as citizens?

OBJECTIVES

By the end of this unit you should be able to:

- appreciate that all teachers are engaged in influencing students' values;
- think about how moral education relates to values education more generally;
- describe the recent challenges to the concepts of citizenship and citizenship education;
- identify similarities and differences in the way citizenship education is delivered in different countries;
- identify ways in which your teaching could contribute to citizenship education;
- reflect on some of the teaching issues associated with citizenship education.

VALUES EDUCATION

Educational *aims and values*

Many people believe, or may at least say they believe, that teaching values is more important than teaching any particular parts of the curriculum. Look for instance at this passage from the Qualifications and Curriculum Authority's (QCA) preamble to the National Curriculum online documentation for England and Wales, which comes under the heading 'About the school curriculum':

> Education influences and reflects the values of society, and the kind of society we want to be. It is important, therefore, to recognise a broad set of common values and purposes that underpin the school curriculum and the work of schools. Foremost is a belief in education, at home and at school, as a route to the spiritual, moral, social, cultural, physical and mental development, and thus the well-being, of the individual. Education is also a route to equality of opportunity for all, a healthy and just democracy, a productive economy, and sustainable development. Education should reflect the enduring values that contribute to these ends. These include valuing ourselves, our families and other relationships, the wider groups to which we belong, the diversity in our society and the environment in which we live. Education should also reaffirm our commitment to the virtues of truth, justice, honesty, trust and a sense of duty.
>
> (QCA, 2004)

**Reflective task 12.1
Values and purposes
underpinning the school
curriculum**

Consider carefully how far you would yourself endorse everything in the statement of 'common values and purposes' quoted above. Does everything in it seem obvious, or are some elements controversial? For instance:

- Can you attach any clear sense to the idea of spiritual development?
- Is it right for schools to promote social aims such as social justice and a productive economy?
- Do you see it as part of your own role as a teacher to promote 'truth, justice, honesty, trust and a sense of duty'?

There are some elements in the statement which it is hard to imagine any teacher dissenting from. For instance, that education is, among other things, a route to the *mental* development of the individual. Any teacher who is trying to get students to acquire certain information, develop certain mental skills (such as doing arithmetical calculations) or expand their understanding is aiming to promote some aspect of the students' mental development.

You might at this point wonder what this has to do with values. Aren't some parts of the curriculum 'value-free'? The point is, of course, that the idea that the mental development of individuals is something worth aiming at is already an expression of values. Though it is difficult to give a precise definition of 'values', there is no need for the idea to be in any way mysterious; we can give examples of values even if we do not have a definition. What we value is what we care about, what we think matters, what we think is good and worthwhile and important. We think that in general it is *better* for people to be in a state of knowledge rather than ignorance (though there is room for judgements about relevance here too), to have understanding of what is going on round them rather than being in the dark, to be able to exercise certain skills for themselves rather than having to rely on others. Most of us also have views about what makes for a good society; if we think that social justice and democracy are good, and if we think that education can do something to make it more likely that our society will be just and democratic, then these values too enter into our thinking about educational aims.

Why all teachers influence students' values

But it is not just that our aims for education reflect what we – teachers, parents, politicians – value. To achieve our aims for education, we also need to influence the values of the people we are educating. Though the idea of influencing students' values may bring up worries about imposing our values or indoctrinating students, it is doubtful whether there are any educational aims that don't involve influencing student's values. Consider mathematics. Is it just a matter of enabling people to do certain things, such as carrying out certain calculations and getting the right answer? Think of the students who have that ability but do not bother to use it; the students who are sloppy in their working out and often get the answer wrong, although they could do it if they tried. Wouldn't the teacher want these students to *want* to get it right? We can want students of maths to *care* about accuracy and carefulness. And probably a teacher of any subject could pick out aspects of their subject that students have to recognise as important, have to care about, if they are to do well in the subject.

So any teaching, at least if it is done well, involves influencing students' values. However, we do not *call* all education 'values education'. That term, if it is to be used at all, helps to focus our attention on education's role in relation to values that might not receive concentrated attention simply as part of the teaching of regular subjects in the curriculum.

Consider again some of the elements in the statement of 'common values and purposes' above. These include 'equality of opportunity for all' and 'a healthy and just democracy'. These are conditions of society which cannot be achieved or sustained just through people acquiring certain knowledge – e.g. about how society works – or certain skills. There have to be enough people who care about equality and democracy, who are prepared to put time and effort into working for equality and into participating in the affairs of their community. This explains both the importance of citizenship education – which is treated in the second part of this chapter – and the fact that citizenship education is one of the parts of the curriculum in which the concern with values is strongest.

Values and spiritual development

But it would be a mistake to think that citizenship education can encompass all of education's concerns with the developing values of young people. The statement above, for instance, refers to 'spiritual development' among other sorts of development. This notion is likely to seem more problematic to many teachers than the idea of citizenship, because spiritual development, whatever exactly it may be, may seem to be tied up with religion or may simply seem too personal to be addressed by teachers within an education system which is not committed to some particular worldview. There is not space here to go into any detail about what might be covered by 'spiritual development' but a good way to approach the idea may be to consider the fact that many people seem to feel a need for some sense of who they are, where they fit into the world and where they are going in their lives. For some people (many worldwide, though fewer in some countries, including Britain, than in others) this need is met through one of the mainstream religions; for some (though perhaps not many in a pluralist and democratic society) the need may be fully met through their own citizenship: that is, through their sense of belonging to and contributing to their community and country. For many others a sense of who they are and where they are going may not come in these ways; the need may not be met at all, and some may never feel the need. The point for teachers is that it would be an odd education that did not do anything to help individuals to make sense of their lives if they feel the need to do so; and since education also has social aims (including the valuing of diversity) it will be important that individuals realise how central the questions of meaning and identity are to other people even if they do not feel (at their present age) the need to address these questions for themselves.

If the area of spirituality is conceived in some such way, then (leaving aside in this context schools which are themselves committed to a particular religion or worldview) it should be obvious that spiritual development is not something that schools can address by presenting to all students one common answer to the 'big questions' in life. Education in this area will have to be about appreciating the force of the questions and understanding something about the range of answers which people have been able to find and the values which these answers have involved.

Two further points follow from this: that many subjects in the curriculum are relevant (though religious education certainly has a role, as does what in England is called PSHE); and that if the educational task is done well, it will certainly not involve imposing a particular set of beliefs on people (see Chapter 4).

Values and moral development

But if the values which may be important in individuals' spiritual development may be very personal, what about the area of moral development? The terms 'values education' and 'moral education' are sometimes used interchangeably. This is understandable, since many people, when they talk about schools transmitting values, may chiefly have in mind that they want schools to turn out people who will do what is morally right. What is included under 'moral' is as open to interpretation as what is included under 'spiritual'. Nevertheless, I would argue that it would be better to see 'moral education' as only one part of 'values education', since (as I hope this section has illustrated) morality is only part of the whole field of values.

So where is the distinction? To try to answer this at all fully would take us deep into moral philosophy, and different philosophers would offer different answers. What follows here is an attempt to offer a workable distinction which teachers can use, and which they can offer to their students in turn. Morality is the area of values which affects how we treat each other, and hence the area of values which in an important sense are *not* optional. It is about what we owe to each other, what we can expect from each other, what we may blame others for not living up to. Because this area of values has to do with how we relate to each other, it is important for avoiding too much conflict in societies; and because of that, it is important that morality contains *shared* values and norms, which everyone, more or less, expects everyone else to adhere to.

Many of the values that people live by, especially in a diverse society in which there is a good deal of individual freedom, are not shared with everyone else. Some people put positive value on a life that involves risk and the constant possibility of the unexpected, and would find a settled predictable life far too dull; for others the reverse is the case. Some people put great value on the freedom to make their own decisions without being bound by too many personal ties; others value more highly their community and family ties and do not want so much independence. Such differences in values are part of what education, in such areas as personal and social education and career guidance, needs to help students understand and appreciate; but it is not the role of education to lay down one particular set of values as the best. *Within limits*, people need to find their own way through the complex web of possible values.

It is the phrase 'within limits' that points to the importance of a shared morality. Morality cannot be a matter purely of personal choice, precisely because – for everyone's sake – it sets limits to what the individual can choose. It says, in effect, that however you choose to live your life, you must have regard to other people's interests, to rights and to fairness. The points mentioned in the final sentence of the extract above – truth, justice, honesty, trust and a sense of duty – do represent a rough view of the values which are central to morality (understood in this way).

This way of seeing morality, as concerning our responsibilities to each other – what we owe to each other – would seem too narrow to some. On some religious views, what we owe to God may be a more important question. And equally on some secular views, we have obligations to other animals as much as to other human beings. And even where what we owe to other people is emphasised, there is a lot of room for dispute as to just what it *is* that we owe to each other. Is it enough, for instance, that we do not directly harm others and we respect their right to make their own choices? Or do we have a moral obligation positively to help others, through giving to charity, for instance, and to campaigning for greater justice in the world?

So taking a view about *moral* values, within the whole broad field of values, does not remove controversy. Nevertheless, it's important for any teacher who is contributing in any way to values education to recognise that not all values can have the same status, and not all values can be seen just as a matter of personal choice. It is possible to argue for different points of view, it is possible to defend one view and object to another, it is even possible and will sometimes be right to try to change someone else's point of view. If these things were not true – if everything in this area really was just a matter of personal choice – there would be little scope for education in the area of values.

Why values education is not indoctrination

To any teachers who are worried that values education cannot avoid indoctrination, or imposing some people's values on others, there are several points that may help:

- If there are some values that really are important for everyone, and because of that cannot be just a matter of personal choice, teaching these values will not be a matter of imposing the values of some people on others.
- If these values are important for everyone it is not too difficult to see *why* they are important – what would a world with no honesty, no justice, no sense of responsibility towards others, be like?
- So the role of schools in relation to these values is not to impose them but to get students to appreciate the importance of these values for themselves.

That means that what teachers need to do in this area is not so different from what teachers do in other areas: not just telling people things, but getting students to think, understand reasons, make connections, look at matters from more than one perspective, and so on.

It also means that responsibility for values education must lie with a whole school, not just with particular teachers, because it is within the school community that students can see both the importance of different values to different people and the importance of shared values to the whole group. So perhaps the first question you need to ask about values education in the school in which you are beginning to teach is: does this school have a shared sense of values, which includes both a sense of respect for diversity, and the expectation that all – teachers as well as students - will take seriously the values which are important to the whole school community?

CITIZENSHIP

Broadly speaking, *citizenship* is the relationship between a political entity, usually a country, and the individuals who are members of that political entity. Citizenship usually confers on the individual a web of rights and responsibilities, relating both to other individuals and to the country as a whole. These vary from country to country but can broadly be classified under Marshall's (1950) headings of:

- *Civil rights*, e.g. rights to protection from individuals and from other nations, rights to legal recourse, property rights.
- *Political rights*, e.g. the rights to vote and take part in governance.
- *Social rights*, e.g. rights to education, health and welfare.

Beyond this somewhat 'legal' definition of citizenship in terms of rights, the concept of citizenship also plays a less formal but important role in helping to define both individual and national identities. This role is not always positive – for example, if the cultural meaning of citizenship is narrowly construed it can lead to the alienation of minority cultures. Indeed, defining citizenship in a way that is pluralistic and reflects not static, but diverse and ever shifting, cultural identities is one of the key challenges facing many societies.

It is also worth noting another dimension to citizenship – its scope and scale. The term 'citizen' is Roman in origin and relates to the city-state political entities of the day, typified by Rome itself. In the modern era, the emergence and dominance of nation states changed the nature of citizenship and recently, transnational groupings such as the European Union have altered the concept further still. Further, transnational concerns such as industrialisation, with its effect on the environment, and globalisation, with its effect upon work and trade, have also given birth to the concept of *global citizenship*, whether as an aspiration, a metaphor or simply as call for a general shift in outlook. The concept of citizenship has changed greatly over the past two decades and has evolved different meanings and roles in the various countries and contexts it is used. Given this rapid change, it is not surprising that the concept and nature of citizenship education has also undergone much analysis and revision in recent times.

CITIZENSHIP EDUCATION

Citizenship education is a 'topical' curriculum subject (Kerr, 1999). Many countries, as they routinely review their curricula, are seeking to adapt, amend or introduce elements of citizenship education – often in response to some of the global challenges outlined above. This can lead to the impression that it is a relatively new initiative, which is by no means the case. Its roots can be traced to some of the earliest recorded educators, the sophists of ancient Greece, who trained their students in rhetoric, morality and public speaking with a view to preparing them for public life. In the modern era, citizenship education has existed in various guises, from the embedded ideology in the classrooms of the old Soviet Union to the 'preparing for leadership' ethos of British fee-paying 'public schools'. In this new century a whole range of different expressions of citizenship education can be found throughout the world.

However, partly because its 'political' nature makes it highly susceptible to government involvement, citizenship education has had a fairly episodic and sporadic history in some education systems, notably the English. And this chequered history can make it appear to some as if citizenship education is a new subject each time it is introduced. (Crick and Heater [1977] provide an account of the history of citizenship education in England.)

Despite such a long history, there is no agreed definition of citizenship education. Its different formulations throughout history, and the need for the subject to reflect the culture of its own country, prevent any simple generalisations. That said, there are a cluster of key elements that are common to many of its instantiations.

Knowledge base

As discussed above, citizenship brings with it a web of rights and responsibilities. Naturally, an element common to many forms of citizenship education is an examination, critical or otherwise, of these rights and responsibilities, as well as the political system that brings them about and of the legal system that enforces them. Beyond this, the knowledge base for citizenship education may also extend to an examination of other key institutions and practices affecting public life, such as the media, monarchy, the internet, or even the education system itself. Beyond national boundaries it may also extend to exploring wider regional or global issues, such as the conflict resolution or the role of the United Nations (UN).

Skill base

For some countries the knowledge base is the primary focus for citizenship education, whereas in others a more participatory approach is taken. This approach could consist of encouraging different forms of student 'voice' – whether in the classroom, the school, the community or beyond. It could involve creating meaningful opportunities to develop the habits of democracy through referenda or school councils. It could also occur through engaging students in socially constructive activities.

Value base

Another important feature of citizenship education is its relation to the broader area of values education, which was discussed earlier in the chapter. The two areas impact in several ways. Firstly, citizenship education, because of its subject matter, is inherently related to values. Political and social issues concern the question of how we should collectively live, which, at root, is an extension of the basic moral question, 'How should I live my life?' The political is inherently moral. And, although many areas of public life can be taught in a fairly descriptive manner, with an emphasis on facts and figures rather than critical debate, the areas themselves remain value-laden in nature and may often call for sensitive handling.

Secondly, citizenship education relates to values in terms of the general aims of education. Most education systems or curricula have broad aims and objectives. Such aims vary enormously in scope and scale, but common foci include reference to pupils' development as individuals; pupils' future lives in terms of further education or work and the nature – desired or otherwise – of society, cultural heritage and tradition. Most of these aims, implicitly or explicitly, reflect particular values.

Citizenship education may relate very closely to some of these aims, particularly those that are value-explicit, and may be called upon to play a key role in their fulfilment. Consider the following educational aims, taken from Kerr's (1999) comparison of citizenship education in 16 countries:

- Re-establishing a national identity after decades of Soviet rule – *Hungary*.
- To promote patriotism and affection for the continuance and development of national independence, as well as world peace, and to preserve and develop national culture – *Korea*.
- Encourage respect for other languages and cultures – *Switzerland*.

It is apparent that citizenship education might play a greater role than other curriculum subjects in reflecting or helping to deliver such aims. Examples of general aims which embody values closely related to citizenship education might include:

- developing national identity;
- preserving cultural heritage;
- valuing diversity;
- respecting others;
- protecting democracy.

This close relation to values can make some people uneasy about citizenship education. Some may feel less happy than others about political issues being raised in the classroom, perhaps feeling that such areas are the domain of the parent. Others, however, feel that learning about society, its laws and systems, is exactly what schools should be teaching. It is worth noting that although citizenship education may relate closely to values education, this connection is emphasised to varying degrees in different contexts, ranging from the more value-neutral programmes to the more value-laden. A survey of civic education across 24 countries (Torney-Purta *et al.*, 1999: 33) concluded that most countries are at pains to steer clear of anything that might imply indoctrination.

DIFFERENT APPROACHES TO CITIZENSHIP EDUCATION

A recurring theme so far is the wide variation in the different approaches to citizenship education. There are many historical and cultural reasons for this. Indeed, it would be surprising if a subject concerned with society and social living did not vary enormously from country to country. Some of the key variations identified by Kerr (1999) include:

- *Curriculum status*: In some countries citizenship education is statutory (e.g. France and England), in others it is optional (e.g. Germany, Spain).
- *Delivery mode*: Citizenship may exist as a stand-alone subject (Korea, Japan) or may be integrated (Spain, Switzerland). The subject may be taught by specialists or non specialists. The amount of time devoted to the subject also varies considerably.
- *Name*: Although this unit, following much of the international literature, refers to 'citizenship education', this term is rarely used in individual countries, where the subject may appear under such names as: 'social studies' (Sweden, New Zealand and many others), 'civics' (France), 'people and society' (Hungary) or even 'a disciplined life and moral education' (Korea, at primary level).

Some of these factors – the fact that citizenship is commonly integrated, and that few countries train specialists – means that many teachers, particularly of humanities subjects, may be involved in its delivery. Such wide variation also makes it difficult to discuss the subject on a general level, beyond simply making comparisons. The rest of this chapter examines the particular example of citizenship education in England to enable a more detailed examination of some of the key issues.

A CASE STUDY: CITIZENSHIP IN ENGLAND

Citizenship education in England has had an episodic history. In 1997 it existed as a non-statutory cross-curricular theme, and its coverage varied widely from school to school. In that year the newly formed government established an advisory group, under the chairmanship of Professor Bernard Crick, to explore the case for increased provision of citizenship education. The committee's recommendations, known as the Crick Report (Department for Education and Employment [DfEE]/QCA, 1998), noted a series of social trends it perceived as worrying; particularly the lack of interest in party politics, and the low levels of participation, amongst the 18-to-24 age group. To help address these and other concerns the committee set itself an ambitious task: 'We aim at no less than a change in the political culture of this country both nationally and locally' (DfEE/QCA, 1998: para 1.5).

To help achieve this aim the Report set out various recommendations, the first of which is that citizenship should become a statutory entitlement in the National Curriculum. The Report opted for a broad model of citizenship education consisting in the development of important citizenship skills in addition to a base of political knowledge. In doing so the Report adopted a sense of citizenship that is active rather than passive, participatory rather than simply knowledge based. It hoped that by giving students appropriate opportunities to participate they might become actively engaged in the process of citizenship.

The committee's recommendations were incorporated into the National Curriculum and, since September 2002, secondary schools in England have been required to deliver the citizenship programme of study (PoS) (DfES/QCA, 1999).

Reflective task 12.2
What should be included in a citizenship programme of study for 11–14-year-olds?

What would you include in a citizenship PoS for 11–14 year olds? In other words, which elements of knowledge and which sets of skills do you think citizenship education should develop?

Compare your answer with the PoS outlined below. Which areas would you include or omit, and why?

The following details the citizenship PoS for Key Stage 3 (11–14 years old). A similarly structured programme exists for Key Stage 4 (14–16 years old), with different elements of knowledge and different wording for the sets of skills, to allow for a model of progression.

1) **Knowledge and understanding** about becoming informed citizens. Pupils should be taught about:
   a) the legal and human rights and responsibilities underpinning society, basic aspects of the criminal justice system, and how both relate to young people;
   b) the diversity of national, regional, religious and ethnic identities in the United Kingdom and the need for mutual respect and understanding;
   c) central and local government, the public services they offer and how they are financed, and the opportunities to contribute;
   d) the key characteristics of parliamentary and other forms of government;
   e) the electoral system and the importance of voting;
   f) the work of community based, national and international voluntary groups;
   g) the importance of resolving conflict fairly;
   h) the significance of the media in society;
   i) the world as a global community, and the political, economic, environmental and social implications of this, and the role of the European Union, the Commonwealth and the United Nations.

2) **Developing skills of enquiry and communication.** Pupils should be taught to:
   a) think about topical political, spiritual, moral, social and cultural issues, problems and events by analysing information and its sources, including [information and communications technology] ICT-based sources;
   b) justify orally and in writing a personal opinion about such issues, problems or events;
   c) contribute to group and exploratory class discussions, and take part in debates.

3) **Developing skills of participation and responsible action.** Pupils should be taught to:
   a) use their imagination to consider other people's experiences and be able to think about, express and explain views that are not their own;
   b) negotiate, decide and take part responsibly in both school- and community-based activities;
   c) reflect on the process of participating.
   (DfES/QCA, 1999, available online from http://www.nc.uk.net)

Examining the PoS

The PoS contains only a few *explicit* references to values: the importance of resolving conflict fairly, the importance of voting, diversity of identities and the need for mutual respect and understanding. Beyond these, the focus is on descriptive knowledge, participation and discussion with a range of opinions and values being encouraged. The *implicit* model of citizenship that seems to emerge is that of an informed, critical citizenry, playing an active role in society.

The PoS also relates closely to the overall aims of education in England. The entire National Curriculum, containing the details for all curriculum areas, is prefaced by two overarching aims:

- to provide opportunities for all pupils to learn and achieve;
- to promote pupils' spiritual, moral, social and cultural development, and prepare them for the opportunities, responsibilities and experiences of life.

Citizenship makes a key contribution to fulfilling both of these aims, particularly the latter. An important way of promoting students' spiritual, moral, social and cultural development is to provide opportunities for the discussion of spiritual, moral, social and cultural issues, and this is exactly what the PoS specifies (element 2[a] above).

CITIZENSHIP IN SCHOOLS

Although citizenship is statutory, schools have been given freedom to choose how the PoS is developed, and, as a result, a myriad of delivery models have evolved. No two schools approach citizenship in exactly the same way. Some choose to use a dedicated team to teach stand-alone lessons; others merge citizenship with the delivery of PSHE (see Chapter 4). Some schools use their form tutor system; others still adopt a wider cross-curricular approach. And many use a variety of the approaches in tandem. On top of this, various whole-school initiatives such as anti-bullying campaigns, suspended timetable 'immersion days', student councils, school- and community-based projects may also form part of a school's citizenship programme.

The PoS is also quite general, allowing schools further flexibility in delivery. Consider element 1(g) above: 'the importance of resolving conflict fairly'. As this is not elaborated with specific content, schools are able to contribute its delivery in various ways, perhaps through: looking at personal relationships in PSHE; an anti-bullying campaign; examining the founding of the UN in history; a peer mentoring project; analysing key texts in English; or even through discrete citizenship lessons. Such flexibility enables schools to tailor citizenship in schools that follow the English National Curriculum to reflect their local contexts and to match the subject to their school strengths.

Reflective task 12.3
Citizenship in your school

1   Find out how and when citizenship is delivered in your school.
2   Consider what contributions you could make to its delivery through your own teaching.

TEACHING CITIZENSHIP

Teaching citizenship raises several issues, many of which will be common to other humanities subjects, including the points that follow.

Balance

Avoiding bias is crucial when teaching political issues. In England, conscious bias is legislated against. The 1996 Education Act specifies that children should not be presented with only one side of a political/controversial issue, forbids the promotion of partisan political views in the teaching of any subject and requires that teachers try to ensure balanced presentation when dealing with political or controversial issues sections (Great Britain, 1996: Sections 406 and 407). However, unconscious bias can be much harder to eliminate and can occur in many ways, for example: through unbalanced resources; by misrepresenting the views of others; by not considering different sides to issues; through body language. Though a perfectly balanced lesson is unachievable, effort should be taken to eliminate or reduce these factors where possible.

Teacher's voice

When considering open questions – questions where there is no commonly agreed answer, and where the school or curriculum has no established stance – the teacher's opinion is one amongst many, and consequently the pedagogical 'voice' should be considered carefully. Common approaches include:

- *Neutral*: Acting as a chair, facilitating discussion amongst students.
- *Balance*: Attempting to present the major sides of a debate with equal or appropriate weighting. This could also include the use of a 'devil's advocate' approach to provoke reaction.
- *Committed participant*: Making your opinion known. Ideally this should only occur in a context where discussion is encouraged and where students are also encouraged to voice opinion.

To avoid confusion and possible bias, it is important that the students are aware of the role that the teacher is adopting when exploring political or controversial issues.

Controversial issues

Discussing highly controversial or sensitive issues ideally should only occur where there is an atmosphere of psychological safety, which may involve the teacher knowing the students fairly well. Individual schools may have a policy on discussing controversial and sensitive issues and teaching should occur within that framework. If no policy exists, Jerome *et al.* (2003) suggest what such a policy might look like. General guidance for teachers in England is available from the DfES Standards Site at http://www.standards.dfes.gov.uk/schemes2/citizenship/teachersguide. Also available from the same website are the schemes of work for citizenship, which contain a variety of different ideas and approaches for teaching all the various elements of citizenship, as well as guidance on how it can be incorporated in to all curriculum areas.

Student voice

Encouraging different forms of student voice, particularly democratic voice, can be a challenge for schools, which themselves are quite often excellent models of autocratic rule. Despite this difficulty, encouraging meaningful participation and discourse is a key aim of citizenship in England, as it attempts, in part, to reverse the symptoms of political alienation outlined above. Encouraging voice and participation is a large pedagogical field in itself, with various competing approaches that cannot be entered into here.

A further discussion of these and other pedagogical issues surrounding the teaching of citizenship education is contained in Gearon (2003).

SUMMARY

The first part of this chapter has shown that teachers cannot avoid some sort of engagement in values education; and that any teachers seriously concerned with the well-being of their students and their society would not want to avoid it. Teachers who wish to give special attention to this area of their work will find that citizenship education is an important vehicle for doing so, though not necessarily the only one. Indeed, as the second part of the chapter has shown, countries differ in the particular ways in which the concern with the developing values of citizens is related to other areas of the curriculum which also deal with values.

Overall we can see that citizenship education is not a 'tidy' curriculum subject and can take many forms and guises. Although its status, compared to other subjects, is relatively low it is becoming an increasingly discussed and researched area as governments seek new ways to prepare students for the complexities and challenges of modern society.

As a teacher, citizenship education can be a challenging experience; however, it can also be extremely rewarding. It can offer teachers the opportunity to engage students with interesting, relevant and topical issues using dynamic and interactive methods – the kind of teaching opportunities that attracted many to the profession in the first place.

FURTHER READING

Values education

Haydon, G. (1997) *Teaching about Values: A New Approach*. London: Cassell. See Chapter 2 for more on the way in which educational aims necessarily involve values, and Chapters 11 and 12 for more on teachers' roles in values education.

Bramall, S. and White, J. (2000) *Will the New National Curriculum Live up to its Aims?* (IMPACT paper 6). London: Philosophy of Education Society. A case study, in relation to the English

National Curriculum, of whether the details of the curriculum requirements are likely to promote the values and aims which (as in many national curricula) are set out in broad terms in the preamble.

Smith, R. and Standish, P. (1997) *Teaching Right and Wrong: Moral Education in the Balance.* Stoke-on-Trent: Trentham. A series of lively and sometimes controversial discussions about how teachers and schools should see the task of moral education.

Citizenship education

Jerome, L., Hayward, J., Easy, J. and Newmanturner, A. (2003) *The Citizenship Co-ordinator's Handbook.* Cheltenham: Nelson Thornes. A practical book that guides the reader through all the different aspects of managing and delivering a citizenship programme in English secondary schools.

Gearon, L. (ed.) (2003) *Learning to Teach Citizenship in the Secondary School: A Companion for the Student Teacher of Citizenship.* London: RoutledgeFalmer. Explores the different aspects of teaching citizenship in England from both a theoretical and practical viewpoint.

DfEE/QCA (1998) *Education for Citizenship and the Teaching of Democracy in Schools: Final Report of the Advisory Group on Citizenship* (the Crick Report). London: QCA/98/245 (available online at http://www.qca.org.uk). The key document that outlined the vision for citizenship education in England and led directly to its introduction as a statutory entitlement.

The website of the Citizenship Foundation at www.citizenshipfoundation.org.uk.

13 Using ICT in the Classroom and for Administration

Marilyn Leask

> Every student needs a grandparent to link them to the past and a PC to take them
> into the future.
>
> (Headteacher in Leask and Kington, 2001)

The headteacher making this comment was leader of one of the most innovative schools in terms of information and communications technology (ICT) in England, where all teachers had laptops and ICT use was integrated across the curriculum (Organisation for Economic Cooperation and Development [OECD], 2002). Your pupils can expect to work in environments where familiarity with the use of computers is taken for granted and a high level of skill is expected. There can be few occupations now which are unaffected by ICT – records are kept on computer, equipment and supplies are ordered by internet and so on. Integrating appropriate forms of e-learning into the learning environment is a major challenge for all twenty-first-century teachers. But what is e-learning and how does it link with ICT?

'If someone is learning in a way that uses information and communications technologies (ICTs), they are using e-learning' (Department for Education and Skills [DfES], 2003b: 6). In this DfES consultation paper on how to achieve a unified approach to e-learning across England, the DfES called on all involved in education to ensure that the benefits of e-learning were available to all learners, not just those in innovative institutions with innovative teachers.

This challenge involves you directly as you make decisions about the teaching strategies and learning approaches which you employ with the pupils for whom you are responsible. Ways in which you use ICT in your teaching, preparation and administration provide models of e-learning for your pupils which helps prepare them for the uncertain future. Writing when personal computers were becoming widespread but before internet, mobile phone and digital video technologies were widely available, Papert identifies this future as being one of constant change in the workplace, and this change applies to teachers as well as to pupils:

> Not very long ago, and in many parts of the world even today, young people would learn skills they could use in their work throughout life. *Today, in industrial countries, most people are doing jobs that did not exist when they were born.*
>
> (Papert, 1993a: vii, my emphasis)

During your career you can expect that ICT will be used to make schooling more individualised with assessment strategies and teaching styles increasingly being adapted to include individualised resources, learning and assessment opportunities. Ways of providing teachers with appropriate data about individual pupils' achievements in order to support your teaching and each pupil's learning are being improved and you can expect to be held accountable for your use of such data.

So in deciding what to teach and how to teach it, you as the teacher are preparing pupils for a future that the pupils themselves will make by building on the foundations that parents, teachers and society have laid for them.

Papert (1993a: vii) makes the point that:

> The most important skill in determining a person's life pattern has already become the ability to learn new skills, to take in new concepts, to assess new situations, to deal with the unexpected ... The competitive ability is the ability to learn.

In using the term ICT we include both computer-based systems and electronic communications systems such as internet and email supported by satellite and cable communication systems and telephone, radio and television.

In the United Kingdom (UK) there has been substantial investment in ICT infrastructure, hardware and software over a sustained period since the mid-1990s. Experiments in electronically networking communities in different parts of the UK and around the world (Department for Education and Employment [DfEE], 1995) took off in the mid-1990s; free training was provided for all teachers in the UK in the use of ICT in their subject areas during the period 1999–2003 (Leask, 2002); a rolling programme of providing laptops for teachers has developed and there has been investment in online materials and access to software (e.g. the Curriculum Online initiative and TeacherNet at http://www.teachernet.gov.uk). As a result of this, availability of equipment and access in schools is increasing. The annual survey of ICT in UK schools allows you to compare what you are experiencing in your school with the national average (see, for example, DfES, 2003a). Longitudinal research findings (from the Impact2 studies listed in the 'Further reading' at the end of the chapter) and Office for Standards in Education (OFSTED) findings (see the OFSTED reports on ICT at http://www.ofsted.gov.uk) indicate that pupils in technology-rich environments gain on average higher grades than other pupils even when allowances are made for home background and access.

There is still much to be done to ensure that each pupil benefits fully from this investment made on their behalf. Many schools will struggle to maintain ICT resources and to ensure reliable access to teachers when they are teaching using ICT. Teaching assistants, particularly, the higher-level teaching assistant, can be expected to provide high-quality support in these areas.

OBJECTIVES

By the end of this chapter, you should know:

- how you are going to audit the resources in the home and school environment where you are teaching and review the current skill base and knowledge base of the pupils;
- questions to ask to establish whole-school and department ICT policy and practice including administrative systems and management information systems in use;
- which different forms of teaching and learning can be stimulated through the use of ICT and key classroom management issues.

AUDITING YOUR ENVIRONMENT

Self-audit

All teachers trained in the UK are expected to be able to use e-mail, the internet, word processing, presentation (e.g. PowerPoint) and spreadsheet packages as well as software and specific technologies relevant to their subject, so these topics are not dealt with here in any detail. You need to assess you own needs for professional development in these areas and discuss them with the mentor in your induction year in order to develop a plan for your ongoing professional development (see Table 17.1, which sets out the steps for your professional development profile).

As well as drawing on support from staff in your own school, you may find advice and support is available from your subject association or local education authority. It may be possible for you to observe another teacher using technology with classes similar to your own. Over a period of time, you should build up a bank of ideas and ICT resources to support your teaching. In many countries, there are government-supported websites for teachers, e.g. in the UK, the government agency British Education Communication Technologies Agency (BECTA) has a key role in supporting the use of technologies in schools (the website http://www.becta.org.uk is packed with advice; research reports on ICT are available on http://www.becta.org.uk/research/reports). Various sites offering support for teachers in particular countries are as follows:

- in England, the DfES TeacherNet site (http://www.teachernet.gov.uk);
- in Scotland, the Learning and Teaching Scotland site (http://www.ltscotland.com);
- in Northern Ireland, the Northern Ireland Network for Education site (http://www.nine.org.uk);
- in the US, the askERIC service provides online support (http://www.askeric.org) on general education issues;
- across Europe, the European Schoolnet provides resources and opportunities to make links with schools in other countries (http://www.eun.org);
- many Commonwealth countries have schoolnets and they can be found on the Commonwealth of Learning website (http://www.col.org/cense).

School and department resource audit

What ICT resources are available in your new school? The availability and use of ICT in schools varies considerably so in each school in which you teach you need to audit the resources before undertaking detailed planning for schemes of work and lesson plans. Table 13.1 provides an example of an audit tool which you could use to give an overview of the resources available to you and how you can access them.

Familiarity with computer-based equipment comes with experience and you are unlikely to gain this if you are restricted to using such equipment during the school day. Research (Leask and Younie, 2002) shows that the ethos of schools where ICT is most embedded in classroom and general professional practices is likely to be supportive and collaborative. Ideally ICT expertise should be held by staff within all departments and not just concentrated in the ICT department, so that the 'just in time learning' of individual staff trying out new methods of working with ICT can be supported. Reflective tasks 13.1 and 13.2 suggest ways of auditing the resources of your school.

Reflective task 13.1
Auditing the ICT available in your subject area

Using the audit tool in Table 13.1, find out about access to the internet in your school and the availability of e-mail. Ask about the availability of different forms of ICT, CD-ROMS and computer software to support your area of the curriculum. The school library or your department may have a budget for buying resources you wish to use. Consider using pupils to help you find and evaluate such materials for your teaching programme. Find out if your school has the facilities for multimedia production and see what has been produced so far. Plan to incorporate the resources available into your teaching, over time. You can expect to have to negotiate with other staff for access to various resources and as a new member of staff you should expect to adapt to the existing ways of deploying limited resources.

Auditing home access and the skill and knowledge base of pupils

Successful teaching and learning is more likely to occur when the teacher builds on what the children already know. In the case of ICT, you are likely to find pupils in your classes who have access through family members to top-of-the-range ICT resources. Such access is not necessarily directly related to income. Some refugee families and other immigrants whose children I have taught prioritise ICT access at home as a means of keeping in touch with friends and relatives in the countries left behind. Local communities that are mono-cultural and on low incomes may lack access to the local pool of problem-solving skills held within a community which facilitates home access and enables families to keep the technology working. Some schools acknowledge this and take on the role of providing ICT support for the local community, sometimes in conjunction with local colleges.

Clearly identifying the skill and knowledge base of pupils is a necessary prerequisite to using ICT in the classroom that requires hands-on pupil use. A brief pupil questionnaire

Table 13.1 Auditing school and department resources: ICT audit tool

ICT type	Person responsible for maintenance and bookings	Booking procedure	Availability: booking will usually be necessary	Do you need training or practice to be able to use this confidently? How can you get this?	Notes: e.g. access codes, location of keys, passwords, pupil access notes, teacher access notes, rules for use, common problems, problem-solving notes, availability of help from technicians or other adults, your training needs
Laptops for teacher use					
Laptops for pupil use					
PCs for teacher use					
PCs for pupil use					
Scanners					
Data projector					
Interactive whiteboard					
Internet					
Intranet					
Printers (colour?)					
Digital camera: still					
Digital camera: video					
Virtual learning environment for in-school use and across region use					
Departmental website including homework website					
CD-ROMs/DVDs/video and audio resources					
Equipment for making CD-ROMs					
Subject-specific ICT such as: digital microscope data loggers					
Management information systems					
Other ...					
Other ...					

asking pupils about their experience with and access to the different forms of technology you wish to use is probably the quickest and easiest way to identify this knowledge and skill base. Questions you might pose include:

- What ICT resources do you have at home that you are allowed to use?
- Which of the following resources can you use now and which do you need training to use? For example:

School ICT resource	Tick if you can use it now	Tick if you need training

As well as the technical skills your pupils may need, skills of critical evaluation are particularly required where electronic information sources, e.g. CD-ROM and internet, are to be used, so that pupils are able to evaluate the quality of information that they are receiving. These skills of critical evaluation must be taught. This is discussed later in this chapter.

SCHOOL AND DEPARTMENT ICT POLICY AND PRACTICE

Gaining an overview of the kinds of ICT-related projects which have been done in your department and other departments in the school in previous years gives you an understanding of what pupils are likely to be able to do and an understanding of accepted practice in your school. Some schools have extremely high expectations about the level of ICT use in the work of departments; other schools may not be able to support the level of practice you would wish to achieve personally. Variations between schools and departments in their ICT policy and practice are huge. In schools using ICT effectively you can expect to find a departmental intranet site packed with electronic resources and ideas for lessons which you too should expect to use and add to, and well-established systems for the maintenance of equipment and for sharing access to equipment.

In your classroom, you need to ensure that 'ground rules' are established for working with ICT, for example for internet and e-mail use; inappropriate use needs to be defined, e.g. no bullying e-mails. Pupils need to be aware that records can be kept of the sites they visit and the e-mails they send. When pupils store their files on the school intranet they need to be aware of security issues and that interfering with other pupils' files is a serious offence. I have found young pupils are not as careful to keep their passwords private as are older pupils.

Administration, including pupil achievement tracking

As research has been done on how ICT can benefit education, a priority has become developing ways in which the technology could support teachers in their administration, including planning, monitoring pupil achievement and record keeping.

In England, from the late 1990s a major priority for government funding was on providing

Reflective task 13.2
Auditing school and
department ICT policy and
practice

As well as knowing what ICT resources are available and how you can access them, you need to know about school and department policy and practice about the use of resources. You may wish to:

- check the procedures governing pupil access to ICT resources;
- find out about school and department ICT policies, including policies on posting lesson plans and homework on the school website for home access by pupils and parents, as well as breakages, losses and how use is monitored;
- ask about the kinds of ICT-related work that pupils regularly undertake in your own department and other departments, e.g. production of a CD-ROM following visits or field trips; international collaborations on projects with other schools using e-mail or video conferencing;
- review the resources available on the departmental intranet and find out how you can contribute to building this shared professional resource;
- check the processes for monitoring, recording, analysing and reporting pupil achievement – schools can be expected to have management information systems in place to handle this data and to give you as an individual teacher feedback about individual pupils' achievement over time.

access to laptops for teachers as the particular value that technology brings to the teachers' work outside the classroom was recognised:

- Lesson plans and schemes of work worksheets can be stored and shared electronically where once hard copies would been kept in filing cabinets, perhaps never shared or used until they become increasingly dog eared before having to be reproduced over again. Electronic versions can be easily accessible to all teachers and easily adaptable to different pupil needs. The availability of syllabi and supporting materials as downloadable files on the websites of examination boards makes teachers' planning electronically of courses leading to national examinations much easier than was previously the case.
- Electronic mark books created through, for example, spreadsheet software allow the production of graphs showing pupil progress over time at the touch of a button so that individual pupil data is easily available to the teacher. Where schools have management information systems, data on the individual pupil can be used to compare their performance across subjects and throughout their school career. The data can be mapped against their expected outcomes. Evidence from the OECD ICT and whole-school improvement project (OECD, 2002) suggests that pupils can be motivated when this type of data is discussed with them as individuals.
- Individual contact by e-mail with pupils and parents is part of the work of some teachers but this has to be managed carefully because of work overload implications for the teacher. In addition some schools have policies about the procedures to be followed for home–school communication.

TEACHING AND LEARNING USING ICT

The ICT we are now dealing with is an extension of the type of ICT that has been available for decades (video, audio, computer technologies), and the understandings developed through this research on computer-based education and media studies provides a solid foundation for the ongoing development of pedagogies which use new forms of ICT to aid teaching and learning. The major pedagogical change which will come in the next decades is expected to be the focusing on the individualisation of learning supported by ICT. The cheapness of ICT, including that which gives low-cost access to school and expert communities around the world, provides scope for this individualisation of the curriculum.

The role of the teacher

How does ICT affect the role of the teacher? The vision of the teacherless learner sitting in front of a computer screen is prevalent but as knowledge of how effective learning is supported by ICT has developed so has a new role for teachers as e-learning mentors providing individual support at the time of the learners' need. This support is very time-intensive and, as mentioned above, you need to consider your workload carefully if there are elements of e-mentoring within it, e.g. feeding back on drafts which are submitted electronically, providing individual help via e-mail. It is advisable to focus this support on targeted groups for short periods of time, at least at the beginning until you get a sense of how much time you have available for this work. In contrast, the time taken to post in advance lesson plans and homework on the departmental or school website is a sound investment. Teachers report gains in pupil learning as pupils are more easily able to revisit lessons in which they may have had difficulties or which they missed, and they also see the progression that is planned for their learning as well as the relevance of the homework linking in with the overall learning programme.

Those who believe that interaction with material is an important part of learning find ICT offers pupils tremendous opportunities to explore the world and to undertake projects under the teacher's guidance. Daily contact can be made with pupils, schools and communities around the world – joint history, art and science projects can provide immediate insights into the life experiences and environments of others. Experts in different fields can sometimes be involved in such projects through online contact – e-mail or video conferencing.

Pupil learning

As always, the role of the teacher is to understand the learner and to construct situations that allow the learner to learn – scaffolding new learning experiences on what is known already. (See Chapter 5: 65, for discussion about scaffolding.)

Research into the use of ICT in classes confirms that there is increased motivation for many pupils, and 'significant learning gains' for both high- and low-ability pupils have been identified (National Council for Educational Technology [NCET], 1994: 19; OECD, 2002; Impact2 studies (2001–3), see the BECTA reference in 'Further reading'). No significant differences in 'learning gains' between boys and girls are reported.

Active learning approaches

These play a central role in most teaching programmes that integrate ICT, i.e. the approach to lesson planning is underpinned by activity learning theory – learning by doing – as opposed to acquisition learning theory – learning through acquisition of facts. Those whose view of teaching is that the pupils passively receive knowledge from the teacher have a limited view of how computer-based systems might be used in the classroom - i.e. for drill and practice routines. This view is based on a limited understanding of learning theory – that acquisition of knowledge is the end point.

Learning to Teach in the Secondary School, 3rd edition, identifies dimensions of active learning which includes: meaningful learning, giving a sense of ownership, personal involvement in learning, valuing of pupil ideas, problem solving, questioning, incorporating talk and debate, resource-based learning, collaboration with other learners and negotiation over content of and focus for learning. Teaching sessions using ICTs can be structured to include active learning approaches. In designing lessons that incorporate pupil use of ICTs, teachers apply the same principles that they use when planning all lessons.

Depending on the required outcomes, pupils may work as individuals, groups or teams and on the same or different tasks. Your lesson objectives, which indicate the outcomes you desire and the teaching strategies you use to achieve these, may, for example, include problem solving, group work, planning research, analysis and reporting skills. Approaches to learning which can be adapted to a teaching environment using ICT include independent pupil-centred learning, enquiry or active learning, cooperative or collaborative learning. Internet research projects can be designed so that they require active interaction with data collected: e.g., where e-mail links are made with other schools, pupils could be collecting, sharing *and* analysing data rather than simply writing to each other. Such e-pal (pen-pal) activities, whilst useful at one level are more likely to be sustained if they are linked with collaborative projects: e.g. pupils could be directed to produce a report with their e-pal on, for example, an aspect of their local area such as population characteristics, their occupations and so on.

In carefully constructed situations ICT can be used to provide opportunities to develop higher-level cognitive skills: 'Effective learning requires the development of thinking skills. Teachers need to create situations and tasks which encourage pupils to think hard in order to make progress' (National Commission on Education, 1993: 85).

Table 13.2   Examples of the opportunities available through ICT

- Pupil presentations of work as web pages, CD-ROMs or PowerPoint presentations – developing creativity as well as skills.

- Resource-based learning – information retrieval from the internet, CD-ROMs, DVDs.

- Partnerships with experts and networking with individuals and institutions around the world – through e-mail links and video conferencing.

- Virtual environments – you can 'stroll' through art galleries around the world or undertake virtual field trips linking the experience with direct questions to pupils in schools living in such environments.

- Access to services: health and careers advice, information about revision guides online and subject specific sites.

If higher order thinking is to be developed in pupils through the use of new ICT then careful planning is essential. The construction of the learning environment is crucial if learning outcomes are to be maximised and planned outcomes achieved.

Skills in critical evaluation

The internet in particular contains information from sources which have not undergone the degree of scrutiny and quality assurance that traditionally published paper-based sources have and so it is particularly important that pupils learn to critically evaluate information they find on the internet. They need to routinely consider questions such as:

- Who is providing this information?
- What do they hope to achieve by providing this information?
- Are they in a position to provide accurate information?
- In what way might the information be biased or inaccurate?

Pupils must be made aware that information on the internet is produced for particular purposes as is that in the press and on television, to which they are exposed daily, so it may be unreliable and biased. Whilst some providers may have education as a priority, other providers want to sell products or to influence recipients' thinking.

Galligan (1992) highlights the need to develop critical faculties in pupils so that they can effectively evaluate software and information providers they come across. She lists these critical skills as a number of processes. Pupils need to be able to:

- identify and consider the values embedded in software;
- assess the effect of the structure of software on meaning;
- evaluate computer mediated information for bias, accuracy, credibility and underlying assumptions;
- recognise the ability of software to amplify, ignore, simplify or reduce aspects of real life;
- appreciate the aesthetics of computer mediated images, text and sound; and
- discriminate between information and ideas, quantity and quality of information.

(Galligan, 1992: 2)

Classroom management issues

Management of necessarily limited ICT resources so that all pupils are treated equitably requires careful planning. Arrangements for computer access in classrooms vary widely, from hubs (i.e. groups of computers in an open area serving groups of classrooms giving pupils access during all lessons), to mobile sets of computers which might need to be booked, to full rooms of computers available on a much more restricted basis. In some schools all classrooms have at least one intranet/internet point of access allowing, for example, the teacher to project material for the whole class to see.

Interactive white boards bring a range of advantages to the teaching situation. Whole-class brainstorming results – for example, around an essay topic – can be recorded on the board then saved as a file on the intranet from which it is then available for all pupils to work on individually. The BECTA website has many ideas for the use of different forms of technology to achieve different pedagogical outcomes (see 'Further reading' below).

The use of the internet in the classroom poses a number of challenges. In secondary schools, if it is used for resource-based learning, pupils may need longer than the traditional teaching periods of around an hour to achieve useful results, even if the teacher directs their search to some extent. Logging onto the school network and logging off can take a significant amount of lesson time and there will often be one or two pupils who experience difficulty – e.g. their password doesn't seem to work – which can disrupt the lesson. The problem of speed of access to internet sites may hinder the use of the internet during lessons in some schools. Downloading files from different internet sites in advance of lessons is one solution that some teachers propose but is there something intrinsically motivating for a learner to have access to an open-ended resource? The open-ended nature of the internet as a resource does mean that the path of learning is less predictable and some teachers may find this difficult to manage. Many schools have resource centres which pupils can access outside of class time. So where all pupils can access the internet outside lessons, it may be appropriate to set internet-based tasks for homework. Traditional library searches can sometimes be quicker and yield more high-quality information than internet searches and these should be normally included in such work as well.

Plagiarism

This takes on new dimensions as pupils can now download materials from CD-ROMs or the internet straight into their assignments. Pupils need to be alerted to the unacceptability of including text written by others in their work unless they attribute the source of such text. It is suggested that when referencing internet sources pupils should state the internet address together with the date and time of access as well as any other identifying features.

Equal opportunity issues

On the plus side, the advantages offered by ICTs for learners with various impairments are significant – library access and opportunities for interpersonal communication are just two ways in which new ICTs may benefit such pupils. You should naturally monitor issues of access, whether related to gender, ability or background.

Access to inappropriate material

There is concern among educationalists and parents about the access young people have on the internet to information which is considered inappropriate for them. However, it is possible to block access to certain sites and schools have their own policies on this. The downloading of inappropriate material perhaps at home and its subsequent passing from pupil to pupil is to be anticipated. Schools normally make the rules for using the internet completely clear and they have procedures to deal with misuse, such as informing parents and withdrawing a pupil's privileges.

As young people whose homes and schools are connected to the internet may have easy access to material that schools or parents find unsuitable, teachers may wish to take steps to help them develop ways of dealing with the material to which they are likely to be exposed.

CONFRONTING TECHNOPHOBIA

Whatever your own feelings about the use of ICT, as a professional you have a responsibility to the pupils you teach to prepare them for the future. It is not uncommon for teachers and some pupils to feel out of their depth when it comes to the use of ICT. As with any teaching and learning situation, the problems need to be identified and strategies put in place to remedy them.

Not being familiar with ICT is hardly an option for teachers working in the twenty-first century. At a fundamental level, ICT allows you to use your time much more effectively – for administration, for keeping up to date and in the searching for information related to subject areas. The quality and quantity of the work of those not able to use such ICTs will be increasingly seen to be unacceptably limited. Take, for example, the art teacher. Why should pupils be limited to examining printed or prerecorded material about artefacts from different cultures when, with the use of the internet or CD-ROMs, they can roam the galleries of museums of the world, incorporating directly into their own projects images of what they find. In the case of science teachers, if they are teaching about space, why not use the latest information from NASA?

SUMMARY

Using ICT in the classroom does not ensure that more effective learning takes place – so many other factors come into play. What we are suggesting is that using ICT is an integral part of the learning experience of pupils in the twenty-first century and you are responsible for ensuring that such opportunities are provided for your pupils. To ensure that you are addressing their needs, you should review your teaching strategies regularly and be ready to assimilate new methods of proven worth into your teaching.

In the first year of your teaching, you are likely to be very busy getting to know the school and the pupils and developing and consolidating your teaching skills. The texts which follow in the further reading section below provide useful material for you to draw on when you have time to reflect and when you are extending your work using ICT.

FURTHER READING

BECTA Research Reports are available on http://www.becta.org.uk/research/reports and represent the outcomes of some of the most detailed studies on the use of ICT in classrooms undertaken in the UK. A few examples are given below.

BECTA (2001) *Computers for Teachers: Phase 1 Report.* London: Department of Education and Skills and BECTA (2002) *Computers for Teachers: Phase 2 Report.* London: Department of Education and Skills. This research reports on the government schemes for providing laptops for teachers.

BECTA (2000–2) IMPACT2 reports. This series of reports covers topics such as: *Learning at Home and School: Case Studies; Parents' and Teachers' Perceptions of ICT in Education; The Impact of ICTs on Pupil Learning and Attainment.* Full copies are available on the website given above.

Lachs, V. (2000) *Making Multi-Media in the Classroom: A Teachers' Guide.* London: Routledge Falmer. Source of useful ideas about making multi-media for the classroom teacher.

Loveless, A. and Ellis, V. (eds) (2001) *ICT, Pedagogy and the Curriculum.* London: Routledge Falmer. Provides further ideas about ICT practice in the classroom and includes a range of perspectives on ICT use in different subject areas.

Leask, M. (ed.) (2001) *Issues in Teaching with ICT.* London: Routledge. This edited text brings together ideas and explores tensions in the use of ICT in teaching and learning.

NATIONAL CONFERENCES AND EXHIBITIONS

The British Education and Training Technology (BETT) Exhibition takes place over several days including Saturday each January and is advertised in the *Times Education Supplement.* Free tickets are available for teachers. This is a huge exhibition which includes software and hardware suppliers and publishers. There is a considerable focus on software and other resources to support each subject area including special educational needs software. See http://www.besa.org/BETT for details.

Subject associations provide advice about conferences and ICT applications. In the UK, accessing TeacherNet http://www.teachernet.gov.uk and searching for subject associations will lead you to the list of UK associations.

14 Preparing Pupils for Public Examinations

Developing Study Skills

David Balderstone and Sheila King

Since the 1980s, assessment and reporting of pupils' achievements have been placed near the top of the educational and political agenda. The National Curriculum (NC) for England, introduced through the Education Reform Act in 1988 (ERA, 1988), brought with it statutory assessment procedures. Monitoring standards of achievement through assessments of pupils aged 7, 11, 14 and 16, and now at ages 17 and 18, have increasingly become a focus for parents, teachers and others involved in education as well as for media attention, as schools are compared through local and national performance ('league') tables. The Qualifications and Curriculum Authority (QCA) website (http://www.qca.org.uk) provides details and should be studied for any updates in arrangements for assessment. Recent changes in curriculum and assessment in England, known as Curriculum 2000, have responded to pressure to reform the post-16 qualifications, introducing changes to the structure of the General Certificate in Education at Advanced level (GCE A level) and introduced new vocational courses (Department for Education and Employment [DfEE]/QCA, 1999).

This chapter introduces you to the three different national assessment patterns used for NC Key Stage 3, the General Certificate of Secondary Education (GCSE) and GCE AS (Advanced Subsidiary) and A2 level, explaining briefly how each has developed in recent years. Examples of study skills that you can use to raise the achievement of your pupils in those examinations are discussed.

OBJECTIVES

By the end of this chapter you should:

- know the types of assessment undertaken at Key Stage 3, GCSE and GCE A level;
- be aware of the importance of external examinations on the school curriculum;
- be aware of some of the study skills that you can be use to improve your pupils' performance in examinations.

UNDERSTANDING THE REQUIREMENTS OF THE NC

The development of assessment within the NC

In 1987 the government announced that there would be national systems of assessment to accompany the NC in England and Wales and the blueprint for this was the report of the Task Group on Assessment and Testing (TGAT) (Department of Education and Science [DES], 1988). This report identified teacher assessment as the main assessment device with a summative test, the Standard Assessment Task (SAT), to support and moderate the teachers' assessment. Assessment tasks which were originally proposed included practical, oral and group tasks as well as more conventional pencil and paper tests. Although teachers were dubious about the time and logistical pressures the new methods of testing would bring, they welcomed the new-style tasks and felt they were educationally beneficial. From 1989 the first assessment programmes were introduced for Key Stage 3 but gradually the mode and style of assessment moved away from those suggested in the TGAT report because they were not appropriate for testing the hundreds of statements of attainment required by most subjects. As a result of public, professional and political pressures, the structure of testing in 1996 looked rather different from those in earlier years. The widespread boycotting in the mid-1990s of the NC tests by many teachers suggested that the assessment process at the end of Key Stages 1, 2 and 3 needed to be re-examined. Consequently, in 1995 the report on the assessment of the NC (Dearing, 1994) replaced statements of attainment in each Attainment Target, with eight level descriptions plus an additional level for exceptional performance. These amendments were widely approved by teachers. Aspects of these developments are described in more detail in Chapter 8 and in *Learning to Teach in the Secondary School*, 3rd edition, Units 6.1, 6.2 and 7.3

Types of assessment at Key Stage 3

The QCA develops the statutory assessments to be taken at the end of Key Stages 1, 2 and 3. There are currently two types of assessment used at Key Stage 3. The first type applies only to the core subjects of English, mathematics and science. These three subjects have end-of-Key-Stage tests which are externally marked. The key features of these tests are:

- paid markers are appointed by external marking agencies;
- external agencies operate quality assurance procedures in order to ensure accuracy and consistency of marking;
- there is a review procedure for re-marking where this is necessary;
- test results must be reported to parents, along with the results of classroom-based tasks and teacher assessment, by the end of the summer term; schools must also provide the marking agencies with the results of their school-based assessments in order that they may make comparisons with the external test results;
- unlike GCSE, the external tests are free to pupils.

Written tests are used only to assess pupils who are achieving at NC Level 4 and above in English and at Level 3 and above in mathematics and science. Below this level, with lower-performing pupils, classroom-based tasks are used and these are administered and marked by teachers within their schools. Differentiation is achieved in mathematics and science largely through tiered papers, mathematics having four tiers and science two tiers. Tiered papers are designed to assess pupils across a limited range of levels, with overlap of levels occurring between adjacent papers in the tier. All three subjects have an optional extension paper which allows the award of Level 8 and the recognition of an exceptional performance grade (8★).

The second type of assessment is teacher assessment which is used throughout all subjects. At the end of Key Stage 3 you assign a level grade to each pupil in your subject. The grade relates to the appropriate level description and is seen as the 'best fit' for each individual pupil. Level descriptions are to be found in the Attainment Targets section of the NC document for your subject. The current concern of teachers is how to use the level descriptions and how consistency in interpretation from one school to another can be achieved. Arriving at a rounded judgement to find the level which best fits a pupil's performance in each Attainment Target is now the main assessment concern at Key Stage 3.

Improving pupils' performance using level descriptions

An understanding of the level descriptions for your subject is vital to making effective judgements on the attainments of individual pupils. Although intended for use 'in the round', most teachers recognise that the different components of knowledge, understanding and skills initially have to be unpacked and examined. One of the key points to emerge from detailed analysis of the level descriptions is that, in order to judge the level of pupils' attainment, you must use every opportunity to assess them by providing appropriate tasks. This consideration obviously informs the schemes of work and lesson planning in which you are engaged. As a result of your understanding of the level descriptions you should introduce appropriate skills to pupils in order to help them maximise their performance.

Examples of how this understanding can be applied in three different subjects are described below.

1   In geography, pupils must be provided with opportunities and freedom to pose questions for investigation and to select and choose how they present their findings. A pupil working at Level 7 would be showing an ability to select skills in order to present and investigate, whereas pupils working at a lower level would be told the relevant skills.

2   In design and technology (making) at Level 8, pupils' design plans must allow for alternative methods of manufacture, whereas earlier levels do not require this skill.

3   History pupils working at Level 7 begin to reach substantiated conclusions independently and teachers must therefore provide opportunities for pupils to demonstrate this.

You need to develop a range of teaching and learning strategies to ensure that your pupils demonstrate their abilities in all areas. These strategies include:

- practical tasks
- group tasks
- written work completed in class
- homework tasks of several types
- school examinations and class tests.

Study skills are increasingly being taught through a whole-school approach, often during tutor group sessions. The trend in schools has been to delay such teaching until GCSE but many study skills are appropriate to younger learners. Therefore you could introduce at Key Stage 3 some of the skills discussed later in this chapter as appropriate for GCSE and GCE A level. In particular, you should:

- encourage your pupils to take more responsibility for their own work;
- design enquiry-based learning experiences which may or may not have predefined outcomes;
- provide strategies for remembering factual work;
- provide opportunities for your pupils to demonstrate their knowledge and under-standing from one lesson to a similar but different situation in another;
- encourage your pupils to redraft their work;
- make explicit in advance what you will look for when you assess the pupils' work.

Further ideas for supporting learning skills can be found in Chapters 5, 6 and 10.

PREPARING PUPILS FOR THE GCSE

The development of the GCSE

The GCSE examination was introduced in 1986 after a prolonged period of feasibility studies, trials and political discussion. Teachers and parents had been asking for a single examination at 16+ for many years and this pressure was heightened in 1974 by the raising of the school-leaving age to 16 and the increasing transition from a tripartite system of schooling, with grammar, secondary modern and technical schools, to a comprehensive system. Full details of the merger of GCE O-level with the Certificate of Secondary Education (CSE) and the development of GCSE can be found, for example, in Nuttall (1984) or Youens (2001).

The GCSE examination has a number of features which differed from previous examination systems. These features include:

- a requirement for general and subject-specific criteria upon which to base the specifications;

- a requirement that all pupils study similar specifications constructed from the same framework;
- a requirement that all pupils take the same examination, where differentiation is achieved through tiered papers and/or questions;
- the requirement that course work is undertaken by pupils as an integral part of their assessment;
- grade criteria which link levels of pupils' competence to specific GCSE grades;
- the award of seven pass grades, A–G.

As a result of the introduction of a NC for England, new GCSE specifications were needed. Although revised draft criteria for these were published in 1994, it was subsequently decided that the GCSE specification in each subject at Key Stage 4 would not be so tightly tied to the NC and therefore a second set of criteria was published and developed from the Key Stage 3 programmes of study. As a result, new specifications, written from new general and subject-specific criteria, were introduced into schools for the first time in September 1996 for examination in 1998 (see Youens, 2001).

GCSE as it is today

The main general features of GCSE include:

- Tiered papers which allow for differentiation. Mathematics has three tiers while most others have two: a foundation tier, covering grades G–C, and a higher tier covering grades D–A. Art, music, history and physical education are recognised as subjects where pupils can respond effectively at their own level and these subjects do not have tiered examination papers.
- A balance between terminal examination and course work. Each scheme of assessment includes an externally set terminal examination, the weighting for which varies between subjects. Art, design and technology and information technology, for example, are at the upper end of the scale for course work, which counts for 60 per cent, while mathematics and history, with up to 20 and 25 per cent for course work respectively, represent the other end of the scale.
- An additional grade description, A★, is awarded to candidates who perform at an exceptional level above grade A.

Another change which could have a significant impact on the curriculum at 16+ is the introduction of short courses. These free-standing, accredited courses have half the content of a full GCSE and may be taken over one year, (described as 'short and fat'), or over two years ('long and thin'). In addition, combined subject GCSEs have been developed in subjects, so that business studies, for instance, can be combined with subjects such as design and technology, information technology and a modern foreign language.

GCSE course work

Course work is a central feature of the GCSE, so it is important for you to invest time and effort in understanding your role in this part of the examination. You need to construct course work which is interesting and motivating to pupils; this requirement may be a tall order for a newly qualified teacher, yet this task is central to the whole concept of effective school-based assessment. The course work your pupils carry out should be attainable at some meaningful level, challenging and educationally worthwhile.

There are several skills which you can assess more effectively through course work than by a written examination. These include practical skills, oral skills and skills in writing in an extended form. Good course work allows your pupils to demonstrate positive achievement: that is, what they know, understand and can do; it endeavours to make what is important measurable (rather than make what is measurable important) and so increase the validity of the assessment process (Mobley *et al.*, 1986: 77). Examples of the types of course work from a range of subjects are shown in Figure 14.1.

One of the benefits of course work is that it enables your pupils to spend as much time as they need to complete their work, by contrast with the very limited constraints of written examinations. The disadvantage of course work is that your pupils can spend huge amounts of their time, often inefficiently, producing their work. This situation is exacerbated when numerous pieces of course work for several subjects are being worked on at the same time. It is essential, therefore, that you know about whole-school planning of course work in order to minimise overloading your pupils at any one time.

Parents in particular may find it difficult to understand the exact nature of a course-work task. Such tasks include, e.g. a fieldwork enquiry in geography, a portfolio of selected class work in information technology, an oral exercise in French or an investigation into spatial properties in mathematics. Course-work assignments are set by the teacher and usually provide written guidance for the pupil in the form of a plan of action. For example, a piece of course work for media studies may be set on the topic of the game show on television, requiring the candidates to devise a new game show. Teacher guidance may include:

*   a set of questions probing the understanding of the genre and the nature of its appeal to the public;
*   a set of procedures identifying the steps to be taken to develop the game show;
*   evidence of development of the task through, for example, reports, sketches, research, video and trials;

Figure 14.1   Some examples of types of coursework

Written assessments	Practical assessments
Short-answer queston	Controlled experiments
Structured questions	Short practical test
Data response questions	Observation/aesthetic tasks, working to a brief within a set time period
Objective tests	
Open-response questions	
Open writing/essays	
Reports	
Decision-making exercises	
Critical evaluation	
Problem-solving exercises	
Investigations	

Note: some individual coursework assignments may contain several of these types of assessment

- the ways in which the finished product should be presented together with the evidence for the viability of the proposed game show.

The finished product must meet the criteria laid down by the awarding body for coursework.

Reflective task 14.1
Coursework assignment

Discuss with your subject mentor how GCSE coursework assignments are supported in your subject at GCSE. Using the school's guidance for a current selected assignment, relate that guidance to the specification laid down by the awarding body for such assignments. Prepare brief notes for your own guidance in supporting your pupils in such a coursework assignment.

Course work across the various subject areas makes very different demands on teachers and pupils. Even within one subject the amount and type of help offered by the awarding bodies varies. As well as giving teachers starting points for course work tasks, the guides show how work is assessed, thus setting standards of moderation. Helpful timetables and diagrams of procedures are often given within specifications.

Specifications from awarding bodies may give helpful steps for coursework development which teachers and pupils can work through, allowing coursework to maintain focus. Advice for setting up a study for geography coursework might include a sequence such as:

1   Identify the topic for study through observation, discussion, reading or previous study. Present the study to candidates as an extended piece of investigative writing which is couched in terms of an hypothesis.
2   State the objectives of the study in specific terms. It is helpful if your candidates clearly recognise that the study involves a consideration of a number of specific problems or questions.
3   Share the assessment criteria with your candidates.
4   Make decisions about
   - what evidence is relevant to the study;
   - how evidence can be collected.

Your candidates should:

5   Collect the evidence.
6   Present the evidence in the form of maps, diagrams, etc.
7   Interpret and explain the evidence.
8   Develop conclusions relating them to the original objectives.
9   Evaluate their work and present it.

You may give pupils guidance up to step five in the steps listed above but beyond that stage the only advice that can be given is on the techniques of recording that the pupil proposes to use. The addresses of awarding bodies in England and elsewhere from whom you can get details of syllabuses and guidance are in Appendix 1.

The role of the teacher in course work assessment

Your role in assessing the school-based component of your GCSE subject may be daunting to you as a newcomer to the profession. This is particularly true when the course work component contributes a high percentage to the overall grade, such as in design and technology or in physical education. The high time element involved, not only in the setting, supervising, marking and moderation of assignments, but also in the administrative dealings with the examination boards and attending external standardisation meetings, aroused considerable feelings amongst teachers and teaching unions. The fact that many teachers are prepared to take on this extra work load shows their commitment to the benefits of course work.

TEACHING AND PREPARING PUPILS FOR GCE A LEVEL

There has been a rapid increase in the number of pupils moving into post-compulsory education in the last decade. The enrolment rate in year 2000 in further education in all institutions in the United Kingdom at 16 is high, just over 80 per cent, but drops to around 50 per cent by age 18; see Chapter 15, Figure 15.1. Achievements at GCSE have certainly increased pupils' motivation and willingness to continue in education. There has been a corresponding increase in the uptake of the GCE A-level examinations and the standards achieved have continued to rise. The growth in post-16 education is discussed in Chapter 15.

The GCE AS (then called Advanced Supplementation) examination was introduced in 1987 in an attempt to broaden the curriculum at GCE A level. As a result of the review of the qualifications for 16–19-year-old pupils (Dearing, 1996), GCE A level underwent further changes. Vocational courses replaced General National Vocational Qualifications (GNVQs) and were introduced at GCE A level in an attempt to give parity between academic and vocational qualifications. The GCE A level was split into two parts, the Advanced Subsidiary (AS) for year one of the course and the A2 in the second year. The final award and grading of GCE A level is based on performance in both courses (see Chapter 15). The standards expected by your pupils in the AS examination are as demanding as those in the corresponding GCE A2-level subject but the content to be covered is intended to be half that of a GCE A2-level specification. One concern of teachers is that the AS content must be taught in only two terms and that within this short time pupils also need to adjust to the more advanced way of working.

The introduction of new modular specifications has helped increase choice and flexibility for pupils, schools and colleges. With module results being valid for four years after the module is taken, your pupils can complete A2 and AS qualifications over a longer period of time. Module examinations can also be retaken on any number of occasions before presenting them finally for a subject award of a GCE A-level pass. A further indication of the flexibility provided by the new arrangements is that a pupil of yours working towards GCE AS-level qualifications can add further modules to obtain a full GCE A-level. Likewise, any pupil who is unable to complete a full GCE A-level course may be able to 'cash in' three of the six modules to obtain an AS qualification. Each module has to be assessed at full GCE A-level standard, irrespective of the point in the course at which the module is taken.

In addition to these modular arrangements, GCE A2- and AS-level specifications have had to satisfy the QCA regulations and Code of Practice (School Curriculum and Assessment Authority [SCAA], 1994). These regulations require that externally assessed terminal examinations should contribute at least 30 per cent of the total assessment for a final subject award. In most subjects, internally assessed course work is limited to a maximum of 20 per cent of the total available marks. The exceptions include subjects like art and design where special arrangements allow a maximum allocation of up to 60 per cent of the total marks for course work.

When you prepare to teach GCE A-level and AS-level courses it is clearly essential that you should become very familiar with your subject specification and its assessment arrangements. You should consider the following questions:

- What is the rationale, focus or main approach of the specification?
- What is the structure of the specification and how much choice is available?
- Is the specification linear or modular?
- What is the subject content and how is it organised?
- How is it assessed and when?
- What are the weightings of the assessment objectives?
- What is the nature of the course work assessment?
- What forms of assessment are used in the examination papers?

Once you know the content and approach of the specification, you should think about the skills that your pupils have to develop and the knowledge and understanding they have to acquire in order to succeed in the various forms of assessment. You should consider these questions:

- When is the pupils' course work to be produced and assessed?
- What skills do your pupils need to produce good course work?
- How and where can these skills be developed in the pupils' course of study?
- What support can I provide (study material and guidance), and when?
- What skills do my pupils need to develop to succeed in their externally assessed examinations?
- How and where can these skills be developed?

DEVELOPING STUDY SKILLS IN YOUR PUPILS

General principles

There are many books dedicated to the teaching of study skills and some schools run courses for their pupils to teach techniques and to assist the planning and development of pupil working patterns. Such skills become particularly important at GCSE when pupils begin to take on more responsibility for their own work. This chapter can do no more than touch on some practical suggestions which may assist you in preparing pupils for GCSE examinations. More general study skills such as note making, reading and home studying are not discussed here. Additional readings, some directed at specific study skills, suitable for you and your pupils are listed under 'Further reading' at the end of this chapter.

The term 'study skills' is understood by some teachers but others find it confusing. You could consider study skills to comprise the following ideas (adapted from Irving, 1982: 4):

- formulating and analysing the range and nature of information to be gathered;
- identifying and appraising the most likely sources of information;
- tracing and finding the sources of information;
- examining, selecting and rejecting from what is found;
- using or interrogating resources;
- making notes or otherwise recording any information found;
- interpreting, analysing, synthesising and evaluating the information;
- presenting and communicating your findings in an organised way;
- evaluating personal performance to improve future efficiency.

Reflective task 14.2
Developing examples of
revision cards

Choose a suitable topic which is studied in your GCSE specification. From the notes that your pupils have on that topic:

- reduce the notes to a set of essential points (postcard size);
- use the key word of each point to produce a suitable mnemonic.

Describe and discuss this method with your pupils and encourage them to do the same for their next revision test.

Study skills for GCSE examinations

Pupils embarking on their GCSE courses often meet for the first time the need to introduce some sort of discipline into their working patterns, particularly concerning their homework and course work. The amount of work and its academic content seems to rise suddenly in Year 10 and your pupils' attitudes to their study often becomes more focused as they accept that these examinations 'matter'; and that they are for 'real life'.

You can help your pupils acquire study skills in a variety of contexts. Within your day-to-day teaching there are skills such as pupil research, note making, writing and time management that you can you foster. You might consider also the following suggestions to help develop your pupils study skills. You should:

- encourage your pupils to apply newly learnt knowledge, skills and understanding to situations similar to those in which they were learnt;
- encourage accuracy at all times;
- not dismiss a learning homework, with a follow-up short test, as unimaginative teaching – there is a body of knowledge to be learnt in most subjects;
- produce a glossary of terms for your pupils as you teach;
- give pupils details of the specification which they are following and some guidelines as to what are the main content, skills and assessment.

You can have an impact on your pupils' success in coping with the actual examination and the preceding revision. Practical suggestions to help your pupils include:

- using helpful shortcuts to memorise information: for example, the use of mnemonics. Encourage pupils to make up their own mnemonic;

- utilising past papers at all stages of teaching, not just for 'end-of-unit-of-work' tests. Many examination resources are excellent for incorporating into lessons. Get your pupils used to the terminology of the examination paper and the way that the examination questions are set out;
- giving advice on their use of time in both studying and in the examination itself. However, after advice is given, only practice can drive this point home;
- providing a study guide for the examination. If no such guide exists, you could suggest ways in which the school might prepare one by drawing up a departmental guide yourself. See 'Further reading';
- fostering a way of getting pupils to ask for your help, especially during the spring term of Year 11. Arrange surgeries or lunch-time clubs; and be explicit about when and where you can be found.

Reflective task 14.3
Helping pupils to interpret
examination questions

Examine a range of past examination papers for your subject. Write down all the key words which drive the nature of the question, e.g. describe, compare, outline, analyse, etc. With the help of your pupils, prepare a guide to distinguish between these words and how the differences direct the writing of answers to examination questions.

Developing study skills for pupils at GCE AS level and A2 level

One of the main objectives of teaching study skills in post-16 education is to help your pupils to progressively take on greater responsibility for their own learning. However, the development of their study skills should go beyond training in the use of specific study techniques. If your pupils are to develop into effective, independent learners they 'need help at the strategic level throughout all their work' (Waterhouse, 1983: 55). As well as helping pupils to develop specific study skills, you should provide personal support and guidance so that they can 'learn how to learn' through experience and practice. This approach to study skills is summarised in Figure 14.2.

It has been argued that while the mechanics of study skills should be developed in earlier years, the 'sixth form pupil should be committed to thinking about his thinking and learning about his learning' (Hamblin, 1981: 135). Although hard work and intelligence are important, success at this level and in higher education also depends on your pupils' style of thought and method of problem solving. Their work often requires them to assess evidence, to reason deductively and to appraise the strengths and weaknesses of arguments or particular techniques. It is therefore worth helping your pupils to reflect on their learning and cognitive style and to encourage them to move away from the idea that there is a right answer, or that there is a correct way to study.

You can help your pupils to do this by introducing them to a variety of study techniques and giving your pupils opportunities to use them in real tasks in your subject. Pupils should be encouraged to evaluate the strategies used to complete the tasks and to identify their own learning. Tutorial support and guidance is important to help pupils to reflect on their

Figure 14.2   Learning how to learn: developing study skills and promoting pupil autonomy

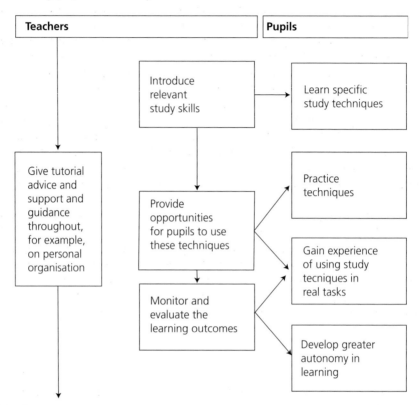

approach to study. Thus guidance can be given through individual or small group discussion and your pupils' progress reviewed through profiling. This aspect of pupil development is discussed further below, under 'Coursework'.

The learning processes that your pupils engage in should help them to develop their critical thinking skills and creativity. The learning skills of your pupils could be improved by focusing their study in the following areas:

- planning skills
- information skills, research and processing
- interpretation of ideas and evidence
- questioning assumptions and evidence
- developing logical arguments
- creative thinking
- understanding and using problem–solving techniques
- communication skills
- self-evaluation.

You could, for example, help your pupils identify the discrete stages in planning an essay, investigation or piece of research. The first time that pupils are required to carry out such a task, it is well worth working through each stage with them, highlighting the skills that are being developed in the process. The steps in this process are discussed in the section below called 'Essays'.

The implication of this suggestion is that through 'thinking about thinking and learning about learning' (Hamblin, 1981), your pupils can begin to make conscious choices about the strategies they use in tackling problems. This process is often referred to as 'metacognition' and is a common feature of courses in thinking skills (see Chapter 5 for further discussion of metacognition). Such an approach requires you to encourage pupils to discuss how they have tackled problems and to view the lesson as a learning experience.

Even though changes in learning and assessment styles at GCSE have contributed to more pupils being motivated to pursue post-16 education, it is clear that many pupils find the transition to GCE AS- and A2-level study challenging. Schools may not give enough attention to supporting pupils to make this transition effectively. Induction into post-16 education should do more than simply providing information about course content and assessment, going further to advise on their role in learning and of the study skills needed to succeed.

For most of your pupils there is a gap of nearly three months between the end of their GCSE examinations and the start of their GCE AS- and A2-level courses. You could provide, with help from colleagues, a flexible learning package to help bridge this gap. Such packages should be self-contained and aim to both stimulate your pupils' interest in your subject and introduce them to learning styles relevant to your subject. You could also use this strategy as an indication of your pupils' commitment to further study in your subject. The work required of your pupils should not be excessive; about five hours is appropriate.

Essays

In many subjects the success of your pupils at GCE AS- and A2-level examinations is still determined by their ability to write essays. However, do you provide suitable opportunities for your pupils to develop the skills needed to write good essays? Indeed, are your pupils even aware of the skills that are required? Very often teachers assume that pupils develop these skills by writing essay after essay. Clearly practice is important but your pupils also benefit from exploring with you ways of writing effectively. You could break down the writing of essays and reports into stages, as follows:

- analyse the question or title;
- brainstorm and explore ideas;
- research:
  - identify and select information,
  - retrieve information (read and take notes),
  - analyse and evaluate the information;
- plan:
  - the structure,
  - the introduction and conclusion,
  - the paragraphs;
- draft and check the essay;
- present the essay;
- self-evaluate your work;
- have your work evaluated and assessed by your teacher.

Within the context of your subject, you should develop activities to help your pupils explore strategies that could be used in each stage of essay writing. For example, you could introduce the principles of effective note taking and encourage your pupils to try out different techniques in groups, by using the same piece of reading, lecture or video presentation. These techniques could then be evaluated so that your pupils can decide which approach is appropriate for them (see, for example, Mckeown, 1991).

Your pupils could explore structuring and paragraphing essays by taking a copy of a short article and dividing it up into its constituent parts or paragraphs. Ask your pupils to give a heading or theme for each paragraph and then to arrange the paragraphs into a logical order which could then be checked against the original article.

Your pupils should also find it useful to assess examples of other people's work. Give your pupils essays for them to assess and comment upon. With your help, the feedback could be used to establish the criteria for a good essay which then become more readily understood by your pupils. A similar activity could be used when preparing your pupils for course work assignments, such as projects and investigations (see Henderson, 1996).

Course work

Course work is still an important feature of GCE AS-level and A2-level examinations although its contribution to the final marks varies between subjects. For many pupils course work involves independent research and investigation, often over an extended period of time. Course work can also involve practical and oral work.

As well as helping your pupils to develop the skills needed to produce their course work, you should provide them with appropriate tutorial support and guidance. This guidance may include reviewing their progress and setting targets at a series of interim stages to support their process of action planning. Your pupils should also be made fully aware of the criteria upon which their course work is assessed. Where involvement is constructive and welcomed, parents could be made aware of course-work requirements and deadlines and of ways in which they can help their daughter or son.

Revision

Although the style and structure of examinations can vary considerably between subjects, there are certain common principles that can guide the way that you prepare pupils. However, as argued earlier, it is important that your pupils at this level are encouraged to develop strategies that work for them. Revision, for example, is a very personal activity, although your guidance about ways of making it a more efficient, effective and conscious process helps to improve their understanding.

Your pupils should be encouraged to view revision as an active and critical process that helps them develop the understanding and skills they need to succeed in examinations. Too often revision is passive, e.g. simply reading through large volumes of notes may give your pupils a limited view of their subject. A passive revision technique makes it difficult for your pupils to answer questions effectively.

To guide the preparation of your pupils for examinations you could:

- ensure that revision is a continuous process that is not left until the end of a course of study – encourage your pupils to review their work throughout the course;
- ensure that revision for terminal examinations is part of a planned programme that includes a final intensive period of preparation;
- ensure that your pupils encounter examination questions and activities throughout the course;
- provide your pupils with examples of examination papers at an early stage and introduce them to ways of using them to revise (this process should normally take place before any practice examinations);
- ensure that your pupils identify and practise subject-specific examination skills and include them in a revision study guide;
- encourage your pupils to rework notes into a more concise and understandable format, e.g. as revision cards;
- remind your pupils that regular review and recall helps to improve understanding and memory;
- give your pupils examples of 'model' answers in order to familiarise them with assessment criteria, i.e. what a good answer might look like;
- ask pupils to make short presentations on a topic as revision; their response to questions you set can provide another indication of their understanding;
- encourage peer support among your pupils, e.g. help them to establish small revision groups;
- give your pupils regular assessment and feedback, e.g. in response to practice questions and tasks;
- explore with your pupils strategies of time management during the revision period and in the examination itself.

There are numerous resources available in book form and on the internet for supporting revision for GCSE and GCE; many schools and colleges produce their own guides. The growth of vocational courses in 14–19 education in England has led to the development of a whole range of materials for supporting and guiding study, as has the introduction of Basic Skills and Key Skills.

Internet sites provide some support for study and revision, such as the BBCi websites (BBCi 2003a and 2003b) and How to Study (2003). Further guidance on the use of ICT in supporting learning can be found in Johnson (2002) and Leask and Pachler (1999); see particularly, in the latter, Chapters 8 and 14. See also the 'Further reading' section of this chapter.

SUMMARY

While few people would deny that external examinations are a necessary and valuable part of education, many would argue that the present system has significant flaws. While debate continues amongst parents, teachers and politicians about the merits, costs and time element involved in different forms of assessment, you as a classroom teacher must get on with the task of preparing your pupils for examinations. Research has shown that pupils can be taught study skills which enable their examination performance to improve. Developing your understanding of the examination system and knowing the range of strategies which help your pupils improve their examination performances is an essential requirement for you to become an effective and successful teacher. The foundation of good practice of study skills is of great benefit to your pupils as they move into adult life. Further developments in England in academic and vocational courses offered to pupils aged 14–19 are imminent (DfES, 2002a), and with it changes in assessment practice, but the task of helping pupils to become autonomous learners will remain.

FURTHER READING

Drew, L. and Bingham, R. (1996) *Student Skills: Tutor's Handbook*. Aldershot: Gower Publishing. A series of booklets to help pupils develop study skills and employment skills. Each skill pack is set out at two levels and has learning outcomes defined for each topic.

Hamblin, D. (1981) *Teaching Study Skills*. Oxford: Basil Blackwell. An activity-based programme of guidance which helps pupils to analyse ways of thinking and methods of problem solving. Chapter 6 ('Thinking about thinking and learning about learning') is of particular relevance to this chapter.

Hamblin, D. (1983) *Guidance: 16–19*. Oxford: Basil Blackwell. A good introduction to the constructive teaching of study skills in the secondary school. It includes practical activities designed to help pupils investigate and develop their own style of learning.

Henderson, P. (1996) *How to Succeed in Examinations and Assessment*. London: Collins Education for the National Extension College. Part of a series on 'learning skills', this book addresses the variety of assessment strategies in use and offers guidance on approaching the process. Comprises 13 units including units on using course work, writing essays and revising for examinations.

Irving, A. (ed.) (1982) *Starting to Teach Study Skills*. London: Edward Arnold. A book which discusses, in a practical way, how study skills programmes can be incorporated into the curriculum in secondary schools.

Lewis, R. (1992) *How To Write Essays*. Cambridge: National Extension College. Useful materials and activities to support the development of essay-writing skills.

Mckeown, S. (1991) *Developing Learning Skills: An Activity Based Manual*. Cambridge: National Extension College. A useful resource with activities for developing learning skills within subject and class teaching. Target group 14–19 years.

Montgomery, M. (1991) *Study Skills for GCSE and GCE A Level*. Scotland: Charles Letts. A comprehensive handbook on general study skills for pupils.

15 The School Sixth Form and the Growth of Vocational Qualifications

Judith Brooks and Norman Lucas

This chapter is an introduction to the bewildering curriculum changes that have occurred for sixth-form students in the last few years. We place these changes within a wider context by tracing the introduction of a vocationally orientated curriculum for 14–19-year-olds. The main focus of the chapter is on recent reforms as they affect school sixth forms as well as some reforms in sixth form and further education (FE) colleges. Each qualification offers fresh challenges to teachers. This chapter is an introduction to sixth-form vocational qualifications and we advise the reader interested in more detail to use the contacts and further reading given at the end of the chapter. In this chapter we use the term 'student' to refer to learners in schools and colleges. Elsewhere in this book we use the term 'pupil' to refer to learners, mainly aged 11–16. Abbreviations used in the chapter are listed in Appendix 1.

OBJECTIVES

By the end of this chapter you should be able to:

- understand the changing 14–19 curriculum and its impact on schools and colleges;
- understand the vocational and academic choices available at age 14 and the importance of seeking advice on possible study pathways;
- appreciate some of the differences in teaching, learning and assessment between vocational and academic courses;
- appreciate the changing context and debates concerning a new 14–19 curriculum framework.

THE WIDER CONTEXT

Traditionally sixth forms in schools were places where a minority of 16-year-old students stayed on to study A-levels, mostly with the aim of going on to university. For the overwhelming majority who left school at age 16 the choices were employment (or unemployment), some form of youth training or a course at a local further education college.

During the 1980s and 1990s governments were faced with four basic problems. Firstly, they were faced with rising youth unemployment, which prompted the development of a whole range of courses for the young unemployed such as the Youth Training Scheme. Secondly, employers and politicians complained that our education system had lost touch with the 'world of work' and argued that more work-related studies should be introduced. Thirdly, as traditional manufacturing disappeared and new businesses emerged the argument was made that new areas of employment required more young people to have higher levels and broader ranges of skills and knowledge than hitherto. Finally, throughout the 1980s and 1990s, comparisons were made between participation rates and education achievements of British 16–19-year-olds and those in other countries. Figure 15.1 illustrates this point by comparing enrolment rates between different countries in the year 2000 for 16-, 17- and 18-year-olds.

In response to these problems there were many proposals; the Confederation of British Industry (CBI) called for a 'Skills Revolution' (CBI 1989) and during the late 1980s and early 1990s a general agreement arose, cutting across political divisions, that something had to be done to include more people in education and training if the UK was going to be economically competitive with other advanced industrial countries.

In 1990 the British education system was characterised as having low staying-on rates

Figure 15.1   Percentage net enrolment rate in public and private institutions by level of education at ages 16, 17, and 18 in various countries (as at year 2000)

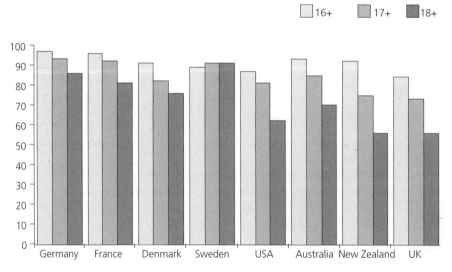

Source: OECD/DfES, 2003.

**Reflective task 15.1
Comparing participation rates
in the UK with other countries**

Figure 15.1 shows that the staying-on rates for 16-year-olds is quite low in the UK and drops markedly at ages 17 and 18. This is particularly the case when compared with European countries.

Why do you think the staying-on rates drop? Could it be that we do not offer the right curriculum to this age group? Is our system too selective? Is the prospect of gaining employment more attractive then staying on and gaining qualifications that are not valued? What reasons can you offer why so many 16-year-olds leave education and so many 17-year-olds drop out after only one further year? What could be done about this?

and a divided system between a minority of academic pupils that followed one set of curricula and others who followed a vocational course, if they were lucky (Finegold *et al.*, 1990). The authors argued that students following General Certificate in Education Advanced levels (GCE A-levels) undertook a specialised narrow academic route and students following vocational courses experienced a narrow job-specific focus which was pitched at a low level and was badly co-ordinated and undervalued. In other words, in the 1990s the British system for 16–19-year-olds was described as a 'narrow, early-selection, low-participation education and training system' and to remedy these limitations a baccalaureate approach was advocated.

Most 14–16-year-olds currently take six to ten General Certificates in Secondary Education (GCSEs), including mathematics, English and other 'core' subjects. This means the curriculum is content heavy and for the student it leaves little space for other activities. Beyond 16 (if the student goes on to do A-levels) the opposite occurs: there is no common curriculum and students can drop important subjects such as English, mathematics and science and follow three or four subjects in the first year of A-levels and three (perhaps two) in the second year. The argument could be made that 16-year-old students who stay on choose a narrow and often incoherent set of either academic or vocational qualifications.

Furthermore, only about half of all 16-year-olds in England succeed in achieving five A★–C grades at GCSE, the basic threshold for progression to advanced level study. This means that the other 50 per cent do not progress to advanced level and as a consequence find it difficult to stay on in a school sixth form. Many of these students opt for employment if there is any, company training schemes, modern apprenticeships or a course at a further education college. The suggestion by many policy makers is that such a system not only fails half the students at 16, but that the educational experience of those that succeed is far too narrow and too heavily examined, with no room to develop the broader skills needed for further study and employment. It is largely in response to these sorts of criticisms that 16–19 qualifications were reformed: to broaden the curriculum and offer wider choices for young people.

RECENT REFORMS

Curriculum 2000

The educational debate in the last decade or so has prominently featured the question about what 14–19-year-olds should study. This has focused on broadening choices at age 16 and increasing the numbers of those staying on in education and training. While many school sixth forms have continued to offer traditional GCSEs and GCE A-levels, the structures of these qualifications and their alternatives have undergone big changes.

The Dearing Report (Dearing 1996) made a series of far-reaching proposals for the reform of the post-16 qualifications framework. These recommendations were echoed in New Labour's 1996 election manifesto, called *Aiming Higher*, which suggested broadening GCE A-level, upgrading vocational qualifications, introducing Key Skills (see below) and making the A-level curriculum more accessible to a wider range of students (Labour Party 1996). This initiative, when implemented, became known as 'Curriculum 2000'. Three important changes took place. The first was to split GCE A-levels into two 3-unit blocks called Advanced Subsidiary (AS) and A2. This way, students are able to broaden their study to achieve four 3-unit AS subjects in the first year and three full A-levels, which are completed in the second year. Secondly, alongside these changes, the General National Vocational Qualification (GNVQ) advanced qualification was reformed in order to align it with GCE A-levels. This qualification became the Advanced Vocational Certificate in Education (AVCE), which was designed in six unit blocks, similar to A-levels. Finally, the Key Skills qualifications were introduced in an attempt to raise standards and to improve the employability of all young people.

Key Skills

It is generally agreed that the changing nature of employment in the twenty-first century demands skills that are significantly different from those associated with the dwindling heavy manufacturing industries that once dominated the British economy (DfES, 2002a). The emphasis is increasingly on generic and transferable skills, such as communication, problem solving, the ability to work independently and in collaborative groups, all underpinned by literacy, numeracy and ICT competence. These Key Skills, as they are known, have been part of GNVQs since 1992, but the Curriculum 2000 qualification reforms uncoupled them from their vocational parent qualification and made them free-standing, with the aim of enabling students on a wide variety of programmes to develop their key skills at the appropriate level.

The government has been very keen to ensure that all 16–19-year-olds reach certain levels of key skills alongside other qualifications. Key Skills have had a bumpy ride since they were introduced in 2000, although most people, from employers to teachers and university lecturers, believe Key Skills to be 'a good thing'. However, there have been problems with delivery and assessment, some universities do not value them and many schools do not teach them at all. They are more widely taught in FE colleges, where most students following vocational programmes also take one or more Key Skills. The specifications are currently being revised by the Qualifications and Curriculum Authority (QCA) to accommodate some of the criticisms levelled at them by teachers, assessors and students.

Reflective task 15.2
Thinking point

We cannot accurately predict the world that our schoolchildren will be living and working in by the time they are, say 25 or 30 years old. Therefore, we need to ensure that we equip them for a rapidly changing society.

What skills do *you* consider young people (14–19) should be taught and encouraged to develop in order that they can confidently meet the challenges that will lie ahead?

How does the current curriculum address such skills and what changes might be necessary?

Curriculum reforms at 14+

Most teachers are aware that some learners become disengaged from their school studies as they go through adolescence; frequently the National Curriculum subjects hold little appeal for many 14–16-year-olds, who would rather be engaged on preparation for work and adult life. The education initiatives following the Curriculum 2000 qualifications reform acknowledged these difficulties and aimed to provide young people with a coherent alternative to the traditional academic route to employment and higher education. These young learners are increasingly participating in a range of vocational options offered by schools and colleges, where the focus is on breadth and flexibility.

At the end of 2002, the government proposed a strategy to address these problems. One possible solution to pupil disaffection with the curriculum could lie, it was suggested, in strengthening the links between schools, colleges and the workplace, in order to provide learning programmes that reflect the local community, e.g. urban or rural, manufacturing or service industries, etc. Within such a strategy, young people would choose a range of subjects from a wide number on offer, combining school, college and work. The constraints (or opportunities) offered by a broad National Curriculum would be replaced by a series of pathways, negotiated between the student, the school or college, the workplace and other outside agencies, such as the Connexions service (http://www.connexions.gov.uk). The learners would continue to follow programmes in English (or communication), mathematics (or application of number) and such core subjects as information and communication technology (ICT), citizenship and physical education.

Most school and college-centred curriculum choices fit within a national qualifications framework developed during the 1990s. Table 15.1 shows a simplified version of that framework outlining the choices and levels of qualifications. For example, level 2 qualifications show the choices equivalent to GCSE level. You may like to refer to Table 15.1 during the discussions that run throughout this chapter; it is a useful aid to understanding the various levels of qualification.

Central to vocational provision is the general vocational pathway, which identifies the possibilities open to young people who decide to opt for a vocationally oriented curriculum. This choice of direction, to be decided by the learner in negotiation with parents and teachers, is now possible from the age of 14, at the beginning of Year 10 (see Table 15.2).

Most schools also offer GCSE and GCE AS/A-levels in vocational subjects such as ICT,

Table 15.1 National qualifications framework

Level	General education	Key skills	General vocational
Levels 4 and 5	Degree level	N/A	Foundation Degrees, HND, HNC
Level 3 Advanced	AS/A Level	Key skills communication, application of number and information technology	AVCE BTEC National Diploma
Level 2 Intermediate	GCSE grade A–C	Key skills communication, application of number and information technology	GNVQ Intermediate Vocational GCSE
Level 1 Foundation	GCSE grades D–G	Key skills communication, application of number and information technology	GNVQ Foundation

* There are also vocational qualifications known as NVQs at each level, which are not usually offered in school sixth forms

Table 15.2 Vocational courses that are most frequently offered by a typical medium-sized school sixth form

GNVQ	Health and social care – Foundation and Intermediate
AVCE*	Health and social care
GNVQ	Art and design – Foundation and Intermediate
GNVQ	Business – Foundation and Intermediate
AVCE	Business

Source: The prospectus of a school in the London area 2002–3.

performing arts and business studies. Schools that have been awarded specialist school status in, for example, ICT or performing arts usually offer a wide range of courses around that curriculum specialism.

GCSE choices

GCSE replaced GCE O levels and the Certificate in Secondary Education (CSE) in the mid-1980s and since that time vocational subjects, like business studies and ICT, have been added to the subject list. Since September 2002 it has been possible to take a range of GCSEs in vocational subjects and these courses offer a broader range of possible vocational options, in many cases from Year 10 onwards. Vocational GCSEs can be taken alongside traditional GCSEs, like mathematics, English and science, over two years. These new qualifications are available in art and design, applied business, engineering, health and social care, applied ICT, leisure and tourism, manufacturing and applied science. The subjects are assessed by a combination of coursework and examinations and are graded from A*–G. Pupils taking these courses may be encouraged by their school to follow key skills in communication, application of number and ICT, all of which are included as an underpinning to the vocational curriculum content of the qualification.

Table 15.3 Vocational courses frequently offered by a typical sixth form college

GNVQ	Health and social care – Foundation and Intermediate
GNVQ	Art and design – Foundation and Intermediate
GNVQ	Business – Foundation and Intermediate
GNVQ	ICT – Intermediate
AVCE	Health and social care
AVCE	ICT
AVCE	Business
AVCE or BTEC	National Diploma in Media (in addition to, or instead of GCE A-level media studies)
AVCE	Travel and tourism
CACHE	Nursery nursing

BTEC, Business and Technology Council; CACHE, Council for Awards in Children's Care and Education.
Source: Prospectus of a sixth form college in the London area 2002–3.

GNVQ

A possible general vocational pathway can be seen to progress through GNVQ at Foundation (level 1) or Intermediate (level 2) which could then lead towards A-level study and even higher education, where appropriate (see Table 15.1). The key word to these new qualifications is *flexibility*, indicating that the possibilities for changing direction are always kept open throughout the pathway.

There are 14 vocational areas available at GNVQ, although most schools only offer the most popular, such as business, health and social care and ICT. Sixth form colleges also offer GCSE and AS/A-levels in vocational subjects such as ICT and computing, performing arts and business studies. Many such colleges offer courses to meet a local need in, for example, child care (see Table 15.3).

Further education colleges, with their more vocationally oriented staff and realistic workplace environments (workshops, hair and beauty salons, kitchens and restaurants, etc.), are better placed to teach a wider range of vocational areas, such as engineering, construction and the built environment and retail and distributive services (see Table 15.4 below).

AVCE

Students who successfully complete their GNVQ at Intermediate level often progress to a level 3 vocational course, usually the AVCE, which replaced Advanced GNVQ in the Curriculum 2000 reforms. The AVCE is also available in 14 similar vocational areas to GNVQ and in 6-unit and 12-unit forms. These subjects are equivalent in unit size and level to one A-level (6 units) or 2 A-levels (the 12-unit double award). A 3-unit AVCE (equivalent to AS level) is also available, currently in only four curriculum areas. Many schools offer AVCEs in business, health and social care, ICT and art and design; the more vocationally specialised AVCEs such as engineering, media production or travel and tourism are again more frequently taught in FE colleges.

One of the central aims in the introduction of the AVCE was to give vocational education a parity of esteem with A-level. However, recent research indicates that many learners (and their parents and teachers) still perceive vocational courses to be for less able students than the traditional A-level route (Savory *et al.*, 2003). This view is reinforced, perhaps by the low retention achievement rates in the first years of this new qualification. Some schools and colleges encourage learners to take mixed programmes: that is, to combine the 6-unit AVCE with two more traditional GCE A-levels, e.g. AVCE business with GCE A-level mathematics and economics, or AVCE art and design with GCE A-level history of art and English. The combinations that are offered in school sixth forms are often limited by student numbers, staffing availability and the constraints of the timetable.

Reflective task 15.3
Curriculum planning activity

Three 6-unit AVCEs are engineering, hospitality and catering, and media. Suggest coherent programmes that could combine each AVCE with two traditional GCE A-level subjects.

Draft a rationale for each combination you choose; you may want to offer the student a vocationally oriented package, or you may decide to keep their options open for as long as possible.

Problems with the AVCE stem largely from the drive, in most ways laudable, for parity of esteem with A-levels (Savory *et al.*, 2003). The demise of GNVQ Advanced level was seen as an opportunity to introduce a new level 3 vocational qualification with increased academic rigour. The entry qualifications for AVCE were suggested to be four or five GCSEs at grades A★–C, but many schools and colleges, in order to offer a progression route to their level 2 students, allow entry to the courses with far lower grades and, as a result, many of these learners cannot cope with the demands of the advanced course. The reason given for many students not coping with the course is the largely academic approach to course content and structure, accompanied by increased external testing, which has resulted in a return to traditional teacher-centred delivery. Many anxious teachers consider it necessary to coach the learners for the tests, in order that students can succeed.

As these vocational courses tend to attract students who have not done well at their GCSEs and are unsuited to the GCE A-level style of assessment, the dropout rate has been high in the first years as learners have become discouraged by the difficulty of the courses. Many teachers feel that the (now defunct) GNVQ Advanced courses were more suited to the needs of their less academic learners, as they were more practical and assessed in a less formal way.

The AVCE offers a general vocational education but some learners are very focused on their intended pathway and want to follow a specialised course with a clear vocational outcome. The Business and Technology Council (BTEC) National Diploma is offered in a range of subjects (e.g. art and design, graphics, media, some engineering subjects) by many FE colleges, but is rarely found in schools, as it demands a dedicated teaching environment and specialist staff with industrial experience. The BTEC route is often preferred to AVCE, but is only appropriate for learners who have a clear vision of their educational future and who have received advice and guidance about the possible pathways open to them. The

Table 15.4 The range of vocational courses offered by a typical general further education college

Art, design, graphics	GNVQ, GCE A level, AVCE, BTEC National Diploma
Building and construction	GNVQ, City and Guilds, BTEC National Diploma
Business and management	GNVQ, GCE A level, AVCE, BTEC National Diploma
Catering and hospitality	GNVQ, BTEC National Diploma, City and Guilds
Engineering	GNVQ, BTEC National Diploma, City and Guilds
Hair, beauty and complementary therapies	BTEC National Diploma
Health and social care, child care	BTEC, CACHE
Horticulture and floristry	BTEC
ICT	GNVQ, GCE A level, AVCE, BTEC National Diploma
Performing arts and media	GNVQ, GCE A level, AVCE, BTEC National Diploma
Sport and Leisure	GNVQ, GCE A level, AVCE
Travel and tourism	AVCE, BTEC National Diploma

Source: The prospectus of an FE college in outer London.

BTEC National Diploma has long been favoured in areas such as art and design and related areas. A trawl through the admissions data of any art college reveals that a significant number of students have come up via this route.

A general FE college can offer a wide range of vocational opportunities to young people, often in partnership with local business and industry (see Table 15.4). Colleges are encouraged to be responsive to local needs, so very specialised courses on, for example, horticulture or aspects of engineering may be offered.

In addition to the courses indicated in Table 15.4, students also have the opportunity to enter Modern Apprenticeship Schemes at Foundation or Advanced level, but this is a specialist area of provision and outside the remit of this chapter (the Learning and Skills link on the DfES website – http://www.dfes.gov.uk – has up-to-date information on Modern Apprenticeships).

OPPORTUNITIES OR CONFUSION?

One interesting consequence of the Curriculum 2000 reforms is the apparent duplication of qualifications in the same or similar subject. For example, a learner interested in following a level 3 business programme could opt for GCE A-level business studies, AVCE business or a BTEC National Diploma in business. This presents problems for the learner and the institution, as courses tend to compete with each other for students, not only across institutions, for example a school sixth form and a local FE college, but also within institutions. Many courses are under intense pressure to fill their places and adopt very sophisticated marketing strategies to attract prospective students. Table 15.5 compares three different business studies syllabuses from the awarding body Edexcel to show the similarities and differences between the three qualifications.

By looking at the range of vocational courses offered by schools, sixth form colleges and FE colleges, it becomes immediately apparent that the widest opportunities for specialist courses are available for learners who choose to study at FE colleges. However, a recent study of school sixth forms and an FE college in one London borough showed that the

Table 15.5 A comparison of three Edexcel syllabuses for business studies to show the similarities and differences between the various pathways

Title of qualification	A level business studies: frequently taught in schools	AVCE business: taught in some schools	BTEC National Diploma in business: offered by colleges, rarely by schools
Size of qualification	AS = 3 units A level = 6 units	AS VCE = 3 units AVCE = 6 units Double Award = 12 units	18 units
Core or compulsory units	AS: Unit 1 Business Structure, Objectives and External Influences Unit 2 Marketing and Production Unit 3 Financial Management A2: Unit 4 Analysis and Decision Making Unit 5 Business Planning Unit 6 Corporate Strategy	AS: VCE Unit 1 Business at Work Unit 2 The Competitive Business Environment Unit 3 Marketing AVCE: All the above plus Unit 4 Human Resources Unit 5 Business Finance Plus one optional unit Double Award: All the above plus Unit 6 Business Planning Plus six optional units	1. Introduction to Business 2. Business and Management 3. Creative Product Promotion 4. Presenting Business Information 5. Business Enterprise 6. Business Online plus twelve optional units
Optional units	None	18 optional units, including: • ICT in Business • Business law • E Commerce • Sales	12 specialist optional units, including: • Introduction to Accounting • Marketing Research • E Business and Internet Marketing • Human Resource Management • Business Ethics N.B. These units offer the opportunity for students to follow specialist pathways
Method of Assessment	Unit 1 Exam Unit 2 Unseen Case Study Unit 3 Exam Unit 4 Exam Unit 5 Unseen Case Study or Coursework Unit 6 Pre-seen Case Study	Unit 1 Portfolio Unit 2 External Test Unit 3 Portfolio Unit 4 Portfolio Unit 5 External Test Unit 6 Portfolio. In addition, for the Double Award, two optional units are externally assessed and four are internally assessed	Unit 1 Internally assessed Unit 2 Internally assessed Unit 3 Externally assessed by integrated assignment Unit 4 Internally assessed Unit 5 Externally assessed by integrated assignment Unit 6 Internally assessed All other units internally assessed

Source: Business Studies Syllabuses, Edexcel, 2003.

Reflective task 15.4
Qualifications comparison
activity

Compare the qualifications in Table 15.5. In what ways do they appear similar and how are they different?

Try to determine the target market for each qualification. What sort of course does each provide for learners wanting to follow a level 3 programme with a business flavour?

nature of the courses was not the only, or even the main, reason for learners choosing where to continue their post-16 studies (Brooks *et al.*, 2003). Many young people stay at school, following a general education course (usually GCE A-levels with perhaps one AVCE), because they are settled at school, the environment is familiar and friendly and they know and like their teachers' styles of teaching. Some learners do choose the FE route in order to access the specialist courses on offer, while recognising that they will need to adapt to a more adult, less structured environment.

Advice and guidance to prospective students

It is increasingly important for learners to be given good, accurate and up-to-date advice and guidance because of the many ways in which courses can be combined to construct a programme at levels 2 and 3. All young people receive careers guidance at school as part of their National Curriculum entitlement, but sometimes they need more detailed information than their careers teacher can give them. This advice and guidance can now be provided to young people by the Connexions Service (http://www.connexions.gov.uk).

Connexions was set up in 2000 to bring together several strands of provision and its aim is to offer all young people impartial advice and guidance about continuing with learning or entering employment. However, unlike its predecessor, the Careers Service, Connexions can also offer help with other areas of a young person's life that may be causing problems and interfering with learning, such as disability, leaving care, drugs or financial problems. The young person is linked with a personal adviser or careers adviser, who may be based at a local school or college, or at a Connexions Centre. The adviser can help by giving information about educational progression, employment and training opportunities, planning a career and looking for jobs, writing curriculum vitae and preparing for interview and, where appropriate, accessing specialist help and support.

The three case studies below represent three different, yet typical, learners, with a range of backgrounds and aspirations.

Case Study 1: Anji, aged 15

Currently: At school in Year 11 taking eight GCSEs.
Ambition: To go into management, perhaps retail.
Possibilities: Anji will go further in management with a university degree, so it is a good idea

to plan for higher education. Anji's school offers GCE A-levels and AVCE business, so Anji hopes to follow A-levels in psychology and communication studies, together with AVCE business studies. She can then decide whether to apply to higher education to do a course in, say, retail management or join the management training course of a large retail group. With her particular combination of GCE A-levels and AVCE, she is keeping her options open for other possible courses in higher education.

Case Study 2: George, aged 16

Currently: Just completed Year 11 with four GCSEs at grades A–C. Has a pass in English at grade C but obtained only a grade D for mathematics.

Ambition: something artistic.

Possibilities: George may like to consider a general course in art and design, either an AVCE or a BTEC National Diploma. However, most schools and colleges prefer students to have five GCSE passes at grade A–C to qualify for these courses and George is likely to be advised to resit GCSE mathematics. He could investigate also a specialist sign-based course such as graphics or fashion. If his school or college considers that he has the ability to succeed at this level despite his having only four GCSE passes with good grades, an alternative route would be to take a mixture of GCE AS-level subjects, including art and design, together with a resit of GCSE mathematics. This choice would depend largely on his attitude, motivation and what his predicted grades were.

Case Study 3: Louise, aged 14

Currently: about to enter Year 10, but her teachers predict that she will struggle with her GCSEs as she is not very motivated and has some difficulty with reading and numeracy.

Ambition: Not sure, possibly working with children in a nursery.

Possibilities: Louise is not keen on academic work but likes children and would be better motivated if she could see a vocational point to her studies. She will need to continue with mathematics and English, although she is unlikely to attain a good GCSE grade in those subjects. She may be well advised to take a GNVQ Intermediate course in health and social care, which will provide a general introduction to the care sector. She could then take a more specialised course, e.g. a CACHE course at her local college. She will also need to take Key Skills in communication, application of number and ICT as an underpinning to her course.

SUMMARY

Curriculum choices for pupils at age 14 or 16 are not easy to make either for them, their parents or their teachers. The increased number and variation of vocational courses has exacerbated the difficulties of decision making. On the one hand, there is no point in putting students on to programmes in which they cannot succeed, as they will become demotivated and likely to drop out. On the other hand, the range of available qualifications is valued differently and traditional GCE A-levels remain the 'gold standard', despite attempts by many policy makers to offer parity of esteem to vocational courses. For example, it is still unlikely that AVCEs will be acceptable to some universities and, for many people wishing to go to university, A-levels remain their first choice. The problem is that as long as academic GCE A-levels continue all other options will be seen by students and parents as second best. It is difficult to get parity of esteem between different curriculum options, especially between academic and vocational choices where course content is so varied. Furthermore, employers may know the value of GCE A-levels but are not always aware of qualifications such as GNVQs or AVCEs. This position is in many ways regrettable, as there are innovative and varied ways of achieving a vocational ambition. Governments and educators need to continue to work towards a high-quality vocational education and training provision for all learners who wish to access that route.

New qualifications and curriculum pathways always take time to become established and the Curriculum 2000 reforms have been particularly controversial. The debate continues and new initiatives are announced by government with alarming frequency; there is little wonder that even the practitioners in schools and colleges often remain unaware of current developments. Many teachers and other interested parties believe that an emphasis on skills will drive down the standard of general education; others believe that a vocational curriculum at 14+ is the most effective way of re-engaging disaffected learners. However, with careful and considered advice from teachers and Connexions advisers, young people today can enjoy a wide range of possibilities to help them to achieve their intended goal, whether that is a job, a place at university or further training on a Modern Apprenticeship scheme.

FURTHER READING

Hodgson, A. and Spours, K. (2003) *Beyond A Levels: Curriculum 2000 and the Reform of 14–19 Qualifications*. London: Kogan Page.

Lumby, J., Briggs, A., Wilson, D., Glover, D. and Pell, T. (2002) *Sixth Form Colleges: Policy, Purpose and Practice, Nuffield Research Project*. Leicester: University of Leicester.

Phillips, G. and Pound, T. (eds) (2003) *The Baccalaureate: A Model for Curriculum Reform*. London: Kogan Page.

USEFUL CONTACTS

Assessment and Qualifications Alliance (AQA); Edexcel Foundation; Oxford and Cambridge Regional (OCR); Qualifications and Curriculum Authority (QCA): see Appendix 1.

Learning and Skills Development Agency. Regent Arcade House, 19–25 Argyll Street. London W1F 7LS.

Part IV

Moving On

16 Using Research and Evidence to Inform your Teaching

Ruth Heilbronn

When you reach the end of your period of induction you will be looking forward to moving on into your early professional development activities. At this stage more than ever becoming research literate is helpful to your development as a teacher, because you can design your teaching and develop your own practice based on previous studies in your field, or on an area of teaching and learning. Your own work then builds on a sound basis of previous work. Research in the context of teaching can be defined in several ways, for example teachers use particular research skills when they work on curriculum development, prepare lessons, resources, schemes of work. Schools are research-rich institutions. Teachers are full-time researchers in one sense, but might not realise this. The process of checking the quality and effectiveness of your teaching requires hypothesising, collecting data, assessing the hypothesis against the data, evaluating, then applying the findings to your teaching. We could so describe the cycle of lesson planning, delivery and evaluation, or writing a scheme of work and evaluating it. In *Learning to Teach in the Secondary School*, 3rd edition, observation schedules and paired observation techniques, work on lesson planning, keeping a reflective journal and evaluating lessons are described as helpful techniques for beginning teachers to use in examining their classroom practice (see particularly Chapters 2.2 and 5.4).

Other kinds of relevant and informative research takes place in schools, for example some members of staff will be engaged on specific research projects, for their own further study, for a course of higher education, such as an MA, or simply to follow their own interests. There may also be specific research projects undertaken by others outside the school, such as a partnership higher education institute, using the school as a source of data. The school management team will routinely use research methods, gathering data on pupil performance for example, as a tool for school improvement, to contribute to raising the quality of teaching and learning. Outside partners, such the local education authority (LEA) and school boards, support much research in the context of schools in order to raise the quality of teaching in schools.

Policy to change educational practices and the promulgation of pedagogical initiatives and strategies often carry a claim to an underlying research base. Therefore, it is important to be an informed user of research, able to judge the validity of the claims made for various initiatives and changes. Recently, networks for practitioners have developed, which support teachers to access and to use research and also to undertake their own small–scale research projects. Being 'research literate' and able to evaluate good from bad research is an important skill for teachers, as practitioners and users of educational research.

OBJECTIVES

In this chapter you will:

- learn more about investigating your own practice through your own practitioner research;
- find out about why it is important to become research literate and how to go about it;
- investigate sources of information and teacher networks for relevant practitioner research;
- find out about teaching as a research- and evidence-informed practice and where to find such research and evidence to inform your practice.

WHAT COUNTS AS RESEARCH?

Earlier it was suggested that many activities which are undertaken in school can be called educational research and it is useful to clarify what research is. Ron Best (2002: 4–5) has suggested that something counts as research to the degree that it:

- seeks to establish the truth (or 'truths') about something;
- is undertaken in a systematic (not haphazard) way;
- is rigorous and is not casual;
- is undertaken by someone whose intention it is to seek or establish truth(s) in a systematic and rigorous manner (i.e. someone who has adopted the perspective of a researcher);
- makes findings open to public tests of truth; and
- makes its methodology transparent.

The Hillage Report on *Excellence in Research on Schools* (Hillage, 1998) pointed out that there is no one definition of good research in the educational field. It used the term 'fitness for purpose' as a key concept. This means it recognised that there is diversity in methods and context in educational research (National Educational Research Forum [NERF], 2000).

One example of the use of research in schools is the evaluation of school policies. Schools function on the basis of policies and procedures which have been drawn up to assure the smooth running of the school community and to take into account principles such as those of equal opportunities. If these policies and procedures are not to become mere paper exercises the school must respond to changing circumstances. To take one common example from the past years, one year's examination results show that a particular group in the school community is underachieving. The senior management team want to know why this has happened and what can be done to change the situation for the following year. They need to gather data systematically, analyse it, evaluate the findings and make recommendations. Consultation should take place at various points, if the school teams are to be engaged. The recommendations then need to be disseminated and on the basis of the enquiry a policy is formed for the following year, or the existing policy is amended.

**Reflective task 16.1
How are school policies devised?**

Reflect on a school policy you have implemented in the classroom, e.g. behaviour management, sanctions and rewards, anti-bullying, special educational needs (SEN), child protection, differentiation, monitoring and assessment.

Investigate how the policies were devised. Which type of research method was used to collect, analyse and publish the data? Did it produce a good working document, i.e. one which was successfully implemented? Are there any further questions to ask which the policy does not cover?

Another way in which research can be used in school is individual teachers investigating and evaluating their own practice. You may be engaged in this form of research when you want to find out, for example, if teaching in a specific way will raise achievement for one particular group in your class. You may want to understand why one particular class is unresponsive to methods you use successfully with another, parallel class. Another topic might be to understand if you are favouring one type of pupil over another, e.g. the noisy over the quiet, the boys over the girls.

The term 'action research' refers to the activity of teachers investigating their own practice (see particularly *Learning to Teach in the Secondary School*, 3rd edition, Chapter 5.4). The concept was developed principally by Stenhouse (1975). Broadly, Stenhouse viewed much educational research as unable to 'get at' the complexity of what goes on in the classroom, because of its distance and its framing of research questions in the form of objective and external questions. A teacher may fruitfully investigate his or her own practice and develop useful ideas to improve this practice, and this knowledge will come from inside the situation. The claim for scientific objectivity in the research, i.e. the researcher as an outsider, cannot apply. Thus action research may not be subject to the same rules as scientific/empirical research. Also, the methods used in the practitioner's inquiry are themselves experimentally developed in the course of actual inquiries. They develop naturally to fit the question under investigation, 'and are tested and improved in the course of doing' (Dewey, 1960: 124).

More recently, action research has become part of a wider involvement by teachers investigating the teaching and learning process and the term 'practitioner research' is in widespread use. Practitioner research can be a powerful tool for raising achievement in one area of your practice and the following section will suggest ways in which you might begin such a project.

Undertaking a small-scale practitioner research project

In any piece of practitioner research the first step is to clearly define what is to be investigated. You need to first frame the research question by asking 'What do we want to know?' This is a crucial step and there is a suggested method for doing this in the Reflective task 16.2. You need to make sure that you have a research question which you can answer, i.e. that you have chosen something manageable and practical, given the time and the resources available to you, and that it will yield enough data to enable you to draw reliable conclusions, which can lead to recommendations for you and other teachers to implement.

Reflective task 16.2
Framing a research question

- Think of an investigation or an initiative or innovation you wish to make which will directly impact on your classroom practice. It does not matter if you are going to carry out this investigation in the near future.
- Write a few lines about the investigation or initiative you wish to undertake and turn this into a question, for example: 'I wish to investigate whether individual support to teach vocabulary learning techniques will help Year 7 SEN pupils to become more confident learners.
- Give your question, but not your background notes, to a colleague and ask them if they understand what you will be investigating. Is the question clear? Can they suggest ways for you to collect data?
- Reformulate your question and suggest ways of collecting the data. (Data are usually collected through observing or talking to participants, through questionnaires, or through analysing documents.)

If you are doing any formal research as part of a higher degree or for an outside funder there will be range of areas to consider and some training will be needed in research methods. Useful sources of information on doing research can be found in the books mentioned at the end of this chapter. Care needs to be taken in designing the research and in building in time and practical methods for analysing the data, so that the results are useful. It is therefore advisable to have a research advisor. This would normally be the case if you are working in a team in your school to examine a school initiative, or if you are working as part of a higher degree.

Introduction to small-scale research methods

If you are undertaking a small-scale piece of practitioner research in order to investigate an area of practice you may find the following helpful. Having precisely framed your research question so that it is clear what it means, you need to answer the following questions (adapted from 'An action research framework' in *Learning To Teach in the Secondary School*, 3rd edition, p. 279):

1   Who has or where are the data needed to answer the question?
2   How much time and what other resources can be devoted to exploring this issue?
3   How are we going to collect the data?
4   When do we need to collect the data?
5   What ethical questions arise from the collection and use of these data?
6   How are we going to analyse and present the data?
7   Are we prepared and able to make changes in the light of the findings?
8   How will we disseminate the findings?

Collecting data

For sociologists and other educational researchers, this choice of method is usually related to their theoretical position or perspective. Those taking a scientific approach use large-scale quantitative methods of collecting data and use this to test a hypothesis. Those taking a more interpretive approach use qualitative methods. However, it is also possible to be methodologically pluralist and use a variety of methods. You should select a small range of methods which complement each other and provide you with as much validity as possible. Having data on the same question coming from two or more sources is good practice, and is known as triangulation.

Here are some methods of collecting data suitable for small-scale educational research:

Qualitative methods

Focus Groups: This involves bringing together a small group of pupils or teachers, in a non-threatening environment, to discuss a selected topic. It could be a whole class or tutor group, but a group of four to 12 is more manageable. The researcher prepares some questions or issues to discuss with the whole group. These provide the opportunity to explore respondents' attitudes, feelings and perceptions. Encouraging a good, lively discussion and utilising the interactions can produce rich data. The focus group can be taped and then transcribed. Focus groups are useful in exploring issues in the early stage of research or to provide ideas for a questionnaire. Successful groups need a good facilitator to draw in those who don't participate and to probe sensitively what people say. It is a good idea if the questions are discussed beforehand with a colleague.

Content analysis: Sociologists use this method to analyse the content of the media. It can also be used in school settings. Feminists have used it, for example, to count the frequency of traditional gender roles in school textbooks. This method allows the researcher to measure or simply add up the frequency of a given message. A coding scheme or a list of categories to look for can be drawn up. This could be used to consider how the language and central concerns of school documents have changed over time (e.g. prospectuses or minutes of meetings).

Participant observation: Your classroom observations have involved this method, i.e. observing and recording pupil interactions in natural settings. You will have kept notes of your observations. Extracts from these notes can be included in your report (e.g. whether or not the disciplinary policy worked in reality, or how group work was organised in different classrooms, or whether or not male pupils dominate classroom interaction). You would need to observe a range of different lessons before making any claims.

Interviews: One or two in-depth interviews with members of staff or students about an issue can produce very interesting data (e.g. how resources can be best employed to develop staff or student ICT skills). You will need a list of open-ended questions to guide you. The interviews can be taped and transcribed. This method can also be useful in exploring issues in the early stage of your research or to provide ideas for a questionnaire.

Diaries: Asking teachers or pupils to keep a record or log of their activities over an agreed period of time can also be a useful source of data. They need to be willing and the instructions need to be very clear. Extracts from the diaries can then be used in your report.

(Adapted from Institute of Education, 2002: 20–1)

Quantitative methods

Statistical analysis: An important source of secondary data is official statistics collected and published by the government. School statistics can be usefully compared to national data (e.g. how General Certificate in Secondary Education [GCSE] pass rates for a range of subjects compare to national figures). Your school can be expected to have mechanisms for providing you with individual pupil achievement data collected over a pupil's school career. These data should enable you to identify underachieving pupils and to closely monitor their progress.

Questionnaires: These can be a useful method of collecting data if you want a larger sample and to generate your own statistics. You need to be clear about exactly what it is you want to find out. This can be done by using some of the above methods at an early stage to discover what the key issues are. This should help you to draw up your questions, which are normally closed to make coding easier. You need to pilot them carefully to make sure they are unambiguous. School registers provide a good sampling frame. Care needs to be taken over the distribution and collection to ensure a good response rate. After coding the data, findings can then be presented. There are software packages to help with the analysis of such data.

What is presented above is a simple account of some research methods. You will need to do more reading before using them effectively. Alongside those methods some teachers have found it useful to keep a diary of how their projects are going, which include musings, reflections and daily interactions which form the background to the research. Keeping this kind of reflective research journal, which later forms the basis of an analytic commentary, can be a useful adjunct to other methods used, as outlined above. The journal forms a narrative of the process of the research. This form of narration can be useful, in conjunction with later critical evaluation and reflection, to gain knowledge and understanding of the processes involved within the complex situation of variables which is your classroom, and within which your research-based understandings have developed (Hiebert *et al.*, 2002).

Ethical issues

It is crucial to consider the ethical issues involved in doing research. Gaining the consent of all those involved and making data anonymous is important. You also need to consider questions of representativeness, reliability and validity. Ethics and professionalism require that researchers are diplomatic, tactful and trustworthy. The following important considerations are based on a professional code of ethics for researchers, developed by the British Psychological Society (1991). There are also specific guidelines for educational research which can be found on the website for the British Educational Research Association (BERA) (http://www.bera.ac.uk).

Issues to consider when researching in the school are:

- relationships between researcher and other teachers, other members of staff, pupils, parents, etc.;
- the importance of evidence/analysis to back up any claim made;
- respect for all who contribute to the research.

These are some guidelines which you must follow:

- treat all information in confidence and do not name anyone, i.e. schools, teachers or pupils. When writing up the results refer to roles, e.g. 'the information and communications technology (ICT) co-ordinator' or anonymise in other ways, e.g. Pupil X, School A;
- negotiate access to participants and observe protocol by speaking to all concerned, such as senior teachers, to gain permission from parents, etc., and get permission first for the project outline;
- involve participants by explaining what you are doing and why, and feed back any results to them when possible. Thank them for their participation. Assure them of confidentiality, i.e. that they will not be named or identified in any way;
- verify all statements you make in the report and on any surveys, etc.;
- think carefully about the audience for your surveys and interviews and make appropriate questions and statements;
- be honest about your purpose;
- show your appreciation for any participation;
- consult within the school if in doubt about procedures.

Keeping a reflective research journal, which later forms the basis of an analytic commentary, can be a useful adjunct to other methods used, as outlined above. The journal forms a narrative of the process of the research. This form of narration can be useful in conjunction with later critical evaluation and reflection, to give more information and insights into the processes involved in the research situation. This situation will encompass a complex of variables in which new understandings have developed (Hiebert *et al.*, 2002).

Good teaching is a result of a process of investigation and reflection and doing some research can benefit your teaching, if you wish to improve in an area, for example, or to implement a new initiative.

ACCESSING RESEARCH AND RESEARCH NETWORKS

To form a firm foundation for a piece of small-scale practitioner research it is advisable to first find out what else is being done in your area. Here the websites mentioned below will be useful. You need to ask what has already been published recently on your initiative. Research the background and the context. You do not need to go into the area in great detail and in many cases this will be evident to you as the topic will arise out of your direct classroom context.

A useful website for networks and partnerships for teachers undertaking research can be found on the Teachernet site (http://www.teachernet.gov.uk/Research/networksand partnerships/). The site points out that collaborating by using or undertaking research with other teachers, schools and LEAs may be useful. For example, it may mean you can check findings from research undertaken in your school against that of others. Networks of teachers interested in research operate in some local authorities and regions and there are links to further networks such as those being developed by the Department for Education and Skills (DfES) through the 14–19 Pathfinders, which started in January 2003 (http:// www.dfes.gov.uk/14-19pathfinders).

The journal *TOPIC*, commissioned and published for many years by the NFER (http:// www.nfer.ac.uk/research/), is dedicated to practitioner research.

There are a number of associations and support networks which give details of education and practitioner research. The URLs for their websites are given at the end of the chapter. They include BERA and the British Educational Leadership, Management and Administration Society, two active national networks which hold annual conferences, where current educational research is presented. Other networks include the Collaborative Action Research Network (CARN) and the Evidence Based Education Network. The National Grid for Learning (NGfL) also provides a list of online educational networks in other countries. Through the European Schoolnet Partner Networks, access to over 20 other national networks is given on the Schoolnet website. The Commonwealth of Learning Electronic Network for Schools and Education also lists school networks in many Commonwealth countries. It is certainly worth exploring these sites if you are undertaking practitioner research.

BEING RESEARCH LITERATE

There are many occasions when your work as a teacher will be based on the findings of educational research, for example if you are implementing a policy on pupils' preferred learning styles you may be referred to the research in the area (see Chapters 5 and 6). As a 'consumer' of research it is important to be able to discriminate and to know that the findings and the recommendations of the research you are using are secure. Brooker and McPherson (1999) have suggested that researchers address the following questions when designing, reading and writing up research:

1   Is there an explanation of the context of the research?
2   Is the researcher's personal position explained?
3   Is the purpose of the research clear?
4   Is the research design clear and relevant?
5   Are the research methods explained adequately?
6   Does the research identify the data sources?
7   Does the researcher make explicit how the data have changed into a credible account of the research?
8   Does the researcher make reasonable suggestions about the applicability of the research?
9   Are there clear suggestions about how the research might be taken forward?
10   Has the research been summarised in the form of a fuzzy generalisation?

The last question is based on a phrase formulated by another writer on educational research, Bassey (1998). This implies that the results carry an element of uncertainty, framed in language such as 'indications show that …' or 'increased use of ICT has a strong correlation with … and might result in …'. The notion that research results are open to question is an important one.

Using these guidelines will help you to critically evaluate the range of factors which can influence the validity of the research, i.e. to understand its value, the impact it might have, its benefits and its limitations. If you engage in your own research, particularly with the support of an experienced research mentor, you will develop your capacity to engage with the methodologies, including an understanding of the applications of different approaches to research from an informed position.

Reflective task 16.3
Evaluating a research project

Choose a research report on an area which interests you. You can access reports on some of the websites given above. You might want to look at some of the short reports from the Teacher Training Agency (TTA) Best Practice Research Scholarships, which are action research reports written by practising teachers, published on the Best Practice Research Scholarship (DfES) website (http://www.teachernet.gov.uk/professionaldevelopment/resourcesandresearch/bprs/)

Apply the Brooker and McPherson criteria (outlined above) to the report. Can you tell whether the research gave valid and reliable results? Is the quality of the report indicative of the quality of the research?

TEACHING AS AN EVIDENCE-BASED PRACTICE

Teaching is a practice, which has a body of theory and research underpinning it. The practice changes to accommodate changing circumstances, and policy and theory are promulgated to promote change. The need for change and the characteristics of the new practices should be based on evidence, i.e. capable of being justified in a way that stands up to scrutiny according to the criteria outlined above (Best, 2002). The promotion of teaching as an evidence-based practice is a development of the late 1990s, following the practice in medicine. Since the early 1990s there has been a database of evidence-based practice in medicine, called the Cochrane Foundation. This is an online resource which consists of reviews of already existing research in the field of medicine and health care, under key topics. This database can be accessed by practitioners, who can search for key terms on an area in which they need up-to-date information. This gives them access to what are known as systematic reviews of all the relevant research in their topic, giving them an overview of the issues and the current state of understanding of the area under investigation. The reviews are done by leading authorities.

The analogy between education and medicine, as practices similar enough to warrant an analogous approach to research, was most famously made by David Hargreaves in the 1996 inaugural lecture of the TTA. Here he stated that educational research, at the time he was speaking, was poor value for money in terms of improving the quality of education provided in schools (Hargreaves, 1996: 1).

He criticised educational research on several counts. He said that:

1   It is usually done in isolated portions, i.e. it is 'non-cumulative', unlike medical research which builds on previous evidence.
2   It is of little relevance to improving classroom practice.
3   It is often partisan, taking place in a context of methodological controversies which only interest academics.
4   There is a great deal of second-rate research, which does not make a serious contribution to fundamental theory or knowledge.

The Hargreaves lecture was seen as an onslaught on academic educational research. He wanted to situate the focus of functional knowledge about education within schools, with the practitioners themselves, on the analogy with medical research. There is a debate about whether teaching is like medicine and a further debate about how to give teachers the skills and the time to access the research (Hammersely, 1997). However, as a new teacher you are in a better position than previous generations of teachers, both to access educational research and to undertake research on your own practice or an area of school-wide practice. There is much good educational research to inform your work as a teacher and convenient means of accessing the information.

FUNDED INITIATIVES

The education section of the Evidence for Policy and Practice Information and Co-ordinating Centre (the EPPI-Centre) was set up in 2000 in the Social Sciences Research Unit, within the University of London Institute of Education. The EPPI-Centre is currently engaged on creating systematic reviews that are pieces of research in their own right. They have a particular emphasis on 'user involvement'. Depending on the research review, users could include parents, teachers and other school staff, governors, LEAs and policy makers. These users 'can be involved in the development of research strategies, the review protocols, the reviews, and their effective dissemination' (Torgerson *et al.*, 2001). Further information is available on the EPPI-Centre's website (http//:www.eppi.ioe.ac.uk/).

The EPPI-Centre is not the only centre aiming to produce high-quality systematic reviews, based on the Cochrane model. The Campbell Collaboration (http://www.campbell. gse.upenn.edu/) is beginning a similar programme in the fields of crime and social welfare.

> The goal of the international Campbell Collaboration is to produce, disseminate, and continuously update systematic reviews for students of the effectiveness of social and behavioural interventions, including education interventions. The object is to produce systematic reviews of evidence that are useful to policy makers, practitioners and the public … This is to ensure that high quality information on what works, what does not work, and what is promising is readily accessible to people who must make decisions – policy makers, practitioners, and the public.
> (Boruch *et al.*, 2001: 1)

Systematic reviews should provide information useful to a wide range of users, who will be able to learn about the major issues in a topic of interest, where the relevant research had been done and what the main findings were. Until a range of systematic reviews of this kind exist and are easily accessible, anyone wishing to access the research which underlies educational policies and strategies has to rely on the guidance given by 'authorities' (e.g. the Qualifications and Curriculum Authority [QCA], TTA, Department for Education and Employment [DfEE] and the Office for Standards in Education [OFSTED]). Alternatively she needs access to a first rate education library and also needs time for the task. Practitioners currently have to rely on statements such as 'research shows that …', without being able to see which research, nor to place the research in the context of debate and discussion. The British Library offers a service in providing research articles which is available to all, and texts can be ordered through local libraries, so those who wish to keep up to date should be able to do so.

Teacher Research Panel (DfES and TTA)

Following on David Hargreaves's speech the TTA set up the Teacher Research Panel to provide a way for teachers to be nationally involved in promoting and developing teaching as a research and evidence-based profession. The teachers on the panel were able to comment on research which is of direct use to teachers and on dissemination methods which enable that research to reach teachers and to routinely seek clarification and evaluation of the sources of research.

SUMMARY

This chapter has pointed to some of the benefits of becoming research literate. This term implies understanding the range of relevant research and some of the criteria for judging good from bad research. A brief overview of the context and methods of action/practitioner research has been outlined, with a guide to some areas for further development. It is always advisable to seek the support of a research mentor and to read further and some suggestions are given at the end of the chapter.

The importance of understanding what the term 'research- and evidence-informed practice' and the notion of 'research capacity' have been outlined. A brief overview has been given of some of the new developments in this area and the range of websites available. Using research to further your own practice as a teacher, both to inform and to develop your practice, is now more than ever a possibility and there are a variety of ways in which you will be able to take this further in the coming years.

FURTHER READING

Bell, J. (1993) *Doing your Research Project: A Guide for First time Researchers in Education and Social Sciences*, 2nd edition. Buckingham: Open University Press. This book is designed for those who are undertaking small-scale research projects. It provides a good basic introduction to educational research.

Pring, R. (2000) *Philosophy of Educational Research*. London and New York: Continuum. The book discusses key issues in the philosophy of educational research. Chapter 6, on action research and practitioner research, is particularly recommended.

Robson, C. (1993) *Real World Research: A Resource for Social Scientists and Practitioner-Researchers*. Oxford and Cambridge, MA: Blackwell. An excellent and comprehensive book which can be a self-study guide to research methods for practitioners or, as the author says in his introductory recommendations: 'alternatively you could jump straight in and use it more as a "how to" cook book'.

Scott, D. (2000) *Reading Educational Research and Policy*. London and New York: Routledge Falmer. If you are interested in sharpening your ability to read research critically, this is a readable and accessible book.

The websites mentioned in text are:

Best Practice Research Scholarship (DfES) website at http://www.dfee.gov.uk/bprs/index.cfm.

British Educational Leadership, Management and Administration Society at http://www.shu.ac.uk/bemas.

British Educational Research Association (BERA) at http://www.bera.ac.uk.

Collaborative Action Research Network(CARN) at http://www.did.stu.mmu.ac.uk/carn/

Commonwealth of Learning Electronic Network for Schools and Education at http://www.col.org/cense/school.htm.

Evidence for Policy and Practice Information and Co-ordinating Centre (EPPI-Centre) at http://www.eppi.ioe.ac.uk/.

European Schoolnet Partner Networks at http://www.eun.org/eun.org2/eun/countries/countries.html.

Evidence-Based Education Network at http://www.cemcentre.org/ebeuk/default.asp.

National Grid for Learning (NGfL) at http://www.ngfl.gov.uk/.

National Foundation for Educational Research (NFER) at http://www.nfer.ac.uk/research/

Pathfinders at http://www.dfes.gov.uk/14-19pathfinders.

Teachernet at http://www.teachernet.gov.uk/Research/networksandpartnerships/.

17 Continuing Professional Development

Norbert Pachler and Kit Field

WHY SHOULD TEACHERS ENGAGE IN CONTINUING PROFESSIONAL DEVELOPMENT?

We live in a fast changing world. One purpose underpinning teaching must surely be to help to prepare pupils for future adult life. Proponents of lifelong learning rightly recognise that reaching adulthood does not signal the end of learning. As Etienne Wenger (1999: 11) succinctly puts it: 'Learners will inherit the earth. Knowers will find that they inhabit a world that no longer exists.' Change in the world of education and beyond is constant and inevitable.

As a professional, you need to keep up to date with evolving policy agendas as well as fundamental changes in your work environments such as those brought about by developments in technology. For example, until the 1990s the internet was still an unknown quantity in the educational context, until the late 1980s there existed no National Curriculum in England and Wales and in the early 1980s computers had only just started to appear in classrooms. It seems sensible, therefore, to expect that before long there will be other significant changes in the world of education which will require fundamental changes in your professional practice. Continuing professional development (CPD) is an important way of managing the process of keeping in tune with such developments.

Effective schools are increasingly thought of as learning organisations (Senge, 1990; Hargreaves, 1999). It is, therefore, incumbent upon you, as a teacher, to be and remain a learner throughout your career. If you have high expectations of your learners, the suggestion is that you should model good practice and engage in systematic learning yourself.

There are three main reasons why you should maintain your own professional learning throughout your career. These are:

- to contribute to your own level of competence, understanding, job satisfaction and career development;
- to make a positive contribution to improving the quality of learning of your learners, and consequently the work of the institution as a whole;
- to help the education service keep pace with societal change, and to create an education service which is attractive and of benefit to all stakeholders including, importantly, the profession itself.

We discuss these three reasons in this chapter.

OBJECTIVES

This chapter seeks to:

- provide an overview of the impact of government policy and initiatives in relation to CPD;
- discuss why, as a teacher, you should engage in CPD;
- raise awareness of some of the CPD opportunities available;
- provide a possible framework for identifying professional development needs and planning professional learning opportunities.

HISTORICAL BACKGROUND

In England,

> ... continuous professional development has all too often been little more than an eclectic and unrelated assortment of in-service training events, narrowly focussed on frequently changing policy initiatives and externally imposed agendas, pieced together reactively by individual teachers in response to extrinsic priorities rather than sought out proactively according to intrinsic training needs. In other words, the notion of *training* has prevailed which tended to be informed by the need to seek information about how to comply with changes in legislation or demands made by school development plans rather than gain a deeper understanding of issues concerning subject pedagogy or pupil learning. Significant and frequent changes to the educational landscape have meant that there has been little time for teacher professional learning about embedding new approaches, techniques, skills, knowledge, understanding and/or insights into personal practice.
>
> (Pachler *et al.*, 2003: 9)

Other countries will have a different history of CPD to look back on but in view of international demands towards stronger accountability, governments and their agencies increasingly expect there to be a direct link between CPD and the quality of teaching and learning in schools. Whilst it is of course very legitimate for government to expect value for money, we are less sure whether effectiveness necessarily always and only manifests itself in such tangible and relatively easily measurable ways. CPD and professional learning should not only equip you to interpret and respond to the changing demands of practice but should also equip you to exercise your professional judgement in informed and creative ways. Professional learning should also, and maybe even predominantly, be seen as a means for you to rejuvenate your practice, to expand your professional repertoire, increase your self-esteem, self-confidence and enthusiasm for teaching or, for example, your level of criticality and, thereby, achieve enhanced job satisfaction.

There appears to be an increasing realisation on the part of governments that the ability to cope with new initiatives in a climate of continuous change is key to teacher effectiveness, however narrowly or broadly defined.

> Encouragingly, the focus of recent (UK) government policy can be seen to be on strengthening teachers' pedagogical skills, developing their phase- and subject-specific expertise and enabling them to experience the challenges of working across different types of schools through networking and collaboration, to engage in research and enquiry into teaching and learning processes and to begin to develop leadership capacity.
>
> (Pachler *et al.*, 2003: 10)

THE TEACHER'S PERSPECTIVE

Keeping up to date

New methodologies and knowledge are regularly published in professional, academic journals and specialist literature and form the backbone of most higher education advanced courses, and the opportunity to develop and draw on practitioners' interpretations of theory are available, for example, through reading professional journals. New technologies allow easy access to online networks such as Lingu@Net,[1] a discussion list for British modern linguists, and can provide easy access to numerous online journals and articles: see e.g. your subject association, the British Educational Research Association (http://www.bera.org.uk)[2] and the American Educational Research Association (http://www.aera.org), as well as examples of good professional practice, available for instance on the British Educational Communications and Technology Agency's (BECTA's) Virtual Teacher Centre.[3] These all should assist you in developing new practices and ideas. Pupils' out-of-school learning[4] is encouraged and, as a teacher, you are rightly seen more and more as a manager of learning, rather than a mere 'deliverer' of curriculum content.

Motivation and job satisfaction

Learning and teaching are increasingly complex activities, and as new ideas 'hit' the agenda, you have to be ready to 'respond'. A reactive mode is clearly undesirable from the point of view of an extended professional (see Hoyle, 1975) and that is why the development of 'educational literacy' can be seen to be key. In this respect, CPD, like school development, is about capacity building. Moon (2000) notes the benefits of CPD in terms of the enhancement of performance through improved self-esteem. A sense of professional control and personal well-being can be seen to be essential ingredients in job satisfaction.

In order to ensure continued job satisfaction and professional fulfilment, certain types of CPD, in particular participation in award-bearing higher education institute courses, can be particularly valuable and important mechanisms to allow for intellectual development of teachers as well as for analytical and, if necessary, critical engagement with prevailing educational policy leading to a 'healthy' sense of professional agency. It can also lead to an increased willingness of teachers to participate actively in the development of a shared body of professional knowledge rather than a reliance on 'prescribed' knowledge, and, in so doing, teachers develop their own professional identity.

Planning your career path

In the English system, promotion may be dependent in part on the provision of evidence of attainment (and, of course, performance) in relation to national benchmarks and individually negotiated targets. Performance management[5] procedures facilitate self-auditing in relation to national/external standards, target setting and the provision of evidence of professional learning and development. National benchmark data in relation to school effectiveness and pupil performance[6] are being used to quantify the impact of personal professional development as well as that of learners and the school. Engagement and impact, however problematic such measures may be, are seen as a mark of professional competence and CPD is seen by government as a means of increasing teacher and, in turn, systemic effectiveness. In view of this you will need to consider how to collect evidence of and monitor your pupils' achievement over time.

CPD as a professional obligation

Funding may be available through your school and/or local/regional/central government for your individual professional development, and accountability procedures often demand that evidence of participation in, and impact of, your CPD is borne in mind. The demonstration of the fulfilment of national standards during initial training and the induction year in England is a requirement for entering the profession, and only those who have attained the national standards for headteachers through a national professional qualification for headteachers (NPQH)[7] will be able to apply for headship posts.

It is important, therefore, to ensure that CPD activities which you undertake not only relate to your needs and wants in relation, for example, to developing aspects of your subject knowledge, but also to any standards to which you aspire such as, for example, subject leadership. In this way CPD is one means by which you can get greater professional fulfilment and prepare yourself for future promotion.

The notion of CPD as an implicit obligation need not be viewed negatively. Bolam (1986, 1993), for instance, concedes that CPD can serve both the individual and the 'system' (e.g. the teachers and the school/government) at the same time. The key is for us, as teachers, to be proactive, and to respect key principles underpinning CPD. In the context of the CPD strategy for England, these principles include the views that:

* there is a sense of teacher ownership and a shared commitment to, and responsibility for, development (by teachers and schools);
* professional development should be centred on raising standards;
* development opportunities should match different needs;
* new and innovative ways of using time and resources for CPD should be sought;

- information and communications technology (ICT) should be central to CPD;
- planning and evaluation are essential components of CPD; and
- good practice should be shared and disseminated, using ICT.

(Adapted from DfEE 2001: 24)

THE SCHOOL PERSPECTIVE

There is no doubt that CPD can be, and is, used as a management tool.

Accountability

Rhodes and Houghton-Hill (2000) note that CPD is being used by many school leaders to help teachers deal with change prescribed by policy and legislation. Schools in most countries are indeed more accountable today than ever before. In England, the publication of test and examination performance data in the form of league tables, the public access to Office for Standards in Education (OFSTED) reports, the need to meet published targets and to report annually to the parent body are all examples of the type of accountability procedures faced by schools. Therefore, for teachers in England, CPD must inevitably be seen in this context. Teachers' development activities can legitimately be seen to have to make a positive impact on pupil learning and, thereby, on school performance.

Performance management

Pollard (2002) recognises participation in CPD activity as an essential part of the performance management cycle. As a consequence of increased accountability, teachers in many countries are expected to meet clear performance targets, which on the one hand will – and should – be relevant to pupils' learning, and, on the other, will be relevant to personal professional targets, which will, in turn, be expected to relate to priorities contained within the school's development plan.

The school as a location for CPD

'… teachers who collaborate, learn together, share ideas and model best practice are more likely to remain in teaching. They feel valued and supported in their development and in their work' (General Teaching Council for England [GTCE], 2003: 3). Given the large number of schools and teachers it is, at times, financially more feasible to locate CPD in schools. Professional development needs to involve a considerable amount of practical application and evaluation of new methods and approaches. Arguably, a strong practice-orientation is important in order for CPD to be 'effective', i.e. to bring about personal and professional learning.

The draft GTCE professional learning framework (2002), for example, proposed that teachers can expect to learn from and with colleagues in a range of ways; these, according to the GTCE, include:

- working within a learning or study team, perhaps with advice and guidance from a tutor;
- team teaching and planning;
- being mentored;
- observing demonstration lessons;
- attending 'masterclasses';
- close study and evaluation of lessons with colleagues;
- being coached by a peer or more experienced colleague for specific areas of development;
- participating in whole-school or team collaborative inquiry and problem-solving;
- planning and assessing with others;
- developing resources and ideas with colleagues.

Day (1999) is categorical that a school's greatest asset is its teaching staff, and that, therefore, the school must make CPD opportunities available for teacher learning and to assist in the development of a capacity for learning and change amongst the staff. This is, however, not to belittle the value of the contribution that can be made, for example, by higher education advanced courses, which often enable you to engage with important conceptual and theoretical frameworks, to develop informed criticality as well as to act as mediators of access to professional networks of teachers working in other schools.

Ethos and culture

Capacity building is not just about providing access and resources. As Day (1999) notes, the school as an institution must display a predilection for lifelong learning if the staff are to keep pace with societal and technological change. This means linking personal professional learning with school development, to focus on pedagogy and pupil learning and not on the 'delivery' or 'transmission' of curriculum content. Invariably, curriculum knowledge is always in danger of becoming obsolete before pupils can apply it in adult life if, indeed, it ever had such currency in the first place. An important emphasis, therefore, needs to be placed on learning strategies. As a professional working within an educational institution, you have a big role to play in contributing to this culture and ethos.

Schools that take themselves seriously as learning organisations will want their staff to participate in CPD for many reasons and such schools will want them to be successful in their work. A positive attitude of staff towards CPD, in turn, will help the school perform towards the benchmarks it has to achieve. Through a positive engagement with CPD both parties will gain.

THE GOVERNMENT'S PERSPECTIVE

Recruitment

Professional learning and development is motivating for teachers, especially when it is acknowledged and rewarded. At a time when the recruitment and retention of teachers is very challenging, CPD is increasingly used as a way of attracting graduates to and keeping them in the profession. Recent research (National Foundation for Education Research [NFER], 2000) confirms that effective CPD requires a long-term commitment by teachers.

Retention

Some schools unashamedly use CPD as a means of retaining teachers. Some schools demand that teachers commit themselves to staying at their school whilst following long-term MA-level courses and programmes (part)funded by the school. Early professional development is undoubtedly being used as a tool for teacher recruitment and retention and you might well want to find out what, if any, professional development opportunities a school is able to offer you when applying for a job there. In addition, opportunities may also be funded through regional or national initiatives.

Compulsory CPD

In Scotland all teachers now have a requirement to undertake 35 hours of CPD a year written into their contracts. CPD is, therefore, effectively compulsory and needs to be demonstrable, for example in portfolio form.

Embedding target setting and accountability measures

The 'Chartered Teacher' status in Scotland[8] is linked to the attainment of higher education accreditation and yields long-term financial benefits through salary enhancements.

In summary of what has been said so far, part of being a professional, we would argue, is to take control of your own professional development (see also Dreyfus and Dreyfus, 1986). CPD is essential for teachers. A positive attitude towards it is motivating and rewarding. And CPD is not purely a way of developing oneself; it can also be a means by which schools evolve and develop and the government ensures central requirements are implemented.

CPD: SOME TYPES AND ISSUES

Towards a definition of CPD

One important question in the context of the present discussion invariably is: what counts as professional development? In its CPD strategy (DFEE, 2001: 3), the UK government provides the following definition: 'By "professional development" we mean any activity that increases the skills, knowledge or understanding of teachers, and their effectiveness in schools.' Beyond the already noted fixation with 'effectiveness', the new paradigm tries to move teachers away from individual, unrelated in-service teacher education (INSET) events and towards in-house activities.

In-house activities versus wider professional networks

Despite their manifest strengths and appeal, a potential weakness of in-house activities is the narrow model of professional learning and reflection sometimes implicit in it.

In-house activities can cut teachers off from the considerable advantages to be had from accessing wider professional networks of teachers working in diverse contexts. As we have noted above, new technologies can offer considerable potential in supporting in-house activities and in overcoming barriers of time and space for professional networking. Other opportunities for sustained networking (i.e. networks which afford a certain stability over time) can be had by attending courses organised for teachers in a locality or by subject associations. Further networking and funding opportunities such as teacher exchange and school linking programmes or attendance at international courses are available for UK teachers through the British Council.[9]

In-house activities can tend to be based on a particular notion of reflective practice, namely one that remains self-referential and devoid of a wider conceptual and theoretical basis. Despite the ubiquitous presence of notions of reflection in the teacher education and training discourse (and many laudable and generally useful attempts to make distinctions within the given concept – 'reflection in action', 'reflection on action' and so on), without recourse to relevant external sources including, importantly, professional and academic background reading, reflection is in danger of remaining a rather empty concept, 'for it is hopeless for those with responsibility for leading professional development simply to urge practitioners to reflect, reflect again, reflect more and reflect deeper' (Pachler *et al.*, 2003: 13). This 'caricature' serves to illustrate how empty a position can be that denies a body of learned knowledge that could inform and refine professional thinking (see also Lawes, 2003). Exposure to, and engagement with, relevant background literature can, therefore, be seen to be one very important CPD activity for us to engage in throughout our careers. Chapter 16, 'Using research to inform your teaching', provides advice about how to access research and evidence relevant to teaching.

Extended professionalism and professionality

Linda Evans, in the introduction to an article in the *Oxford Review of Education* (2002: 123), charts her own development from practitioner to researcher thus:

> I operated at an intuitive level, with very little rationality underpinning my work. I considered educational theory to be entirely irrelevant to classroom practice. I attended in-service courses – but only those of a practical nature – and I was not in the least bit interested in undertaking long, award-bearing courses.

Whilst unable to pinpoint exactly what triggered her transformation, she is inclined to attribute it to the influence of key colleagues with a more extended notion of professionality and she goes on to note that:

> I left teaching because I felt frustrated and constrained by the irrationality which underpinned most of the decision-making in the schools where I worked and because the values and educational ideologies that I held were seldom shared by colleagues.

This clearly underlines the importance of schools perceiving of themselves as learning organisations and of investment of time and money in a broad range of CPD to ensure the recruitment and retention of high-quality professionals.

Drawing on the seminal work of Eric Hoyle (1975) in defining the concept of 'teacher development', Evans distinguishes between the notions of 'professionalism' and 'professionality', with the former being concerned with status-related elements of teachers' work and the latter with those which constitute the knowledge, skills and procedures teachers use in their work. Evans defines professionality as (2002: 130) 'an ideologically-, attitudinally-, intellectually- and epistemologically-based stance on the part of an individual, in relation to the practice of the profession to which s/he belongs, and which influences her/his practice'.

The process of teachers developing such a stance, in our view, is an important function of CPD.

Entitlement to professional learning

The GTCE professional learning framework for teachers delineates the following aspects of teachers' entitlement to professional learning (2003: 6):

- have time to engage in sustained reflection and structured learning;
- create learning opportunities from everyday practice such as planning and assessing for learning;
- develop their ability to identify their own learning and development needs and those of others;
- develop an individual learning plan;
- have school-based learning, as well as course participation, recognised for accreditation;
- develop self-evaluation, observation and peer review skills;
- develop mentoring and coaching skills and their ability to offer professional dialogue and feedback; and
- plan their longer-term career aspirations.

This list of opportunities in our view offers a very useful baseline for the development of professionality in teachers of all subjects (and phases).

Teachers and researchers: educational research literacy

In recent years there has been a tendency towards trying to inform policy decisions and professional practice at all levels of governance by a secure evidence base (see, e.g. Pachler, 2003). Consequently, teaching has been promoted as an evidence-based profession. In order to achieve this goal, arguably teachers need to possess not only so-called 'educational literacy', i.e. the ability to read and critically engage with educational texts of all descriptions and sorts, but also 'educational research literacy', i.e. the ability to systematically gather evidence and data about learning and teaching (see, e.g. Pachler, 2003). In order to achieve extended professionalism as teachers we need to develop research capacity to carry out practice-based enquiries and teacher research. The GTCE provides a very useful service in the form of the 'Research of the Month' website[10] where you can find a series of research summaries on topics of direct interest to practising teachers. For (funding) opportunities for UK teachers, visit for example, the DfES TeacherNet website.[11]

Accredited CPD

Study towards an award-bearing course continues to be a popular option for many teachers, particularly in view of a new, practice-oriented type of higher degree course that is emerging. For details about award-bearing CPD programmes, contact the higher education provider(s) of your choice.

IDENTIFYING PROFESSIONAL DEVELOPMENT NEEDS AND PLANNING PROFESSIONAL LEARNING OPPORTUNITIES

Newly or recently qualified teachers will be familiar with a portfolio approach to demonstrate evidence against external standards. By completing a career entry and development profile,[12] teachers in England and Wales should be comfortable using evidence to identify personal strengths and aspects of teaching that require further attention. This reflects an approach to identifying needs, planning personal professional development and providing the evidence of successful completion of learning and development, which is suggested in Field's (2002) *Portfolio of Professional Development*. Portfolios should be more than a collection of artefacts and evidence. Importantly, they need to include critical reflection clarifying why individual pieces were chosen and what learning they evidence as well as to foreground progress reflecting the nature and impact of professional development. There is a range of purposes for and external criteria against which portfolios could be used. In each case the reflective/critical narrative accompanying the evidence will need to be adapted to suit each framework. The external sets of criteria include the following:

Professional standards framework

UK government and its agencies as well as the National Association of Inspectors and Educational Consultants have published a raft of standards which provide some clarity in terms of job specifications and expectations. Blandford (2000: 66) notes their purposes:

- to establish clear and explicit expectations;
- to help set targets for professional development and career progression;
- to help focus and improve training and staff development at national, local and school levels;
- to recognise the expertise required of effective headteachers and teachers in school.

The standards for each 'position' enable teachers to audit their own qualities, skills and attributes, and to choose CPD opportunities by building on personal strengths and addressing perceived developmental needs. Use of the standards framework provides one means to plan in a more long-term manner. Standards exist for teachers at various stages of their careers.[13]

The general teaching councils (GTCs)

Separate general teaching councils exist for England, Wales, Scotland and Northern Ireland as well as other (English speaking) countries. In the UK context, as self-regulatory professional bodies, GTCs all have similar missions. They seek to raise the status of teaching and teachers in society by promoting high standards of professional practice and conduct by teachers and to provide independent, representative and authoritative advice to government and advocacy about teaching to relevant stakeholders and the general public. They, too, provide a powerful mechanism for professional networking.

As we noted above, the GTC for England (2003) recently developed a framework which spells out what it deems to constitute CPD. Teachers can use the framework to plan their CPD in relation to personal professional development needs, and evaluate the learning and development which occurs. The GTCE intends that the framework resonates with the professional standards framework as well as the qualifications framework offered by higher education institutions.

Higher education qualifications framework

Many teachers follow MA-degree courses and other award-bearing programmes in education and related topics. The link between professional development and academic qualifications is becoming stronger as professional bodies are increasingly seeking academic accreditation for teachers' engagement with their own 'frameworks'. In this way it is possible to use day-to-day professional experiences as a basis for study.

PUTTING TOGETHER A PORTFOLIO

In Chapter 1 the advantages of keeping a professional development portfolio (PDP) were outlined and the process of keeping one was developed. The PDP is an important vehicle in your continuing professional development. At one level it may be used to demonstrate that targets set through the performance management cycle have been addressed and met. On another level the portfolio can be used for promotional purposes in the form of a record of professional achievement. The portfolio may also be used as a basis for study at MA level or as a means of demonstrating progress and development in relation to a CPD framework.

Field's (2002) *Portfolio of Professional Development* is designed to serve a multiplicity of purposes, on the understanding that the accompanying critical reflection would need to be adapted to suit the particular purpose. The process recommended by Field (2002), for example, consists of nine steps as outlined in Table 17.1.

For other models of professional development portfolios see, for example, Jones (2001).

Table 17.1 Steps in planning your portfolio of professional development

Step	Purpose
Self-audit	To identify strengths and weaknesses, for example, in relation to the relevant set of standards, can act as starting point for professional development and learning.
Initial statement	To articulate and make known to senior staff career aspirations and ambitions facilitates the planning of appropriate development activities.
Identifying professional development targets	The purpose of this step is to link need and aspirations to identifiable and demonstrable intended outcomes.
Planning learning and development opportunities	Planning learning involves the identification of learning and development activities. To maximise the learning outcomes you are encouraged to identify your own preferred learning style.
Writing a personal professional development plan	The personal professional development plan enables the marrying of perceived need to preferred ways of attaining higher standards; it also provides the means for demonstrating and sharing aspects of good practice.
Chronicling professional development activities	This step suggests a way of logging participation in planned development activities, and provides a means of gathering evidence of participation.
Implementing changes and improvement plans	Professional learning is worthless unless it leads to a change and/or development in practice.
Evaluating change and/or improvement	This step involves reflecting upon personal professional learning experiences over an extended period of time.
Measuring the 'impact' of change and/or improvement projects	All professional development activities should – directly and/or indirectly – lead to a positive impact on learners. This step involves showing how personal professional learning has enabled the achievement of pre-stated targets which may include improved pupil performance

Source: Adapted from Field (2002: 19–20).

Although CPD for teachers is presented as an entitlement, it is fast becoming a professional obligation. You are recommended to plan your own professional learning and development as a way of securing a sense of professional autonomy and control. By gathering evidence of planning, implementing and evaluating personal professional development, as teachers, we are able to increase our job satisfaction, and make it known to others that we have made significant professional progress.

**Reflective task 17.1
Planning your CPD**

Find out what opportunities for CPD are available to you through your school and through contacting your regional and national education authorities. These will often be advertised on organisations' websites. Check how these opportunities are accessed and when applications should be made. Add this information to your professional development portfolio as outlined in Table 17.1.

CONCLUSION

In this chapter we have tried to outline briefly, in the context of changing policy, some of the reasons why, as a newly or recently qualified teacher (although this applies equally to more experienced teachers), you need to engage in CPD and teacher learning. We have outlined some of the wide range of CPD opportunities available including ones more and less closely linked to prevailing policies and priorities of the day. We argued that CPD should involve at least some element of personal professional choice and that, unless we are prepared to identify, plan for and actively pursue our professional development needs, we are likely to remain restricted in our professionality, are unlikely to fulfil our professional potential and will be less well able to adapt to an ever-changing educational landscape.

NOTES

1   See http://www.linguanet.org.uk/.
2   All URLs listed in this chapter were available at the time of writing.
3   See http://vtc.ngfl.gov.uk/.
4   For useful advice on organising school trips for pupils, see e.g.
    http://education.guardian.co.uk/Print/0,3858,4637280,00.html and
    http://education.guardian.co.uk/Print/0,3858,4637280,00.html.
5   See http://www.teachernet.gov.uk/management/payandperformance/
    performancemanagement/.
6   See http://www.standards.dfes.gov.uk/performance/.
7   See http://www.ncsl.org.uk/index.cfm?pageid=18. In Scotland there exists a Scottish
    Professional Qualification for Headteachers.
8   See http://www.ctprogrammescotland.org.uk/.
9   See http://www.britishcouncil.org/education/teachers/.
10 See http://www.gtce.org.uk/research/romhome.asp.
11 See http://www.teachernet.gov.uk/professionaldevelopment/opportunities/.
12 See http://www.tta.gov.uk/teaching/induction/cedp.htm.
13 See e.g. http://www.tta.gov.uk/teaching/standards/.

FURTHER READING

Blandford, S. (2002) *Professional Development Manual*. London: Prentice Hall. This loose-leaf file is aimed at supporting those who mange professional development in schools. It provides clear guidance of what constitutes professional development, and how teachers' personal experiences can be galvanised to assist in the development of the school, as well as individuals within it. The work provides straightforward guidance and explanations of the funding, resourcing and administrative details that surround professional development.

Bolam, R. (2000) 'Emerging policy trends: some implications for continuing professional development', *Journal of In-Service Education*, 26(2): 267–80. This journal article provides a political context for developments in CPD. Bolam has identified shifting trends in how teachers have been encouraged through legislation and practice to develop professionally. This socio-political study enables teachers to locate their own development within a broader context. This level of understanding assists teachers to gain a sense of intellectual control of their development.

Evans, L. (2002) 'What is teacher development?', *Oxford Review of Education*, 28(1):123–37. This article explores and clarifies the concept of teacher development by presenting some interpretations and definitions.

Field, K. (2002) *Portfolio of Professional Development: Structuring and Recording Teachers Career Development*. London: Optimus Publishing. This photocopiable file enables teachers at all stages of their career to undertake an audit against relevant national standards and to identify their own preferred professional learning style. Teachers are encouraged to plan and implement a personal professional development plan and to generate evidence of participation and impact for performance management purposes. The file contains templates and examples, and also contains theoretical underpinning.

Moon, B., Butcher, J. and Bird, E. (eds) (2000) *Leading Professional Development in Education*. London: RoutledgeFalmer and Open University. This edited text contains chapters which place different professional learning and development approaches in a broader context. It offers a theoretical and historical account of how evidence-based practice and the concepts of collaboration have emerged in more recent years. Comparisons are made with other public service professions, and how lessons can be learnt from these similar but different experiences. Consideration is given to interactive technology as a professional learning and development tool.

Appendix 1
Useful addresses and websites

GOVERNMENT OFFICES AND OTHER RESPONSIBLE BODIES

Department for Education and Skills
(DfES)
Sanctuary Buildings
Great Smith Street
London SW1P 3BT
Telephone: 0870 001 2345
URL: http://www.dfes.gov.uk

Department for Education and Skills
(DfES) Publications
PO Box 5050
Sherwood Park
Annesley
Nottinghamshire NG15 0DJ
Telephone: 0845 6055 5650
e-mail: dfes@prolog.uk.com

Department of Education for Northern
Ireland
Rathgael House
Balloo Road
Bangor
Co Down BT19 7PR
Telephone: 028 9127 9279
URL: http://www.deni.gov.uk

Her Majesty's Inspectorate for Education
and Training in Wales (OHMCI)
Anchor Court
East Moors Industrial Estate
Ocean Park
Cardiff CF24 5JW

HM Inspectorate for Education in
Scotland
see web addresses

Learning and Skills Development Agency
Regent Arcade House
19–25 Argyll Street
London W1F 7LS

Office of National Statistics
1 Drummond Gate
London SW1V 2QQ
Telephone: 0845 601 3034
URL http://www.statistics.gov.uk

Office for Standards in Education
(OFSTED)
Alexandria House
33 Kingsway
London WC2B 6SE
Telephone: 020 7421 6800
URL: http://www.ofsted.gov.uk

Qualifications and Curriculum Authority
(QCA)
283 Piccadilly
London W1J 8QA
Telephone: 020 7509 5555
URL: http://www.qca.org.uk/index.asp

Awdurdod Cymwysterau, Cwricwlwm ac
Asesu Cymru (ACCAC)
Qualifications, Curriculum and
Assessment Authority for Wales
Castle Buildings
Womanby
Cardiff CF10 1SX
Telephone: 029 2037 5400
URL: http://www.accac.org.uk/
english.html

Scottish Consultative Council on the
Curriculum (Scottish CCC)
Gardyne Road
Boughty Ferry
Dundee DD5 1NY
Telephone: 01382 455 053
URL: http://www.sccc.org.uk

Scottish Executive Education Department
Victoria Quay
Leith
Edinburgh EH6 6QQ
Telephone: 0131 556 8400
URL: http://www.scotland.gov.uk/
topics/?pageID=45

Teacher Training Agency (TTA)
Portland House
Stag Place
London SW1E 5TT
Telephone: 020 7925 3700
URL: http://www.tta.gov.uk

Wales Office Education Department
National Assembly for Wales
Cathays Park
Cardiff CF1 3NQ
Telephone: 029 2082 3207
URL: http://www.wales.learning.gov.uk

ASSESSMENT BODIES

*In England there are now three major unitary
awarding bodies, formed by merging a number of
examination boards. They offer both academic
and vocational qualifications. They are:*

Assessment and Qualifications Alliance
(AQA)
Stag Hill House
Guildford
Surrey GU2 7XJ
Telephone: 01483 506506
URL: http://www.aqa.org.uk

EDEXCEL
Stewart House
32 Russell Square
London WC1B 5DN
Telephone: 020 7393 4500
URL: http://www.edexcel.org.uk

Oxford and Cambridge Regional (OCR)
1 Regent Street
Cambridge
Cambridgeshire CB2 1GG
Telephone: 01223 552552
URL: http://www.ocr.org.uk

OTHER AWARDING BODIES

*NOTE: Awarding bodies provide copies of
syllabuses, past examination papers, and reports
by subject; some also produce support materials,
particularly for teaching GCE A level:*

City and Guilds of the London Institute
1 Giltspur Street
London EC1A 9DD
Telephone: 020 7294 2800
URL: http://www.city-and-guilds.co.uk
(offers vocational qualifications)

Northern Ireland Council for the
Curriculum, Examinations and Assessment
(CCEA)
29 Clarendon Road
Belfast BT1 3BG
Telephone: 028 9026 1200
URL: http://www.ccea.org.uk

Scottish Qualifications Authority
Ironmills Road
Dalkeith
Midlothian EH22 1LE
Telephone: 0845 279 1000
URL: http://www.sqa.org.uk

The Welsh Joint Education Committee
(WJEC)
245 Western Avenue
Cardiff CF5 2YX
Telephone: 029 2026 5000
URL: http://www.wjec.co.uk

University of Cambridge Local
Examinations Syndicate
1 Hills Road
Cambridge
Cambridgeshire CB1 2EU
Telephone: 01223 55 3311
URL: http://www.cie.org.uk
*Provides international school examinations
(CIE), vocational and EFL qualifications*

SPECIALIST (SUBJECT) AND OTHER ASSOCIATIONS

*For subject associations please refer to The
Education Authorities Directory and Annual
(see below), consult appropriate staff, or try
http://www.teachernet.gov*

General Teaching Council for England
344–5 Gray's Inn Road
London WC1X 8BF
Telephone: 0870 001 0308
URL: http://www.gtce.org.uk

Inservice and Professional Development
Association
University College Worcester
Henwick Grove
Worcester WR2 6AJ
Telephone: 01905 85 5055
URL: http://www.ipda.org.uk

TEACHER EXCHANGE AND VISITS

British Council Information Centre
Bridgewater House
58 Whitworth Street
Manchester M1 6BB
Telephone: 0161 957 7755

OTHER ADDRESSES

British Educational Communications and
Technology Agency (BECTA)
Millburn Hill Road
Coventry
West Midlands CV4 7JJ
Telephone: 024 7641 6994
URL: http://www.becta.org.uk/
index.cfm

Centre for the Study of Comprehensive
Schools
University of Leicester Mouton College
Northampton NN3 7RR
Telephone: 01604 49 2337
URL: http://www.cscs.org.uk

Commission for Racial Equality
St. Dunstan's House
201–21 Borough High Street
London SE1 1GZ
Telephone: 020 7828 7022
URL: http://www.cre.org.uk

Dyslexia Institute Ltd
133 Gresham Road
Staines
Middlesex TW18 2AJ
Telephone: 01784 46 3851
URL: http://www.dyslexia-inst.org.uk

Equal Opportunities Commission
Arndale House
Arndale Centre
Manchester M4 3EQ
Telephone: 0845 601 5901
URL: http://www.eoc.org.uk

Health and Safety Executive
Services Sector
39 Baddow Road
Chelmsford
Essex CM2 OHL
Sheffield S3 7HQ
Telephone: 01245 70 6200
URL: http://www.hse.gov.uk

Health Development Agency
7th Floor
Holborn Gate
330 High Holborn
London WC1V 7BA
Telephone: 020 7430 0850
URL: http://www.hda.nhs.uk

National Association for Special
Educational Needs (NASEN)
Nasen House
4/5 Amber Business Village
Amber Close
Amington
Tamworth
Staffordshire B77 4RP
Telephone: 01827 311500
URL: http://www.nasen.org.uk

National Foundation for Educational
Research (NFER)
The Mere
Upton Park
Slough
Berkshire SL1 2DQ

Telephone: 01753 57 4123
URL: http://www.nfer.ac.uk

National Society for the Prevention of
Cruelty to Children (NSPCC)
42 Curtain Road
London EC2 A3NH
Telephone: 020 7825 2500
URL: http://www.nspcc.org.uk

Voluntary Service Overseas
317 Putney Bridge Road
London SW15 2PN
Telephone: 020 8780 7200
URL: http://www.vso.org.uk

FOR FURTHER ADDRESSES

Please refer to:

The Education Authorities Directory and
Annual (published annually)
The School Government Publishing
Company Ltd
Darby House
Redhill
Surrey RH1 3DN
URL: http://www.schoolgovernment.
co.uk/pages/pub/ead.htm

This directory is available from most public
libraries and the website above. It includes
the addresses of: awarding bodies; careers
centres; centres of open and distance learning;
Department of Education, Northern Ireland;
educational psychological services; English
language schools; environmental education;
exchange visits and school travel; further
education colleges; government departments; institutes and colleges of further and
higher education; local education authorities;
public library authorities; pupil referral units;
recognised education and educational
associations; schools and sixth form colleges;
Scottish Executive Education Office; social
services departments; special needs services;
special schools; specialist schools; subject

associations; teachers' unions; teachers' pay and conditions; university and constituent colleges; Wales Office; and other organisations concerned with education and educational publishers and equipment suppliers in England, Wales, Scotland, Northern Ireland, Channel Islands and Isle of Man.

OTHER WEBSITE ADDRESSES

Advanced Skills Teacher (DfES): http://www.standards.dfes.gov.uk/ast
BBC education pages – learning: http://www.bbc.co.uk/learning
British Educational Research Association (BERA): http://www.bera.ac.uk
Department for Education and Science Standards Site: http://www.standards.dfes.gov.uk
Connexions service – advice for 13–19-year-olds (career guidance):
    http://www.connexions.gov.uk
Continuing professional development (CPD) (DfES:Teachernet):
    http://www.teachernet.gov.uk/professionaldevelopment/
Edulinks – education and government resources UK: http://www.edulinks.co.uk
Education website for the *Guardian*: http://www.learningalive.co.uk
Educational resource site, including subject resource links: http://www.topmarks.co.uk
Education resources – ICT: http://www.digitalbrain.com
General Teaching Council (GTC): http://www.gtce.org.uk
HM Inspectorate for Education in Scotland: http://www.hmie.gov.uk.
Her Majesty's Stationery Office (HMSO): http://www.hmso.gov.uk
Induction of Newly Qualified teachers (TTA): http://www.canteach.gov.uk/induction
Key Stage 3 National Strategy (DfES): http://www.standards.dfes.gov.uk/keystage3
Learning and Skills Development Agency: http://www.lsda.org.uk
National Curriculum (NC) online (QCA): http://www.nc.net/index.html
National Curriculum (NC) online resources (DfES):
    http://www.curriculumonline.gov.uk/curriculum+online/cover.htm
National Curriculum (NC) in action – pupils' work: http://www.ncaction.co.uk
National Foundation for Education Research (NFER):
    http://www.nfer.ac.uk/research/research.asp
National Grid for Learning (NGfL): http://www.ngfl.gov.uk/
National Literacy Strategy (DfES): http://www.standards.dfes.gov.uk/literacy
National Numeracy Strategy (DfES): http://www.standards.dfes.gov.uk/numeracy
Special educational needs (SEN): http://www.dfes.gov.uk/sen/ (for specific SEN web resources (e.g. autism) see Unit 4.6 in Starting to Teach in the Secondary School, 3rd edition)
Professional Standards for Qualified Teacher Status in England (TTA): http://www.tta.gov.uk/training/qtsstandards/standards/index.htm
Teachernet – support for teachers: http://www.teachernet.gov.uk/
Times Educational Supplement online: http://www.tes.co.uk
Vocational courses (City and Guilds Institute): http://www.city_and_guilds.co.uk/servlet

Appendix 2
Glossary of terms, acronyms and abbreviations

A2 level   Year 2 of a GCE A-level examination

ADD   attention deficit disorder

Accelerated learning   An umbrella term for practical approaches for enhancing learning which draws on a range of approaches including theories of intelligence, motivation and attention theories and recent developments in the understanding of brain function

Advanced skills teacher   An excellent teacher who achieves the very highest standards of classroom practice and who is paid to share his or her skills and experience with other teachers; see **teachernet**

Aims   The purpose of a lesson, unit or course expressed in broad terms; see also **objectives** and **learning outcomes**

A level   Advanced Level of GCE examination

ALITE   Accelerated Learning in Training and Education; see website http://www. alite.co.uk

AS level   Advanced Subsidiary (year 1 of a GCE A level examination)

AQA   Assessment and Qualification Alliance. An **awarding body**

Autumn Package guidance   Data about the performance of pupils nationally at Key Stages 2, 3 and 4 from the **DfES** in England; it enables schools to compare the performance of their pupils with other groups of pupils and to measure **Value Added** factors; available on the DfES Standards website (see also **PANDA)**

AS AVC   Advanced Subsidiary **AVCE**

AVA   Audio-visual aid

AVCE   Advanced Vocational Certificate of Education

Awarding body   Examination organisations in England (**AQA, EDEXCEL, OCR**) which provide syllabuses for **GCSE, GCE and GNVQ**

Banding   Structuring of a year group into divisions on grounds of general ability and generally taught within the band for most of the curriculum; see also **setting** and **streaming**

Beacon schools   Schools identified as representative of the best practice which can be disseminated to other schools; best practice might focus on a particular area, e.g. school management; see also **Specialist schools**

Bench marking   Part of a process of raising achievement by identifying a standard against which to judge the performance of a pupil or group of pupils, for example the proportion of pupils nationally gaining grade A★–C in GCSE in a teaching subject

Brain gym   Short, sharp exercises designed to improve concentration, alertness and hand-eye coordination

BTEC   Business and Technology Council, now part of **EDEXCEL**

CACHE   Council for Awards in Children's Care and Education

CAD   Computer-aided design

CAL   Computer assisted learning

CEDPDR   Career entry development profile and developmental record

CEDP   Career entry development profile (previously **CEP**)

CEP   Career entry profile (now **CEDP**)

Citizenship   A compulsory subject introduced into the **NC** for England in 2002

COA   Certificate of Achievement: an examination from an **awarding body** designed to provide a qualification to pupils who may not gain a GCSE qualification

Community school   One of three categories of **state school**; admissions and staff appointments controlled by LEA

Continuity and progression   Appropriate sequencing of syllabus content and choice of learning activities to promote pupils' development; continuity refers to curriculum organisation and progression relates to pupil learning

Core skills   Skills required of all pupils following vocational courses

CPD   Continuing professional development

CRE   Commission for Racial Equality

CTC   City technology college

DfE   Department for Education (became **DfEE**)

DfEE   Department for Education and Employment, formerly **DfE** (now **DfES)**

DfES   Department for Education and Skills (formerly **DfEE**)

EBD   Emotional and behavioural difficulties (see also **SEBD**)

EDEXCEL   One of three **awarding bodies** in England

EFL   English as a foreign language

EOC   Equal Opportunities Commission

EPLC   Effective professional learning community

ESL   English as a second language

ESOL   English for speakers of other languages

FE   Further education

Formative assessment   Assessment linked with teaching and learning and used to guide future teaching, i.e. assessment for learning

Foundation schools   One of three categories of **state school**; admission and staff appointments by governing bodies

GCE   General Certificate of Education

GCSE   General Certificate of Secondary Education

GNVQ   General National Vocational Qualification

GTC   General Teaching Council of England; Northern Ireland, Scotland and Wales have similar bodies

HEI   See **IHE**

HLTA   Higher level teaching assistant – an assistant who has undergone specific training for teaching and learning

HMI   Her Majesty's Inspectors of schools in England

HMCI   Her Majesty's Chief Inspector of schools in England

IB   International baccalaureate

ICT   Information and communications technology

IEP   Individual education plan for pupil with **SEN**

IHE   Institute of higher education

IIP   Investors in people

Inclusion   Refers to pupils in England; involves the increased participation of pupils in school activities who otherwise might be subject to exclusionary pressures

Independent school   A private school which receives no state assistance but financed by fees; see also **public schools**

INSET   In-service teacher education (see also **CPD**)

Key skills   Of the **NC** for England: communication, application of number, IT, improving own learning and performance; problem solving and working with others; see also **thinking skills**

LEA   Local education authority

Learning outcomes   Teaching **objectives** that you can assess; see also **aims** and **SMART** learning outcomes

LSA   Learning support assistant

MLD   Moderate learning difficulties

National Curriculum (NC)   A mandatory programme of study for pupils in England from ages 5–16; last revised in 1999

National Induction Standards   Standards that all **NQTs** in England are required to demonstrate by the end of their induction period

Norm referenced assessment   A process in which performance is measured by comparing candidates' responses; individual success is relative to the performance of all other candidates

Normative assessment   Assessment which is reported relative to given population

NQT   Newly qualified teacher

NSG   Non-statutory guidance of the National Curriculum, i.e. not mandatory

NVQ   National vocational qualification

Objectives   Changes expected in knowledge, understanding, skills, awareness or attitudes as a result of a lesson or group of lessons; see **aims** and **learning outcomes**

OCR   Oxford and Cambridge Regional; one of three **awarding bodies** in England

OFSTED   Office for Standards in Education (in England)

PANDA   Performance and assessment data provided by government in England and Wales as part of the **Autumn Package guidanc**e

PDP   Professional development portfolio

PICSI   Pre-inspection context and school indicator; used by **OFSTED** in preparation for school inspections

Pole-bridging   A feature of **accelerated learning**; describing to oneself why you are doing something

Private school   See **independent school**

PSCHE   Personal, social, citizenship and health education

PSE   Personal and social education

PSHE   **PSE** plus health education – some schools include **citizenship** education in this programme; see **PSCHE**

Public school   Independent secondary school not state funded; so called because they were funded by charity at their inception

QCA   Qualifications and Curriculum Authority

QTS   Qualified teacher status

Record of achievement   Cumulative record of a pupil's academic, personal and social progress over a stage of education

Reliability   A measure of the consistency of the assessment or test item; that is the extent to which the test gives repeatable results

SACRE   The Standing Advisory Council on Religious Education in each **LEA** and which gives advice on religious education to the LEA

Scaffolding   The input of focused questions or stimulus materials at appropriate points to support learning

School development plan   A coherent plan made by a school identifying improvements needed in the curriculum, organisation, staffing and resources and setting out action needed to make those improvements

Setting   The grouping of pupils according to their ability in a subject for lessons in that subject; see also **banding** and **streaming**

SEBD   Social, emotional and behavioural difficulties (see **EBD**)

SEN   Special educational needs

SENCO   Special educational needs coordinator

SLD   Specific learning difficulties

Special school   A school which is specially organised to make provision for pupils with special educational needs

Specialist school   Maintained schools in England can apply for specialist school status in a curriculum area such as technology, languages, sports and arts – they are specially funded for their specialism and teach the NC; see also **beacon school**

SMART   Of learning outcomes: specific, measurable, assessable, realistic and time-related

SoW   Scheme of work (of a curriculum)

State schools   Schools supported by public funds: in England there are three types of school: **foundation, community** and **voluntary**

Statement of special educational needs   Provided under the 1981 Education Act to ensure appropriate provision for pupils formally assessed as having **SEN**

Statutory induction   The statutory provision of an individualised programme for newly qualified teachers to monitor, support and assess their progress during their first years of teaching

Streaming   The organisation of pupils according to general ability into classes in which they are taught for all subjects and courses; see also **banding** and **setting**

Summative assessment   Assessment at the end of a course of study, used to rank, grade or compare pupils, groups or schools; it uses a narrow range of methods which are efficient and reliable, normally formal: that is, under examination conditions; cf. **formative assessment**

TA   Teaching assistant; also known as **learning support assistant**

Target setting   Part of a process of raising achievement by setting targets for the improved performance of pupils, both individually and as a group

Teachernet   Online support for **CPD** in England; see DfES website http://www.teachernet.gov.uk/

Thinking skills   Skills, in addition to **Key Skills**, to be promoted across the curriculum (of the **NC** for England)

Traffic lighting   A 'traffic light system' of giving feedback to a pupil about behaviour so that he or she can be involved directly in its own management

TTA   Teacher Training Agency

Validity   A statement of whether an assessment measures what it sets out to measure; it is often determined by consensus, rather than measured

Value added (VA)   The improvement in the performance of pupils above that expected from prior performance and may be expressed, e.g. as the difference in grades expected and achieved at GCSE; the difference may be attributed to improved teaching and learning by the school, i.e. the school has *added value* – the **Autumn Package guidance** is designed to help schools assess value added

Voluntary aided   One of three categories of **state school** in England and Wales; it receives financial assistance from an **LEA** but is owned by a voluntary body, usually religious

World class tests   Devised by government in England for gifted and talented pupils; see **QCA** website

Bibliography

Abel, M.H. and Sewell, J. (1999) 'Stress and burnout in rural and urban secondary school teachers' in *The Journal of Educational Research*, 92 (5), 287–93.

Accelerated Learning (2003) website: http://www.accelerated-learning-uk.co.uk/.

Accelerated Learning in Training and Education (ALITE) (2003) website: http://www.alite.co.uk/.

Accelerated Learning Institute (ALI) (2003) 'What is accelerated learning?' ALI website: www.accelerated-learning.com.

Accelerated Learning Network (2003) website: http://www.acceleratedlearningnetwork.com/.

Adair, J. (1988) *Effective Time Management: How to Save Time and Spend it Wisely*, London: Pan Books.

Adams, E. (2001) 'A proposed causal model of vocational teacher stress' in *Journal of Vocational Education and Training*, 53 (2), 223–46.

Adey, P. (2002) 'Should schools teach children how to learn?' Campaign for Learning Lecture, Royal Society of Arts, London, 24 April 2002.

Adey, P. and Shayer, M. (1994) *Really Raising Standards*, London: Routledge.

Adey, P., Shayer, M. and Yates, C. (2001) *Thinking Science: The Materials of the CASE Project* (3rd edition), Cheltenham: Nelson Thornes.

Adhami, M., Johnson, D.C. and Shayer, M. (1998) *Thinking Maths: The Programme for Accelerated Learning in Mathematics*, Oxford: Heinemann Educational Books.

Andrews, R. (1995) *Teaching and Learning Argument*, London: Cassell Education.

Argyle, M. (1983) *The Psychology of Interpersonal Behaviour*, Harmondsworth: Penguin.

Assessment Reform Group website: http://www.assessment-reform-group.org.uk/.

Atkinson, R.C. and Shriffin, R.M. (1968) 'Human memory: a proposed system and its control processes' in K.W. Spence and J.T. Spence (eds) *The Psychology of Learning and Motivation*, Volume 2, London: Academic Press.

Atwell, N. (1984) *In the Middle*, Upper Montclair, NJ: Boynton Cook.

Ayers, H., Clarke, D. and Murray, A. (2000) *Perspectives on Behaviour*, London: David Fulton Publishers.

Barnes, D., Britton, J. and Rosen, H. (1969) *Language, the Learner and the School*, Harmondsworth: Penguin.

Bartlett, S., Burton, D. and Peim, N. (2001) *Introduction to Education Studies,* London: Paul Chapman.

Bassey, M. (1998) 'Fuzzy generalisation and professional discourse' in *Research Intelligence,* 63, 20–4.

BBCi (2003a) Bitesize website: http://www.bbc.co.uk/schools/gcsebitesize/.

BBCi (2003b) Revision Guide website: http://www.bbc.co.uk/schools/revision/.

BECTA (20002) IMPACT2 reports – including: *Learning at Home and School: Case Studies; Parents' and Teacher' Perceptions of ICT in Education; The Impact of ICTs on Pupil Learning and Attainment.*

BECTA (2001) *Computers for Teachers – Phase 1 Report,* London: Department of Education and Skills.

BECTA (2002) *Computers for Teachers – Phase 2 Report,* London: Department of Education and Skills.

BECTA Research Reports available on website: http://www.becta.org.uk/research/reports.

Belbin, R.M. (1981). *Management Teams: Why they Succeed or Fail.* Oxford: Butterworth-Heinemann.

Best Practice Research Scholarship (DfES) website: http://www.dfee.gov.uk/bprs/index.cfm.

Best, R. (2002) *Pastoral Care and Personal-Social Education.* A review of UK research undertaken for the British Educational Research Association, Southwell: BERA.

Best, R., Jarvis, C. and Ribbins, P. (1977) 'Pastoral care: concept and process' in *The British Journal of Educational Studies,* XXV (2), 124–35.

Best, R., Lang, P., Lodge, C. and Watkins, C. (1995) *Pastoral Care and PSE,* London: Cassell/NAPCE.

Black, P. (1998), *Testing: Friend or Foe? Theory and Practice of Assessment and Testing,* London: Falmer.

Blanchard, J. (2003) 'Targets, assessment for learning, and whole-school improvement' in *Cambridge Journal of Education,* 33 (2), 257–71.

Blandford, S. (1998) *Managing Discipline in Schools,* London: Routledge.

Blandford, S. (2000) *Managing Professional Development in Schools,* London: Routledge.

Blandford, S. (2002) *Professional Development Manual,* London: Prentice Hall.

Bleach, K. (2000) *The Newly Qualified Secondary Teacher's Handbook,* London: David Fulton.

Blix, A.G., Cruise, R.J., Mitchell, B.M. and Blix, G.G. (1994) 'Occupational stress among university teachers', *Educational Research,* 36 (2), 157–69.

Bloom, B.S (ed.) (1956) *Taxonomy of Educational Objectives. Handbook 1: Cognitive Domain,* London: Longman.

Boesel, D. (ed.) (2001) *Continuing Professional Development: Improving Teacher Quality – Imperative for Education Reform.* National Partnership for Excellence and Accountability in Teaching (NPEAT) National Library of Education, Office of Educational Research and Improvement, US Department of Education. Website: http://www.ericsp.org/pages/digests/ConProfDev.pdf.

Bolam, R. (1986) 'Conceptually in-service', in D. Hopkins (ed.) *In-Service Training and Educational Development: An International Survey,* London: Croom Helm, pp. 14–34.

Bolam, R. (1993) *Recent Developments and Emerging Issues in the Continuing Professional Development of Teachers,* London: General Teaching Council of England and Wales (GTC).

Bolam, R. (2000) 'Emerging policy trends: some implications for continuing professional development' in *Journal of In-Service Education,* 26 (2), 267–80.

Borg, M.G. and Falzon, J.M. (1990) 'Coping actions by Maltese primary school teachers' in *Educational Research,* 32, 50–8.

Boruch, R., Bullock, M., Cheek, D., Harris, C., Davies, P., McCord, J., Soydan, H., Thomas, H. and de Moya, D. (2001) 'The Campbell Collaboration: concept, status, and plans', conference paper, Inter-Disciplinary Evidence-Based Policies and Indicator Systems Conference, July 2001. Durham, CEM Centre, University of Durham.

Bowring-Carr, C. and West-Burnham, J. (1994) *Managing Quality in Schools: A Training Manual,* Harlow: Longman Information and Reference.

Bristol University (2000) *Don't Know What Would be a Good Bit of Work, Really.* The LEARN Project. Guidance for schools on assessment for learning, Bristol: CLIO Centre for Assessment Studies University of Bristol.

British Educational Research Association (BERA) website: http://www.bera.ac.uk.

British Educational Leadership, Management and Administration website: http://www.shu.ac.uk/bemas/.

British Psychological Society (1991) *Code of Conduct, Ethical Principles and Guidelines*, Leicester: BPS (mimeo) 29.

Britton, J., Burgess, T., Nartin, N., McLeod, A. and Rosen, H. (1975) *The Development of Writing Abilities, 11–18*, London: Macmillan.

Bronfenbrenner, U. (1979) *The Ecology of Human Development*, Cambridge, MA: Harvard University Press.

Brooker, R. and McPherson, I. (1999) 'Communicating the processes and outcomes of practitioner research: an opportunity for self-indulgence or a serious professional responsibility?' in *Educational Action Research*, 7 (2), 203–20.

Brooks, A., Hodgson, A., Savory, C. and Spours, K. (2003) 'Raising achievement in advanced level provision in Tower Hamlets', unpublished work. For further information contact Judith Brooks at School of Lifelong Education and International Development at the Institute of Education, University of London.

Brown, A.L. (1994) 'The Advancement of Learning' in *Educational Researcher*, 23, 4–12.

Brown, M. and Ralph, S. (1998) *Time Management for Teachers*, Plymouth, Northcote House.

Brown, M. and Ralph, S. (2002) 'Teacher stress and school improvement' in *Improving Schools*, 5 (2), 55–65.

Brumfit, C. (ed.) (1995) *Language Education in the National Curriculum*, Oxford: Blackwell.

Bruner, J.S. (1966) *Towards a Theory of Instruction*, New York: W.W. Norton.

Bruner, J.S. (1983) *Child's Talk: Learning to Use Language*, Oxford: Oxford University Press; with the assistance of Rita Watson.

Bubb, S. (2001) *A Newly Qualified Teacher's Manual: How to Meet the Induction Standards*, London: David Fulton.

Bubb, S., Heilbronn, R., Jones, C., Totterdell, M. and Bailey, M. (2002) *Improving Induction: Research-Based Best Practice For Schools*, London: RoutledgeFalmer.

Burke, C. and Grosvenor, I. (2003) *The School I'd Like*, London: RoutledgeFalmer.

Burke, R.G., Greenglass, E.R. and Schwarzer, R. (1996) 'Predicting teacher burnout over time: effects of work stress, social support, and self-doubt on burnout and its consequences' in *Anxiety, Stress and Coping: An International Journal* (online serial) 9, 3. Website: http://userpage.fuberlin.de/ahhahn/publicat/burke9.htm.

Burton, D. (2001). 'Ways pupils learn' in S. Capel, M. Leask and T. Turner (eds) *Learning to Teach in the Secondary School: A Companion to School Experience* (3rd edition), London: RoutledgeFalmer.

Calvert, M. and Henderson, J. (1994) 'Newly qualified teachers: do we prepare them for their pastoral role? *Pastoral Care in Education*, 12(2) (June 1994).

Cameron, L. (2002) 'Metaphors in the learning of science: a discourse focus' in *British Educational Research Journal*, 28 (5), 673–88.

Campbell Collaboration website: http://www.campbell.gse.upenn.edu/.

Capel, S.A. (1992) 'Stress and burnout in teachers', *European Journal of Teacher Education*, 15 (3), 197–211.

Capel, S., Leask, M. and Turner, T. (2001) *Learning to Teach in the Secondary School: A Companion to School Experience* (3rd edition), London: RoutledgeFalmer.

Carre, C. (1981) *Language Teaching and Learning in Science*, London: Ward Lock Educational.

Carron, A.V. (1982) *Social Psychology of Sport: An Experimental Approach*, Wirral: Mouvement.

Carron, A.V. and Chelladurai, P. (1981) 'Dynamics of group cohesion in sport' in *Journal of Sport Psychology*, 3 (2), 123–39.

Carron, A. V. and Hausenblaus, H. A. (1998) *Group Dynamics in Sport* (2nd edition), Morgantown, WV: Fitness Information Technology.

Carter, R. (ed.) (1990) *Knowledge about Language and the Curriculum: The LINC Reader*, London: Hodder and Stoughton.

Carter, R. J. (1987) 'Teaching: a stressful occupation', *NATFHE Journal*, 12, 28–9.

Cartwright, S. and Cooper, C. L. (1997) *Managing Workplace Stress*, London: Sage.

Chaplain, R. and Freeman, A. (1998) *Coping with Difficult Children*, Cambridge: Pearson Publishing.

Chowcat, J. (2002) 'Education for a high knowledge era' in *Education Review: A Creative Future*, 15 (2), 41–6.

Chris and Keith Johnson Readability website: www.timetabler.com/reading.html.

Citizenship Foundation. website: http://www.citizenshipfoundation.org.uk.

Clark, P. (1998) *Back From the Brink: Transforming the Ridings School and our Children's Education*, London: Metro Books.

Claxton, G. (2002) *Building Learning Power*, Bristol: TLO.

Cockburn, A. D. (1996) 'Primary teachers' knowledge and acquisition of stress relieving strategies' in *British Journal of Educational Psychology*, 66, 399–410.

Cole, M. and Walker, S. (eds) (1989) *Teaching and Stress*, Milton Keynes: Open University Press.

Collaborative Action Research Network (CARN) website: http://www.did.stu.mmu.ac.uk/carn/.

Commonwealth of Learning Electronic Network for Schools and Education website: http://www.col.org/cense/school.htm.

Confederation of British Industry (CBI) (1989) *Towards a Skills Revolution*, London: Confederation of British Industry.

Cooper, P. (1993) *Effective Schools for Disaffected Pupils*, London: Routledge.

Corbett, J. (2001) 'Teaching approaches which support inclusive education: a connective pedagogy' in *British Journal of Special Education*, 28 (2), 55–9.

Coulby, D. and Coulby, J. (1995) 'Pupil participation in the social and educational processes of a primary school' in P. Garner and S. Sandow (eds) *Advocacy, Self-Advocacy and Special Needs*, London: David Fulton Publishers.

Cox, T., Boot, N. and Cox, S. (1989) 'Stress in schools: a problem-solving approach' in M. Cole and S. Walker (eds) *Teaching and Stress*, Milton Keynes: Open University Press, pp. 99–113.

Crick, B. and Heater, D. (1977) *Essays on Political Education*, Ringmer: Falmer Press.

D'Arcy, J. (1989) *Stress in Teaching: The Research Evidence*, Belfast: Northern Ireland Council for Educational Research, Occasional Paper Number 1.

Davies, J. D. (1996) 'Pupils' views on special educational needs practice' in *Support for Learning*, 11 (4), 157–61.

Day, C. (1999) *Developing Teachers: The Challenges of Lifelong Learning*, London: Falmer Press.

Dearing, R. (1994) *The National Curriculum and its Assessment: The Final Report*, London: School Curriculum and Assessment Authority (SCAA).

Dearing, R. (1996) *Review of Qualifications for 16–19 year olds (Full Report)*, London: School Curriculum and Assessment Authority (SCAA).

Department for Education (DfE) (1994) *Guidelines on School Attendance, Policy and Practice on the Categorisation of Absence*, London: HMSO.

Department for Education (DfE) (1994a) *The Education of Children with Emotional and Behavioural Difficulties* (Circular 9/94), London: DfE.

Department for Education (DfE) (1994b) *Pupil Behaviour and Discipline* (Circular 8/94), London: DfE.

Department for Education and Employment (DFEE) (1995) *Superhighways for Education*, London: HMSO.

Department for Education and Employment (DfEE) (1997) *From Targets to Action*, London: HMSO.

Department for Education and Employment (DfEE) (1999) *Social Inclusion: Pupil Support* (Circular 10/99), London: DfEE.

Department for Education and Employment (DfEE) (2000) *The Induction Period For Newly Qualified Teachers* (Circular 90/2000), London: DfEE.

Department for Education and Employment (DfEE) (2001) *Learning and Teaching: A Strategy for Professional Development*, London: HMSO. Website: http://www.teachernet.gov.uk/_doc/1289/CPD_Strategy.pdf.

Department for Education and Employment and Qualifications and Curriculum Authority (DfEE/QCA) (1998) *Education for Citizenship and the Teaching of Democracy in Schools: Final report of the Advisory Group on Citizenship (The Crick Report)*, London: QCA/98/245. Website: http://www.qca.org.uk.

Department for Education and Employment/Qualification and Curriculum Authority (DfEE/QCA) (1999) *The National Curriculum for England. Handbook for Secondary Teachers in England: Key Stages 3 and 4*, London: The Stationery Office. Website: http://www.nc.uk.net/about//about/ks3 ks4.html.

Department for Education and Skills (DfES), Schemes of Work website: http://www.standards.dfes.gov.uk/schemes2.

Department for Education and Skills (DfES) (2001a) *The Code of Practice*, London: DfES.

Department for Education and Skills (DfES) (2001b) The Key Stage 3 Strategy website: http://www.standards.dfes.gov.uk/key stage3.

Department for Education and Skills (DfES) (2001c) *Schools – Achieving Success*, London: DfES. Website: http://www.dfes.gov.uk/achievingsuccess//

Department for Education and Skills (DfES) (2001d) *Special Educational Needs Code of Practice*, London: DfES.

Department for Education and Skills (DfES) (2002a) *14–19 Opportunity and Excellence*, London: HMSO.

Department for Education and Skills (DfES) (2002b) *Key Stage 3 English. Roots and Research*, London: DfES. Author Colin Harrison, date of issue 06/02, Ref. 0353/2002.

Department for Education and Skills (DfES) (2002c) *Key Stage 3 National Strategy: Training Materials for the Foundation Subjects. Module 1 Assessment for Learning in Everyday Lessons*, London: DfES.

Department for Education and Skills (DfES) (2002d) *Research Brief and Report No 338. The Evaluation of the Effectiveness of the Statutory Arrangements for the Induction of Newly Qualified Teachers*, London: HMSO.

Department for Education and Skills (DFES) (2003a) *The UK 2003 Survey of ICT in Schools*, London: DfES. Website: http://www.dfes.gov.uk/rsgateway/DB/SBU/b000421/bweb05-2003.pdf.

Department for Education and Skills (DFES) (2003b) *Towards a Unified E-Learning Strategy*, London: DfES. This was available at the time of writing on the website: http://www.dfes.gov.uk/consultations2/16/.

Department for Education and Skills (DfES) (2003c) *Improving Behaviour in Schools*. Website: http://www.dfes.gov.uk/ibis/case_studies/case_studies.cfm.

Department for Education and Skills (DfES) (2003d) *CPD Partners Newsletter Special 2*, London: DfES. Website: http://www.teachernet.gov.uk/_doc/3698/CPD%20SPECIAL_2.pdf.

Department for Education and Skills (DfES) (2003e) *Behaviour and Attendance: An Initial Review for Secondary and Middle Schools*, London: DfES.

Department for Education and Skills (DfES) (annually), *The Autumn Package*, London: DfES. Website: http://www/dfes.gov.uk.

Department for Education and Skills (DfES) Standards and Effectiveness Unit (2001a) *Key Stage 3 National Strategy. English Department Training 2001*, London: DfEE.

Department for Education and Skills (DfES) Standards and Effectiveness Unit (2001b) *Key Stage 3 National Strategy Literacy across the Curriculum*, London: DfEE.

Department for Education and Skills/Teacher Training Agency (DfES/TTA) (2002) *Qualifying to Teach*, London: TTA.

Department of Education and Science (DES) (1975) *A Language for Life* (The Bullock Report), London: HMSO.

Department of Education and Science (DES) (1987) *The National Curriculum 5–16*, London: HMSO.

Department of Education and Science (DES) (1988) *Task Group on Assessment and Testing (TGAT) Report*, London: DES.

Department of Education and Science (DES) (1989) *Discipline in Schools* (The Elton Report), London: HMSO.

Dewey, J. (1960) *The Quest for Certainty: A Study of the Relation of Knowledge and Action*, USA: Capricorn Editions.

Dochy, F., De Rijdt, C. and Dyck, W. (2002) 'Cognitive prerequisites and learning: how far have we progressed since Bloom? Implications for educational practice and teaching' in *Active Learning in Higher Education*, 3 (3), 265–84.

Doughty, P., Pearce, J. and Thornton, G. (1972) *Language in Use* London: Arnold.

Drew, L. and Bingham, R. (1996) *Student Skills: Tutor's Handbook*, Aldershot, Hants: Gower Publishing.

Dreyfus, H. and Dreyfus, S. (1986) *Mind Over Machine: The Power of Human Intuition and Expertise in the Era of the Computer*, Oxford: Blackwell.

Dryden, G. and Vos, J. (2001) *The Learning Revolution: To Change the Way the World Learns*, Stafford: Network Educational Press.

Dunham, J. (1994) 'A framework of teachers' coping strategies for a whole school stress management policy' in *Educational Management and Administration*, 22, 168–74.

Dunham, J. and Varma, V. (eds) (1998) *Stress in Teachers: Past, Present and Future*, London: Whurr.

Education Department of the Scottish Office (1995) 'What did "good differentiators" do?' in *Interchange*, 30.

Education Service Advisory Committee (1998) *Managing Work-Related Stress: A Guide for Managers and Teachers in the Schools* (2nd edition), London: HMSO.

Edwards, A.D. (1992) 'Teacher talk and pupil competence' in K. Norman (ed.) *Thinking Voices: The Work of the National Oracy Project*, London: Hodder and Stoughton.

Entwistle, N. (1988) *Styles of Learning and Teaching*, London: David Fulton.

EPPI (unpublished) *A Systematic Review of how Theories Explain Learning Behaviour in School Contexts*, Institute of Education: EPPI (personal communication; to be published in 2004).

EPPI-Centre website: http://www.eppi.ioe.ac.uk/.

ERA (1988) *Education Reform Act, 29 July*, London: HMSO.

Eskridge, D.H. and Coker, D.R. (1985) 'Teacher stress: symptoms, causes and management techniques' in *The Clearing House*, 58, 387–90.

European Schoolnet Partner Networks website: http://www.eun.org/eun.org2/eun/countries/countries.html.

Evans, L. (2002) 'What is teacher development?' in *Oxford Review of Education*, 28 (1), 123–37.

Evidence-Based Education Network website: http://www.cemcentre.org/ebeuk/default.asp.

Farber, B.A. (1984a) 'Stress and burnout in suburban teachers' in *The Journal of Educational Research*, 77, 325–31.

Farber, B.A. (1984b) 'Teacher burnout: assumptions, myths and issues' in *Teachers College Record*, 86 (9), 321–38.

Farmer, S. (1999) 'Core Skills in the post-14 Scottish Science Curriculum' in *Education in Scotland*, April: 16–17.

Fazey, J.A. and Marton, F. (2002) 'Understanding the space of experiential variation' in *Active Learning in Higher Education*, 3 (3), 234–50.

Ferguson, P., Earley, P., Ouston, J. and Fidler, B. (1999) 'New heads, OFSTED inspections and the prospect for school improvement' in *Educational Research*, 41 (3), 241–9.

Field, K. (2002) *Portfolio of Professional Development: Structuring and Recording Teachers' Career Development*, London: Optimus Publishing, 19–20.

Finegold, D., Keep, E., Miliband, D., Raffe, D., Spours, K., Young, M. (1990) *A British Baccalaureate: Ending the Division Between Education and Training*, London: IPPR.

Fitz-Gibbon, C.T. (1997) *The Value-Added National Project Final Report:- Feasibility Studies for a National System of Value-Added Indicators*, London: School Curriculum and Assessment Authority.

Fletcher, W. (2001) 'Enabling students with severe learning difficulties to become effective target setters' in R. Rose and I. Grosvenor (eds) *Doing Research in Special Education*. London: David Fulton.

Florian, L. and Rouse, M. (2001) 'Inclusive practice in English secondary schools: lessons learned' in *Cambridge Journal of Education*, 31 (3), 399–412.

Fontana, D. (1993) *Managing Time*, Leicester: British Psychological Society Books.

Galligan, J. (1992) 'Thinking with and about computers' in J. Edwards (ed.) *Proceedings of the Fifth International Conference on Thinking*. Melbourne: Hawker-Brownlow.

Gardner, H. (1983) *Frames of Mind: The Theory of Multiple Intelligences*, London: Heinemann.

Gardner, H. (1993a) *Multiple Intelligences: The Theory in Practice*, New York: Basic Books.

Gardner, H. (1993b) *Frames of Mind: The Theory of Multiple Intelligences* (2nd edition), London: Fontana

Garner, P. and Gains, C. (1996) 'Models of intervention for children with emotional and behavioural difficulties' in *Support for Learning*, 11 (4), 141–5.

Gearon, L. (ed.) (2003) *Learning to Teach Citizenship in the Secondary School: A Companion for the Student Teacher of Citizenship*, London: Routledge.

General Teaching Council for England (GTC) website: http://www.gtce.org.uk.

General Teaching Council for England (GTC) (2000) *Professional Learning Framework: A Draft for Discussion and Development*, London: GTC.

General Teaching Council for England (GTC) (2003). *The Teacher's Professional Learning Framework*, London: GTC. Website: http://www.gtce.org.uk/gtcinfo/plf.asp.

Gillborn, D., Nixon, J. and Rudduck, J. (1993) *Dimensions of Discipline: Rethinking Practice in Secondary School*, London: DfE/HMSO.

Gillies, R.M. and Ashman, A.F. (2003) *Co-operative Learning: The Social and Intellectual Outcomes of Learning in Groups*, London: RoutledgeFalmer.

Gold, Y. and Roth, R.A. (1993) *Teachers Managing Stress and Preventing Burnout*, London: Falmer Press.

Goldstein, H. (2001) 'Using pupil performance data for judging schools and teachers: scope and limitations' in *British Educational Research Journal*, 27 (4), 433–42.

Goleman, D. (1996) *Emotional Intelligence: Why It Can Matter More Than IQ*, London: Bloomsbury.

Graves, D. (1983) *Writing: Children and Teachers at Work*, London: Heinemann.

Gray, J. and Richer, J. (1988) *Classroom Responses to Disruptive Behaviour*, Basingstoke: Macmillan Education.

Gray, P. (ed.) (2002) *Working with Emotions*, London: RoutledgeFalmer.

Great Britain (1996) Education Act, Elizabeth II 1966, London: HMSO.

Greenfield, S. (1997) *The Human Brain: A Guided Tour*, London: Weidenfeld and Nicolson.

Griffith, J., Steptoe, A. and Cropley, M. (1999) 'An investigation of coping strategies associated with job stress in teachers' in *British Journal of Educational Psychology*, 69, 517–31.

Gunther, H. (2001) *Leaders and Leadership in Education*, London: Paul Chapman Press.

Gurnah, A. (1989) 'After bilingual support' in M. Cole (ed.) *Education for Equality*, London: Routledge.

Hall, D. (1995/2002) *Assessing the Needs of Bilingual Pupils* (revised and updated by D. Griffiths, L. Haslam and Y. Wilkin), Chiswick, London: David Fulton.

Hamblin, D. (1981) *Teaching Study Skills*, Oxford: Basil Blackwell.

Hamblin, D. (1983) *Guidance: 16–19*, Oxford: Basil Blackwell.

Hammersley, M. (1997) 'Educational research and teaching: a response to David Hargreaves – Teacher Training Agency Lecture' in *British Educational Research Journal*, 23 (2), 141–61.

Handy, C. (1993) *Understanding Organisations* (4th edition), London: Penguin Business.

Hanko, G. (2003) 'Towards an inclusive school culture – but what happened to Elton's "affective curriculum"?' in *British Journal of Special Education*, 30 (3), 125–31.

Hargreaves, D. (1996) 'Teaching as a research-based profession: possibilities and prospects. Teacher Training Agency Annual Lecture 1996' in B. Moon, J. Butcher and E. Bird (eds) *Leading Professional Development in Education*, London: RoutledgeFalmer and Open University.

Hargreaves, D. (1999) 'The knowledge-creating school' in *British Journal of Educational Studies*, 47 (2), 122–44.

Harris, K.R., Halpin, G. and Halpin, G. (1985) 'Teacher characteristics and stress' in *Journal of Educational Research*, 78, 346–50.

Harrison, C. (2002) *Key Stage 3 English. Roots and Research*, London Department for Education and Skills.

Harrison, C. and Gardner, K. (1977) 'The place of reading' in M. Marland (ed.) *Language across the Curriculum*, London: Heinemann Educational.

Hart, N. and Hurd, J. (2000) *Teacher Stress*, London: Monitor Press.

Hart, P.M., Wearing, A.J. and Conn, M. (1995) 'Conventional wisdom is a poor predictor of the relationship between discipline policy, student misbehaviour and teacher stress' in *British Journal of Educational Psychology*, 65, 27–48.

Hastings, N. and Chantrey Wood, C. (2002) *Reorganizing Primary Classroom Learning*, Buckingham: Open University Press.

Haydn, T. (2001) 'Assessment and accountability' in S. Capel, M. Leask and T. Turner (eds) *Learning to Teach in the Secondary School: A Companion To School Experience* (3rd edition), London: Routledge.

Heath, S.B. (1983) *Ways with Words*, Cambridge: Cambridge University Press.

Heilbronn, R. and Jones, C. (1997) *New Teachers in an Urban Comprehensive: Learning in Partnership*, Stoke on Trent: Trentham Books.

Heilbronn, R., Jones, C., Bubb, S. and Totterdell, M. (2002) 'School-based induction tutors: a challenging role' in *School Leadership and Management*, 23 (4), 371–87.

Henderson, P. (1996) *How to Succeed in Examinations and Assessment*, London: Collins Education for the National Extension College.

Her Majesty's Chief Inspector of Schools (2000) *The Annual Report of Her Majesty's Chief Inspector of Schools: Standards and Quality in Education 1998/99*, London: HMSO.

Her Majesty's Inspectors (1977) *Ten Good Schools*, London: HMSO.

Her Majesty's Inspectors (1993) *The New Teacher in School: A Survey by HM Inspectors in England and Wales 1992*, Great Britain: Department for Education Inspectorate of Schools.

Hiebert, J., Gallimore, R. and Stigler, J.W. (2002) 'A knowledge base for the teaching profession: what would it look like and how can we get one?' in *Educational Researcher*, 31 (5), 3–15.

Hillage, J. (1998) *Excellence in Research on Schools*, Sudbury: Department for Education and Employment.

Hodgson, A. and Spours, K. (2002) *Developing an English Baccalaureate System from 14+*, London: Institute of Education, University of London.

Hodgson, A. and Spours, K. (2003) *Beyond A Levels: Curriculum 2000 and the Reform of 14–19*

Qualifications, London: Kogan Page.

Homework Study Tips (2003) website: http://homeworktips.about.com/cs/studyskills/index.htm.

How to Study (2003) website: http://www.how-to-study.com/tkng_notes.htm.

Howe, A. (1992) *Making Talk Work*, London: Hodder and Stoughton.

Howley, M. and Kime, S. (2003) 'Policies and practice for the management of individual learning needs' in C. Tilstone and R. Rose (eds) *Strategies to Promote Inclusive Practice*, London: Routledge Falmer.

Hoyle, E. (1975) 'Professionality, professionalism and control in teaching' in V. Houghton, C. Morgan, and R. McHugh (eds) *Management in Education: The Management of Organisations and Individuals.* London: Ward Lock Educational for the Open University Press.

Institute of Education (2002) *Secondary PGCE Professional Studies Handbook, 2002–2003* (internal publication), London: Institute of Education, University of London.

International Review of Curriculum and Assessment Frameworks Archive (QCA/NFER) website: http://www.inca.org.uk.

Irving, A. (ed.) (1982) *Starting to Teach Study Skills*, London: Edward Arnold.

Jarvis, P., Holford, J. and Griffin, C. (2003) *The Theory and Practice of Learning* (2nd edition), London: Kogan Page.

Jerome, L. Hayward, J., Easy, J. and Newmanturner, A. (2003) *The Citizenship Co-Ordinator's Handbook*, Cheltenham: Nelson Thornes.

Jerwood, L. (1999) 'Using special needs assistants effectively' in *British Journal of Special Education*, 26 (3), 127–9.

Johnson, G. (2002) *ICT and Study Skills*, Newmarket: Suffolk County Council.

Johnstone, M. (1993) *Teachers' Workload and Associated Stress*, Edinburgh: Scottish Council for Educational Research.

Jones, C. (2001) *The Use of a Professional Development Portfolio Within a Masters Framework. Report on an Escalate Thematic Initiative*, Liverpool: Department of Education, University of Liverpool. Website: http://www.escalate.ac.uk/initiatives/CliffJones.php3.

Jordan, J. (1974) 'The organisation of perspectives in teacher–pupil relationships', unpublished M.Ed. Thesis, University of Manchester.

Joyce, B. and Showers, B. (1995) *Student Achievement Through Staff Development*, New York: Longman.

Kelly, A. (1999) 'The evolution of key skills: towards a Tawney paradigm' in *Journal of Vocational Education and Training*, 53 (1), 21–35.

Kelly, T. and Mayes, A. (1995) *Issues in Mentoring*, London: Routledge.

Kerr, D. (1999) *Citizenship Education: An International Comparison*, London: QCA/NFER. Website: www.inca.org.uk.

Kerry, T. (1999) *Learning Objectives, Task Setting and Differentiation*, London: Hodder and Stoughton.

Kolb, D.A. (1985) *The Learning Style Inventory: Technical Manual* (revised edition), Boston, MA: McBer and Co.

Kutnick, P. and Manson, I. (2000) 'Enabling children to learn in groups' in D. Whitebread (ed.) *The Psychology of Teaching and Learning in the Primary School*, London and New York: RoutledgeFalmer.

Kyriacou, C. (1987) 'Teacher stress and burnout: an international review' in *Educational Research*, 29, 146–52.

Kyriacou, C. (1989) 'The nature and prevalence of teacher stress', in M. Cole and S. Walker (eds) *Teaching and Stress*, Milton Keynes: Open University Press.

Kyriacou, C. (1991) *Essential Teaching Skills*, Oxford: Basil Blackwell.

Kyriacou, C. (1998) *Essential Teaching Skills* (2nd edition), Cheltenham: Stanley Thornes.

Kyriacou, C. (2000) *Stress-busting for Teachers*, Cheltenham: Stanley Thornes.

Kyriacou, C. (2001) 'Teacher stress: directions for future research' in *Educational Review*, 53 (1), 27–35.

Labour Party (1996) *Aiming Higher: Labour's Proposals for the Reform of the 14–19 Curriculum*, London: Labour Party.

Lacey, P. (2001) *Support Partnerships: Collaboration in Action*, London: David Fulton.

Lacey, P. (2003) 'Effective multi-agency work' in C. Tilstone and R. Rose (eds) *Strategies to Promote Inclusive Practice*, London: RoutledgeFalmer.

Lachs, V. (2000) *Making Multi-media in the Classroom: A Teachers' Guide*, London: RoutledgeFalmer.

Lawes, S. (2003) 'What, when, how, and why? Theory and foreign language teaching' in *Language Learning Journal*, 28: 22–8.

Leask, M. (2001) 'Improving your teaching, an introduction to action research and reflective practice' in S. Capel, M. Leask and T. Turner (eds), *Learning to Teach in the Secondary School: A Companion for School Experience* (3rd edition), London: RoutledgeFalmer.

Leask, M. (2002) *Commissioned Report: The New Opportunities Fund ICT Training for Teachers and School Librarians: Progress Review and Lessons Learned Through the Central Quality Assurance Process in England*, London: Teacher Training Agency. Website: www.teach-ttaa.gov.uk.

Leask, M. (ed.) (2001) *Issues in Teaching with ICT*, London: Routledge.

Leask, M. and Kington, A. (2001) *A Case Study of ICT and School Improvement at Greenfield College England: Integrating ICT into Teachers' Practice*, for the OECD 'ICT and the Quality of Learning' research; see also Verensky, R. and Davis, C. (2002). Website: www.oecd.org/dataoecd/60/24/2740089.pdf.

Leask, M. and Pachler, N. (eds) (1999) *Learning to Teach using ICT in the Secondary School*, London: Routledge. Website: http://www.ioe.ac.uk/lie/ict.

Leask, M. and Younie, S. (2002) 'Communal constructivist theory: ICT pedagogy and international-isation of the curriculum' in *Journal for IT for Teacher Education*, 10 (1 and 2), 117–34.

Leask, M., Stephenson, J. and Terrell, I. (1997) 'Your wider role within the school,' in. S. Capel, M. Leask and T. Turner (eds) *Starting to Teach in the Secondary School: A Companion for the Newly Qualified Teacher*, London: Routledge, pp. 120-136

Levine, J. (ed.) (1990) *Bilingual Learners and the Mainstream Curriculum*, London: Falmer.

Levine, J. with Hester, H. and Skirrow, G. (1972) *Scope: Stage 2*, London: Longman for the Schools Council.

Levine, N. (1981) *Language Teaching and Learning in History*, London: Ward Lock Educational.

Lewin, K. (1951) *Field Theory in Social Science*, New York: Harper.

Lewis, R. (1992) *How to Write Essays*, Cambridge: National Extension College.

Lewis, A. and Norwich, B. (2000) *Mapping a Pedagogy for Special Educational Needs*, Exeter and Warwick: University of Exeter and University of Warwick.

Lewis, A. (1992) 'From planning to practice' in *British Journal of Special Education*, 19 (1), 24–7.

Loveless, A. and Ellis, V. (eds) (2001) *ICT, Pedagogy and the Curriculum*, London: RoutledgeFalmer.

Lumby, J., Briggs, A., Wilson, D., Glover, D. and Pell, T. (2002) *Sixth Form Colleges: Policy, Purpose and Practice, Nuffield Research Project*, Leicester: University of Leicester.

Lunzer, E. and Gardner, K. (eds) (1979) *The Effective Use of Reading*, London: Heinemann/Schools Council.

MacMahon, A. (1999) 'Promoting continuing professional development for teachers: an achievable target for school leaders?' in T. Bush, L. Bell, R. Bolam, R. Glatter and P. Rubbins (eds) *Re-defining Educational Management*, London: Paul Chapman.

Mancini, V.H., Wuest, D.A., Clark, E.K. and Ridosh, N. (1982) 'A comparison of the interaction patterns and academic learning time of low-burnout and high-burnout physical educators', paper presented at the Big Ten Symposium on Research in Teaching, Lafayette, Indiana: November.

Marland, M. (1977) *Language across the Curriculum*, London: Heinemann Educational.

Marland, M. (1989) *The Tutor and the Tutor Group*, Harlow: Longman.

Marland, M. (1993) *The Craft of the Classroom*, London: Croom Helm.

Marland, M. and Rogers R. (1997) *The Art of the Tutor: Developing your Role in the Secondary School*, London: David Fulton.

Marshall, T. (1950) *Citizenship and Social Class*, Cambridge: Cambridge University Press.

Maynard, T. and Furlong, J. (1995) 'Learning to teach and models of mentoring,' in T. Kelly and A. Mayes (eds) *Issues in Mentoring*, London: Routledge for the Open University.

Mckeown, S. (1991) *Developing Learning Skills – An Activity Based Manual*, Cambridge: National Extension College.

McMahon, A., Thomas, S., Stoll, L., Bolam, R., Wallace, M. (2002) 'Creating and sustaining effective professional learning communities: a conference paper' in *Book of Abstracts, BERA Conference 2002*, British Educational Research Association.

McSherry, J. (2001) *Challenging Behaviours in Mainstream Schools*, London: David Fulton Publishers.

Metcalf, C. (1998) 'Team building: the key qualities' in *Managing Schools Today*, 7 (4), 34–6.

Mezirov, J. (2000) 'Learning to think like an adult' in J. Mezirov and Associates (eds) *Learning as Transformation*, San Francisco: Jossey-Bass.

Mills, S. (1995) *Stress Management for the Individual Teacher*, Lancaster: Framework Press.

Mind, Body and Soul website: http://www.mindbodysoul.gov.uk.

Mobley, M., Emerson, C., Goddard, I., Goodwin, S. and Letch, R. (1986) *All about GCSE*, London: Heinemann.

Monk, M. and Osborne, J. (eds) (2000) *Good Practice in Science Teaching: What Research Has to Say*, Buckingham: Open University Press.

Montgomery, M. (1991) *Study Skills for GCSE and GCE A Level*, Scotland: Charles Letts.

Moon, B. (2000) 'The changing agenda for professional development in education' in B. Moon, J. Butcher and E. Bird (eds) *Leading Professional Development In Education*, London: RoutledgeFalmer and Open University.

Moran, M. (1999) 'Key skills in advanced science – plain sailing or Exocet?' in *Education in Scotland*, April: 12–13.

Mosston, M. and Ashworth, S. (1994) *Teaching Physical Education* (3rd edition), London: Columbus.

National Association for Pastoral Care in Education website: http://www.napce.org.uk.

National Commission on Education (1993) *Learning to Succeed: A Radical Look at Education Today and a Strategy for the Future*, London: Heinemann.

National Council for Educational Technology (NCET) (1994) *Integrated Learning Systems: A Report of the Pilot Evaluation of ILS in the UK*, Coventry: NCET.

National Curriculum online: http://www.nc.uk.net/about_the_sch.html.

National Foundation for Education Research (NFER) website: http://www.nfer.ac.uk/research/.

National Foundation for Educational Research (NFER) (2000) *Continuing Professional Development: Teachers' Perspectives – A Summary*, Slough: NFER.

National Grid for Learning (NGfL) website: http://www.ngfl.gov.uk/.

National Writing Project (1989/90) *Issues from the National Writing Project*, London: Nelson.

National Educational Research Forum (NERF) (2000) *A Research and Development Strategy for Education: Developing Quality and Diversity*. Nottingham: National Educational Research Forum.

Noble, K. (2003) 'Personal reflection on experiences of special and mainstream education' in M. Shevlin and R. Rose (eds) *Encouraging Voices*, Dublin: NDA.

Norman, K. (ed.) (1992) *Thinking Voices: The Work of the National Oracy Project*, London: Hodder and

Stoughton.

Noss, R. and Pachler, N. (1999) 'The challenge of new technologies: doing old things in a new way, or doing new things?' in P. Mortimore (ed.) *Understanding Pedagogy and its Impact on Learning*, London: Sage.

Nuttall, D.L. (1984) 'Doomsday or a new dawn? Prospects for a common system of examining at 16-plus' in P. Broadfoot (ed.) *Selection, Certification and Control*, Basingstoke: Falmer Press.

O'Brien, T. and Guiney, D. (2001) *Differentiation in Teaching and Learning: Principles and Practice*, London: Continuum.

Office for Standards in Education (OFSTED) (1993) *Access and Achievement in Urban Education: A Report from the Office of Her Majesty's Chief Inspector of Schools*, London: HMSO.

Office for Standards in Education (OFSTED) (2001) *The Annual Report of the Chief Inspector of Schools, 1999–2000*, London: OFSTED.

Office for Standards in Education (OFSTED) (2003) *The Key Stage 3 Strategy: Evaluation of the Second Year*, London: OFSTED.

Office for Standards in Education (OFSTED) (ongoing) *Reports on School Subject Teaching*, London: OFSTED. Website: http://www.archive.official-documents.co.uk.

Office for Standards in Education (OFSTED) (ongoing) *School Inspection Reports*, London: OFSTED. Website: http://www.ofsted.gov.uk.

Organisation for Economic Co-operation and Development (OECD) (2002) 'ICT and the Quality of Learning' research, see Leask, M. and Kington, A. (2001) above and Verensky, R. and Davis, C. (2002).

Organisation for Economic Cooperation and Development/Department for Education and Skills (OECD/DfES) (2003) *Education at a Glance 2002*, London: Analytical Services, DfES. Source of data, drawn from the OECD database.

Pachler, N. (2003) 'Foreign language teaching as an evidence-based profession?' in *Language Learning Journal*, 27, 4–14.

Pachler, N., Daly, C. and Lambert, D. (2003) 'Teacher learning: reconceptualising the relationship between theory and practical teaching in Masters level course development' in J. Gunther (ed.) (2003) *Quality Assurance in Distance-Learning and E-learning*, European Association of Telematic Applications, Krems, Austria.

Papert, S. (1993a) *Mindstorms: Children, Computers and Powerful Ideas* (2nd edition), Hemel Hempstead: Harvester Wheatsheaf.

Papert, S. (1993b) *The Children's Machine*, Hemel Hempstead, Harvester Wheatsheaf.

Parcells, B. and Coplon, J. (1995) *Finding a Way to Win: The Principles of Leadership, Teamwork, and Motivation*, New York: Doubleday Dell Publishing Group.

Parkes, J. (2000) 'The interaction of assessment format and examinees' perceptions of control' in *Educational Research*, 42 (2), 175–82.

Pathfinders website: http://www.dfes.gov.uk/14-19pathfinders.

Pernet, R. (1989) *Notes for Managers: Effective Use of Time*, London: The Industrial Society Press.

Phillips, B.N. (1993) *Stress of Teachers in the Public Schools. Educational and Psychological Perspectives on Stress in Students, Teachers and Parents*, Brandon: Clinical Psychology.

Phillips, G. and Pound, T. (eds) (2003) *The Baccalaureate: A Model for Curriculum Reform*, London: Kogan Page.

Piaget, J. (1932) *The Moral Judgement of the Child*, New York: Macmillan.

Piaget, J. (1954) *The Construction of Reality in the Child*, New York: Basic Books.

Pinker, S. (1998) *How the Mind Works*, London: Allen Lane, The Penguin Press.

Polat, F. and Farrell, P. (2002) 'What was it like for you? Former pupils' reflections on their placement at a residential school for pupils with emotional and behavioural difficulties' in *Emotional and*

Behavioural Difficulties, 7 (2), 97–108.

Pollard, A. (2002) *Reflective Teaching: Effective and Evidence-Informed Professional Practice*, London: Continuum.

Posthuma, B.W. (1999) *Small Groups in Counselling and Therapy: Process and Leadership*, London: Allyn and Bacon.

Pring, R. (2000) *Philosophy of Educational Research*, London: Continuum.

Proctor, J. (1994) 'Occupational stress among Grampian primary teachers' in *Education in the North, New Series*, 2, 46–54.

Putnam, R., and Borko, H. (2000) 'What do new views of knowledge and thinking have to say about research on teacher learning' in B. Moon, J. Butcher and E. Bird (eds) *Leading Professional Development in Education*, London: RoutledgeFalmer and Open University.

Qualifications and Curriculum Authority (QCA) (2001) *Supporting School Improvement. Emotional and Behavioural Development*, London: QCA.

Qualifications and Curriculum Authority (QCA) (2003) qualifications website: http://www.qca.org.uk/nq/ks.

Qualifications and Curriculum Authority (QCA) (2004) *National Curriculum Online*, available at http://www.nc.uk.net/about_the_sch.html.

Qualifications and Curriculum Authority for Wales (QCAAW) (2000) *Challenging Pupils: Enabling Access*, Cardiff: QCAAW.

Qualifications and Curriculum Authority/Department for Education and Employment (QCA/DfEE) (2000) *Assessment and Reporting Arrangements*, London: QCA/DfEE.

Ratcliffe, N. (1989/90) Diagram published in *Perceptions of Writing, National Writing Project (1989/90): Issues from the National Writing Project*, London: Nelson.

Reeves, D.J., Boyle, W.F. and Christie, T. (2001) 'The relationship between teacher assessments and pupils attainment in Standard Test tasks at Key Stage 2, 1996–1998' in *British Educational Research Journal*, 27 (2), 141–60.

Renshaw, K. (1997) 'Symptoms and causes of teacher burnout' in *American Music Teacher*, 46 (4), 57–8.

Rhodes, C. and Houghton-Hill, S. (2000) 'The linkage of continuing professional development and the classroom experience of pupils: barriers perceived by senior managers in some secondary schools' in *Journal of In-Service Education*, 26 (3), 423–36.

Riding, R.J. and Rayner, S. (1998) *Cognitive Styles and Learning Strategies*, London: David Fulton.

Rieser, R. (1992) 'Internalised oppression: how it seems to me' in T. Booth, W. Swann, M. Masterton and P. Potts (eds) *Policies for Diversity in Education*, London: Routledge.

Robertson, L.H. (2000) 'Early literacy and emergent bilingual pupils: the exclusive nature of the National Curriculum and National Literacy Strategy' in G. Walraven (ed.) *Combating Social Exclusion through Education*, Leuven-Apeldoorn: Garant.

Robertson, L.H. (2001) 'Excluded voices: educational exclusion and inclusion' in D. Hill and M. Coles (eds) *Schooling and Equality*, London: Kogan Page.

Rogers, W.A. (1996) *Managing Teacher Stress*, London: Pitman.

Rogoff, B. (1998) 'Cognition as a collaborative process' in D. Kuhn and R.S. Seigler (eds) *Cognition, Perception and Language*, Volume 2 of W. Damon (ed.) *Handbook of Child Psychology* (5th edition), New York: John Wiley.

Rose, R. (1999) 'Pupils with severe learning difficulties as decision makers in respect of their own learning needs' in *Westminster Studies in Education*, 22 (1), 19–29.

Rowland, V. and Birkett, K. (1992) *Personal Effectiveness for Teachers*, Hemel Hempstead, Herts: Simon and Schuster Education.

Rutter, M., Maughan, B., Mortimore, P. and Ouston, J. (1979) *Fifteen Thousand Hours: Secondary Schools and their Effects on Pupils*, London: Open Books.

Sage, R. (2002) 'Start talking and stop misbehaving: teaching pupils to communicate, think and act appropriately' in *Emotional and Behavioural Difficulties*, 7 (2), 85–96.

Sale, J. (1998) 'Take the lead!' in *Managing Schools Today*, 7 (6), 13–19.

Salovey, P. and Mayer, J.D. (1990) 'Emotional intelligence' in *Imagination, Cognition and Personality*, 9 (3), 185–211.

Savory, C., Hodgson, A. and Spours, K. (2003) *The Advanced Certificate of Vocational Education (AVCE); A General or Vocational Qualification? Broadening the Advanced Level Curriculum IOE/Nuffield Series No. 7*, London: Institute of Education, University of London.

Scanlon, M. (1999) *The Impact of OFSTED Inspections*, Slough: NFER.

Schagen, I. and Schagen, S. (2003) 'Analysis of national value-added datasets to estimate the impact of specialist schools on pupil performance' in *Educational Studies*, 29 (1), 3–18.

Schamer, L.A. and Jackson, M.J.B. (1996) 'Coping with stress: common sense about teacher burnout' in *Education Canada*, 36 (2), 28–31.

Schon, D.A. (1995) *The Reflective Practitioner: How Professionals Think in Action*, Aldershot: Arena.

School Curriculum and Assessment Authority (SCAA) (1994) *GCE and AS Code of Practice* (The GCSE examining boards of England, Wales and Northern Ireland), London: SCAA.

Scott, D. (2000) *Reading Educational Research and Policy*, London: RoutledgeFalmer.

Scott, M. (1992) *Time Management*, London: Century Business.

Selye, H. (1956) *The Stress of Life*, New York: McGraw-Hill.

Selye, H. (1974) *Stress without Distress*, New York: Signet Books.

Senge, P. (1990) *The Fifth Discipline – The Art and Practice of the Learning Organisation*, New York: Doubleday.

Sharp, C., Pocklington, K. and Weindling, D. (2002) 'Study support and the development of the self-regulated learner' in *Educational Research*, 44 (1), 29–41.

Simco, N. (1995) 'Professional profiling and development in the induction year' in *British Journal of In-Service Education*, 19 (1), 3–4.

Smith, A. (2001) *Accelerated Learning in Practice*, London: Network Educational Press.

Smith, A. (2003) 'What is accelerated learning?' ALITE website: www.alite.co.uk.

Smith, A. and Call, N. (2002) *The ALPs Approach*, London: ALITE.

Smith, C. and Laslett, R. (1993) *Effective Classroom Management*, London: Routledge.

Steiner, I.D. (1972) *Group Process and Productivity*, New York: Academic Press.

Stenhouse, L. (1975) *An Introduction to Curriculum Research and Development*, London: Heineman.

Sternberg, R.J. (1985) *Beyond IQ: A Triarchic Theory of Human Intelligence*, Cambridge: Cambridge University Press.

Sutton, C. (ed.) (1981) *Communicating in the Classroom*, London: Hodder and Stoughton.

Task Group on Assessment and Testing (TGAT); see Department of Education and Science (DES) (1988).

TBF (2000) *Managing Stress in Schools: Teacherline First Report*, London: TBF, The Teacher Support Network.

Teacher Training Agency (TTA) (2004) *Behaviour4Learning*. Website expected to be operational in May 2004 at www.behaviour4learning.ac.uk.

Teacher Training Agency (TTA) (2002) *Qualifying to Teach*, London: TTA.

Teacher Training Agency (TTA) (2003a) *Career Entry and Development Profile 2003*, London: TTA.

Teacher Training Agency (TTA) (2003b) *Into Induction 2003*, London: TTA.

Teacher Training Agency (TTA), induction website: http://www.tta.gov.uk/induction.

Teachernet website: http://www.teachernet.gov.uk/.

Tennant, G. (2001) 'The rhetoric and reality of learning support in the classroom: towards a synthesis' in *Support for Learning*, 16 (4), 184–8.

Thomas, G., Walker, D. and Webb, J. (1998) *The Making of the Inclusive School*, London: Routledge.

Tinklin, T. (2003) 'Gender differences and high attainment' in *British Educational Research Journal*, 29 (3), 307–25.

Tod, J. and Cornwall, J. (1998) *Individual Education Plans*, London: David Fulton Publishing.

Tollan, J.H. (1990) ' "Stress Aid": an evaluation of the effectiveness for planning and management in the primary school', unpublished MEd Thesis, University of Leicester.

Torbe, M. (ed.) (1980) *Language Policies in Action*, London: Ward Lock Educational.

Torgerson, C., Roberts, B., Thomas, J., Dyson, A. and Elbourne, D. (2001) *Developing Protocols for Systematic Reviews in Education: Early Experiences from EPPI-Centre Review Groups*. Conference paper, Inter-disciplinary Evidence-Based Policies and Indicator Systems Conference, July 2001. Website: http://www.eppi.ioe.ac.uk/.

Torney-Purta, J., Schwille, J. and Amadei, J.A. (eds) (1999) *Civic Education across Countries: 24 Case Studies from the IEA Civic Education Project*, Amsterdam: International Association for the Evaluation of Educational Achievement (IEA).

Torrance, H. and Pryor, J. (2001) 'Developing formative assessment in the classroom: using action research to explore and modify theory' in *British Educational Research Journal*, 27 (5), 615–31.

Travers, C.J. and Cooper, C.L. (1996) *Teachers under Pressure: Stress in the Teaching Profession*, London: Routledge.

Trendall, C.J. (1989) 'Stress in teaching and teacher effectiveness: a study of teachers across mainstream and special education' in *Educational Research*, 32 (1), 52–8.

Upton, G. and Cooper, P. (1990) 'A new perspective on behaviour problems in schools: the ecosystem approach' in *Maladjustment and Therapeutic Education*, 8 (1), 3–18.

Urquhart, I. (2002) 'Communicating well with children' in D. Whitebread (ed.) *The Psychology of Teaching and Learning in the Primary School*, London and New York: RoutledgeFalmer.

Vandenberghe, N. and Huberman, A.M. (eds) (1999) *Understanding and Preventing Teacher Burnout: A Sourcebook of International Research and Practice*, Cambridge: Cambridge University Press.

Verensky, R. and Davis, C. (2002) 'Quo vademus? The transformation of schooling in a networked world – draft report'. For the OECD *ICT and the Quality of Schooling Project*. Website: http://peabody.vanderbilt.edu/ICT/.

Visser, J., Cole, T. and Daniels, H. (2002) 'Inclusion for the difficult to include' in *Support for Learning*, 17 (1), 23–6.

Vygotsky, L.S. (1962) *Thought and Language* (edited and translated by Eugenia Hanfmann and Gertrude Vakar), Cambridge, MA: MIT Press.

Vygotsky, L.S. (1978) *Mind in Society: The Development of Higher Psychological Processes* (edited by M. Cole), Cambridge, MASS and London: Harvard University Press.

Waterhouse, P. (1983) *Managing the Learning Process*, London: The McGraw-Hill Series for Teachers.

Watkins, C. (1992) *Whole School Personal-Social Education: Policy and Practice*, Coventry: National Association for Pastoral Care in Education.

Watkins, C. and Whalley, C. (1993) *Mentoring Close Up; Resources for School Based Development*, Harlow: Longman.

Watkins, O. (1981) 'Active reading and listening' in C. Sutton (ed.) *Communicating in the classroom*, London: Hodder and Stoughton.

Webster, A., Beveridge, M. and Reed, M. (1996) *Managing the Literacy Curriculum*, London: Routledge.

Wenger, E. (1999) *Communities of Practice: Learning, Meaning and Identity*, Cambridge: Cambridge

University Press.

Whitebread, D. (ed.) (2000) *The Psychology of Teaching and Learning in the Primary School*, London: RoutledgeFalmer.

Whitty, G. (2000) 'Teacher professionalism' in *New Times Journal of In-Service Education*, 26 (2), 281–96.

Wigfield, A., Eccles, J.S. and Rodriguez, D. (1998) 'The development of children's motivation in school contexts' in P.D. Pearson and A. Iran-Nejad (eds) *Review of Research in Education: Volume 23*, Washington, DC: American Educational Research Association.

Wilkinson, A. (1971) *The Foundations of Language*, Oxford: Oxford University Press.

Williams, M. (ed.) (1981) *Language Teaching and Learning in Geography*, London: Ward Lock Educational.

Wilson, V. and Hall, J. (2002) 'Running twice as fast? A review of the research literature on teachers' stress' in *Scottish Educational Review*, 34 (2), 175–87.

Wise, S. (2000) *Listen to Me. The Voices of Pupils with Emotional and Behavioural Difficulties*, Bristol: Lucky Duck Publishing.

Wood, M. (1992) 'Teaching talk: how modes of teacher talk affect pupil participation' in K. Norman (ed.) *Thinking Voices. The Work of the National Oracy Project*, London: Hodder and Stoughton.

Woods, P. (1979) *The Divided School*, London: Routledge and Kegan Paul.

Woods, P. (1989) 'Stress and the teacher role', in M. Cole and S. Walker (eds) *Teaching and Stress*, Milton Keynes: Open University Press.

Woods, P. (1990) *The Happiest Days?: How Pupils Cope with School*, London: Falmer Press.

Youens, B. (2001) 'External assessment and examinations' in S. Capel, M. Leask and T. Turner (2001) *Learning to Teach in the Secondary School: A Companion to School Experience* (3rd edition), London: RoutledgeFalmer.

Young, R. (1997) 'How the sixth form seized an armoury and shut a school' in *The Times*, 24 January.

Zander, A. (1982) *Making Groups Effective*, San Francisco: Jossey-Bass.

Index of names

Subject index